The Messenger

The Messenger

Moderna, the Vaccine, and the

Business Gamble That Changed the World

PETER LOFTUS

HARVARD BUSINESS REVIEW PRESS
BOSTON, MASSACHUSETTS

The web addresses referenced in this book were live and correct at the time of the book's publication but may be subject to change.

Library of Congress Cataloging-in-Publication Data

Names: Loftus, Peter (Peter D.), author.
Title: The messenger : Moderna, the vaccine, and the business gamble that changed the world / Peter Loftus.
Description: Boston, Massachusetts : Harvard Business Review Press, [2022] | Includes index.
Identifiers: LCCN 2022001931 (print) | LCCN 2022001932 (ebook) | ISBN 9781647823191 (hardcover) | ISBN 9781647823207 (epub)
Subjects: LCSH: Moderna (Firm)—History. | Vaccines industry—History. | Pharmaceutical biotechnology industry—Economic aspects—History. | Messenger RNA.
Classification: LCC HD9675.V334 M645 2022 (print) | LCC HD9675.V334 (ebook) | DDC 338.4/76153—dc23/eng/20220210
LC record available at https://lccn.loc.gov/2022001931
LC ebook record available at https://lccn.loc.gov/2022001932

ISBN: 978-1-64782-319-1
eISBN: 978-1-64782-320-7

For Eileen, James, Nora, and Luke,

with love and gratitude for

supporting me and each other through it all.

And for Mom, whose love and courage

have guided and inspired me.

Contents

Reporter's Note

This book is based on nearly 300 interviews with more than 150 people. Interviewees include Moderna employees, cofounders, members of the company's board of directors and scientific advisory board, and investors, past and present. They also include people outside of Moderna who were involved in some way in the company's growth and in the Covid-19 vaccine project, as well as in the broader vaccine effort: US government health officials, government scientists, members of government vaccine advisory committees, executives and researchers at other drug companies, academic scientists, infectious disease doctors, vaccine specialists, clinical trial investigators and volunteers, and patent law experts.

Unless otherwise noted in an endnote or other attribution, the information conveyed here is from my own reporting. Many quotes in this book are verbatim from interviews or documents, or they are reconstructed dialogue based on the recollections of interview subjects. Some quotes and information are taken from other sources, including news articles by other reporters, which are cited.

The Messenger

Prologue

Disease X

IN EARLY JANUARY 2020, STÉPHANE BANCEL WAS VACA-
tioning near cool, dry Cannes, France, with his wife and two teenage
daughters. For the forty-seven-year-old CEO of the biotechnology company Moderna, Inc., it was a much-needed break sandwiched between
closing the books on a difficult 2019 and upcoming travel that he hoped
would make 2020 a good year. First, he'd jet to a health care conference
in San Francisco to court investors, then cross the ocean to Davos in the
Swiss Alps for the annual gathering of the global business elite.

Bancel was preparing to tell investors about the massive ramp-up of
his company in Cambridge, Massachusetts, which had promised, for a decade now, to deliver an entirely new way of making drugs by harnessing
the power of genetic information. He would tell them about Moderna's
new manufacturing plant outside Boston, its twenty experimental medicines in the pipeline, and its $1.3 billion in cash and investments—more
than most biotechs without a product on the market, but nowhere near
an average large pharmaceutical company, which spent many times that
on marketing alone.[1]

Bancel had a clear plan for 2020: get Moderna close to having a product by turning the genetic material, known as messenger RNA, into a
vaccine. He wanted to reach new milestones in the byzantine development process all drugs go through.

Bancel knew that many investors probably wouldn't be wowed by this approach. Always dogging Moderna was that fact that no matter what Bancel said in his energetic pitches to raise money, no drug or vaccine using its gene-based technology had ever been approved for sale. Even Moderna's most promising project, a vaccine against cytomegalovirus, was a couple of years away from coming to fruition. Even in biotech, where time-to-market is longer than most industries, investors' patience could wear thin, especially for a ten-year-old startup. And their patience was reflected by Moderna's stock, stuck under $20, a disappointing price that was lower than its initial public offering in late 2018.

Even on vacation, Bancel's ritual was to wake up early and scan the news over a cup of tea while his family slept.[2] One morning he noticed a *Wall Street Journal* article, most likely the one headlined "Health Officials Work to Solve China's Mystery Virus Outbreak."[3]

The *Journal* reported that health authorities in China were racing to identify what caused viral pneumonia in about five dozen people in Wuhan, in central China, and early lab tests were only showing what it wasn't: it wasn't a known flu strain, and it wasn't a known coronavirus that had caused scattered outbreaks before. It wasn't the SARS (severe acute respiratory syndrome), that caused an outbreak in China in 2003 and spread to other countries, killing hundreds before travel restrictions contained it.

Moderna was always looking for chances to prove its technology, and Bancel wondered if this mystery virus was a candidate for a vaccine that Moderna could try to develop. That morning, from France, he sent an email to Barney Graham, the deputy director of the Vaccine Research Center at the federal government's National Institute of Allergy and Infectious Diseases (NIAID) in Bethesda, Maryland, headed by Dr. Anthony Fauci.

Graham, then sixty-seven, was a central figure in the world of infectious diseases and the challenge of finding vaccines to combat them. He had an MD and a PhD in microbiology and immunology and helped run clinical trials of HIV vaccines at Vanderbilt before leaving in 2000 for his current post in Bethesda. The center was created initially to seek an AIDS vaccine but expanded its scope to focus on Ebola and the flu as well. Bancel knew Graham because NIAID and Moderna had collaborated on finding a vaccine for another virus that caused an outbreak, Zika. Although Zika abated and the vaccine efforts lost urgency, the collaboration continued, as Fauci saw promise in the messenger RNA (mRNA) technology Moderna was betting on.

Bancel had seen Barney Graham a few weeks earlier when Graham and his boss John Mascola visited Moderna's new state-of-the-art manufacturing plant, in the shell of an old Polaroid film factory. Mascola recalled Moderna executives being proud of the plant, boasting that they could make a small batch of a new vaccine within sixty days of the medicine's design.

Before Bancel's vacation, the NIAID officials and Moderna executives decided they would put that promise of mRNA to the test by doing what they called a "stopwatch drill." They'd pick a virus to target and say go. NIAID would help Moderna design the vaccine. Moderna would make a batch and hand over the doses to NIAID, which would conduct a clinical trial. How fast could they do this? "It was really because we were thinking about pandemic preparedness prior to Covid," Mascola recalled later. "We were interested in rapid platforms that could be used to make vaccines. We viewed it as a proof of concept."

Moderna's bragging about producing small batches in sixty days was tantalizing enough to the feds that it was worth investigating. Chasing outbreaks with vaccines is a tricky, sometimes fruitless business, often because of a disconnect: the science of developing a cure takes a lot of time, whereas outbreaks in the past tended to flare and then fade before the development process could pan out. Even if someone could design a vaccine quickly, it would take, in the best case, months of testing, first in animals, then in humans, with studies that include placebo controls to determine if the vaccine was working and how well, and then months more to manufacture enough doses.

If the drill worked, it would show the world the disruptive nature of Moderna's technology, how it could develop treatments with unprecedented speed and the flexibility to adapt the process to other diseases as well. If it went poorly, Moderna would absorb the failure, adapt, and continue its march to getting a product on the market.

There was no shortage of candidates for the stopwatch drill, and that's one reason Fauci and NIAID wanted to do it. They were seeing an increasingly steady drumbeat of infectious disease outbreaks, brought on by more and more global travel. In addition to SARS in 2003, there was a swine flu in 2009, MERS in 2013, Ebola in 2014, and Zika in 2016. Sometimes, the virus was brand-new, like SARS. Other times, it was a known virus with an outbreak of unprecedented severity, such as Ebola.

Some of these diseases, like Ebola and Zika, earned a place on the World Health Organization's list of seven high-priority pathogens that should be the focus of effective drugs, vaccines, and diagnostic tests.

Added to the list of seven in 2018 was "Disease X"—shorthand for an unknown pathogen that could cause an international epidemic.[4]

By the time Bancel trekked to Cannes for his family vacation, Moderna and NIAID already had a stopwatch drill ready to go. NIAID decided the best pathogen to start with was the Nipah virus, a deadly bug that can cause fever and difficulty breathing. It was not currently a major threat but was typical of the types of threats the team was most concerned about. If the project showed that an effective mRNA vaccine could be quickly developed against Nipah, the technology might work for other infectious diseases, NIAID reasoned.

Bancel said that the only barrier with his board of directors would be cost, but that it could probably be done for under $1 million and Moderna would be game. Bancel said he would start to seek outside funding for the manufacturing costs.

But when Bancel and Graham saw the news of the mysterious virus in China—the feared Disease X—they thought it could replace Nipah in the drill, as it was a real-world threat, and success would have immediate benefits. A plan began to take shape.

Having infected hundreds and killed dozens, the virus made the leap to the United States in late January when a person who had traveled to China was diagnosed with an infection after he returned home to the

Seattle area.[5] But it still wasn't top of mind for many Americans, who were more focused on President Trump's first impeachment trial in the Senate over allegations that he abused his power by soliciting foreign interference in a US election. Trump himself didn't sound too concerned about the first US case. "We have it totally under control," he told CNBC in an interview. "It's one person coming in from China, and we have it under control. It's going to be just fine."[6]

Bancel didn't agree. He became convinced that the virus was going to spread widely, and that Moderna should go all in on the stopwatch test and pursuing a vaccine. He spent much of January trying to get this vaccine project off the ground, looking for outside help—scientifically and financially. He flew back to Boston from Cannes. Then on to San Francisco for the health care conference. Then to Switzerland, then Washington, DC, then back home.

To help with the financial risk, he turned to Richard Hatchett, an American living in the United Kingdom and serving as head of a Norway-based nonprofit started in 2017, the Coalition for Epidemic Preparedness Innovations (CEPI), whose mission was to fight disease outbreaks by providing quick, early funding for vaccine research. CEPI got much of its funding from foundations, including the Bill & Melinda Gates Foundation, as well as governments, including Norway's and India's.

Hatchett, a trained physician, spent much of his waking hours preparing for worst-case scenarios. As head of CEPI, Hatchett had already started to look for promising potential vaccine projects to fund. On January 20, 2020, he received an email from Bancel with the subject line "NCoV": "Hello Richard. I assume you know Barney [Graham] has been working on a vaccine using moderna mRNA. Is there a way we can do a very quick project to fund the Phase 1 and Phase 2 material with CEPI help? It would of course have to be a grant that gets granted in days if not we won't be able to move fast."

Bancel, still on the stopwatch drill, was hoping to telegraph to Hatchett that if CEPI couldn't cut a check quickly, it couldn't help.

Seven minutes later, Hatchett sent a reply: "Short answer is I think so. Our team was talking to Barney today and he had proposed we cover the

Phase 1 manufacturing." Hatchett said he had to talk to members of his board of directors to let them know. "Our legal team has a quick track agreement they say they think they can get in place in 48 hours."

Both men would see each other face-to-face within days in Davos, Switzerland, at the annual World Economic Forum event that brought corporate and government leaders from around the world to the scenic ski resort village in the Alps.

The featured guests at Davos in January 2020 included President Trump, who said the United States would join an international initiative to plant one trillion new trees, while dismissing climate activists as "prophets of doom." Another featured guest was Greta Thunberg, the teenager from Sweden who urged world leaders to get more serious about the climate emergency.[7] But in the hallways of the conference center and in the cafes of Davos, some attendees were whispering about another brewing emergency: Disease X.

Cases had risen to more than five hundred, resulting in nearly twenty deaths—a shocking 4 percent death rate for a fast-moving pathogen. When Hatchett bumped into other global-health specialists, they would trade comments like "Did you hear this? Oh my God, the number of cases has doubled again."

"The concern that we were dealing with something that could rapidly spin out of control was real," Hatchett said.

Hatchett and Bancel met at coffee bars and other spots across Davos a few times over two days, settling on a plan for CEPI to provide about $1 million to help Moderna manufacture a vaccine batch for testing.

Word began to trickle out that Moderna was embarking on the vaccine project. Anthony Fauci, director of NIAID, told a financial news service that his institute was working with Moderna to get the human study of the vaccine started within a record three-month time frame. The stopwatch drill had morphed into something more than a scientific exercise.[8]

Moderna issued a public statement confirming Fauci's comments, which sparked a 5 percent jump in Moderna's share price the next day, to $21.97, inching it closer to its original initial public offering (IPO) price of $23. It also ratcheted up the pressure on some Moderna employees. Bancel's top deputy, Moderna president Stephen Hoge, had previously assumed the company might be able to run its revised stopwatch drill quietly. But when Fauci disclosed the collaboration publicly, Hoge thought, "Now we're on the clock."

Bancel and Hatchett planned to make their own public announcement from Davos. But the night before they did, Bancel needed to make one last call to clear it.

Back in Boston, Moderna's chairman, Noubar Afeyan, was out for dinner with his daughter to celebrate her birthday when Bancel called from Davos. Afeyan, a venture capitalist who cofounded Moderna, excused himself, to his daughter's dismay, and took the call outside on a freezing night.

Bancel wanted Afeyan's blessing to agree to make vaccine doses available for human testing in exchange for funding from CEPI. "I'm here, they want me to commit to working on it," Afeyan recalls Bancel saying on the phone. "We don't have it in our program, we don't have any capital dedicated to it. What do you think?"

Afeyan told Bancel to proceed. "My rationale was that, given the visibility and the urgency, it would give us a unique opportunity to demonstrate one of the key advantages of our platform, which we had not previously had a chance to demonstrate," Afeyan recalled.

Afeyan's blessing in hand, Bancel signed the contract with CEPI on his iPhone, using DocuSign.

The next day at Davos, Bancel and Hatchett held their press conference. Hatchett said his hope was to start human trials of the vaccine as early as summer 2020.

"Trying to go so fast for a vaccine has never been done before," Bancel added. "We have never done it on a compressed time like we are doing now. Which is why we need to work together."

Bancel had completely pivoted to focus on this project. Rather than go home after Davos, he flew directly to Washington, DC, for meetings with government officials to flesh out the vaccine plans and find more money. He also paid a visit to the Food and Drug Administration (FDA).

The FDA would be responsible for evaluating whether any experimental Covid-19 vaccines worked safely enough for mass use. Two of Bancel's deputies met him at the FDA offices, Chief Scientific Officer Tal Zaks and the head of manufacturing, Juan Andres. They sat across the table from Marion Gruber, director of the FDA's vaccines unit; her superior, Peter Marks, head of the FDA's center for biologics evaluation and research, dialed in.

It was an unusual meeting. The FDA usually follows a rigid process of interacting with the drug companies it regulates. Normally, it can take months for a company to schedule an in-person meeting with the FDA. But in late January, the agency was growing concerned enough about the new coronavirus that an immediate ad hoc meeting made sense.

Bancel asked Gruber: If Moderna were successful in quickly developing and testing a vaccine, would it be possible for FDA to approve its use by the end of 2020?

"I really think that's nearly impossible," Zaks recalled Gruber saying.

"Is it *nearly* impossible or impossible? Because *nearly* impossible doesn't faze him," Zaks, said, referring to Bancel. Gruber responded that there may be ways other than standard FDA approval to get the vaccine deployed, like an authorization of emergency use. Tal Zaks left the meeting with the impression that the FDA was prepared for an unusually close level of interaction with Moderna and any other companies that might pursue Covid-19 vaccines. (Several others were beginning to investigate the possibility, including a German mRNA company called BioNTech SE, which would soon team up with US drug giant Pfizer Inc. on a project.) "That for me was a watershed moment," Zaks said. "Our sense of urgency is being matched by the agency's sense of urgency, and a collaborative way of working."

Despite these early steps, Moderna still hadn't made a full-on commitment to see this vaccine all the way through to the finish line, and not everyone at Moderna was as convinced as Bancel that it should. The executive leadership team was divided about how to proceed, or whether to do this at all. Most of the tension and spirited debate focused on whether this new virus would turn into a major pandemic—or fizzle away like past outbreaks. Bancel himself knew the stopwatch drill carried risk. It cost money and would move resources away from other projects. He had to be thinking about Moderna's difficult experience in 2016 trying to develop a Zika vaccine that never worked and then wasn't needed when the outbreak fizzled. Bancel had said he was "traumatized" by that experience.

Still, Bancel and a few other executives thought Moderna should try for a coronavirus vaccine because they suspected the outbreak would get much bigger. Noubar Afeyan thought making a vaccine would be a chance to show the world what Moderna was capable of. Others, including Hoge, the president, thought it was still quite possible the virus would fade away. And scrambling to make a coronavirus vaccine would divert resources from other promising projects. Should Moderna, a company with eight hundred employees, add yet another project to the twenty drugs and vaccines for various diseases that it was trying to advance in lab tests and clinical trials? It wasn't part of the plan for 2020.

Some executives felt conflicted, and a dearth of hard information about how the new virus behaved didn't help. At one meeting in the company's new manufacturing plant in Norwood, Massachusetts, some executives suggested finding some sort of "off ramp" to quietly exit the project, Bancel recalled, citing the bruising the company took from the doomed Zika effort four years earlier.

"Are we sure we should be doing this?" Hoge asked in one meeting. Would work on a promising vaccine for cytomegalovirus and rare disease treatments freeze if Moderna chose to pursue a Covid-19 vaccine? "My concern through the middle of February was: Are we going to go chasing after a rabbit that's not going to get anywhere in the end, and as a result take our eye off the ball on the thing that people are expecting us to do?" Hoge recalled later. "I was struggling with that."

Moderna's chief financial officer, Lorence Kim, worried about investors. Would they approve of the company shifting gears so quickly to take on a risky new vaccine project? No doubt some executives were thinking about the company's year-plus of disappointing stock market performance. If they went all in on this vaccine and it fizzled, and they found themselves even further off from viable products because they delayed promising projects for this, would the stock take another hit?

Moderna's board of directors also debated whether to proceed. Director Moncef Slaoui, formerly the longtime head of vaccine research at pharma giant GlaxoSmithKline (GSK), had mixed feelings. During his time at GSK, the company quickly scrambled during the 2009 flu pandemic to make a vaccine, but demand cratered when it became clear that the flu strain wasn't as serious as originally thought.

"The opportunity cost of dealing with a pandemic is enormous because you stop your other R&D projects for a year, and you risk going from a leader to a laggard," he said. Moderna was a much smaller company than GSK, and Slaoui thought the risk of taking on a coronavirus vaccine project was even more pronounced.

By early February, the news from China was severely concerning: Chinese authorities built two new hospitals in Wuhan in a matter of days to accommodate the growing number of people sickened by the virus.[9] Moderna should proceed, the board decided, though Slaoui still requested that Moderna try as much as possible to keep its other projects alive and advancing at the same time.

Though ultimately as CEO it was Bancel's decision—with the blessing of his board of directors—he spent more time trying to convince his deputies his decision was right. He knew he would be asking them to work nights and weekends. He wanted buy-in with their "brains and hearts." He tried to impress upon them how much faster this virus was spreading than past outbreaks like SARS and MERS.

Still, he knew that if he was wrong, and the virus faded away like Zika without need for a vaccine, it was his failure. His decision would have set back much of the rest of Moderna's R&D pipeline and he'd take the blame, and possibly the fall, for it.

Stephen Hoge seemed to remain unsure about the strategic decision. In his office in mid-February, Hoge acknowledged Moderna was working on a vaccine for this new coronavirus, but he minimized Moderna's role, perhaps still trying to square his own skepticism with the company's move. He said: "Our narrow part of it is to put our head down, work as hard as we can every day and get a vaccine to the US government so they can run a clinical study. . . . We're just a small part of this."

Bancel—stubborn, confident, impatient—had made up his mind. "This is going to be a big deal, we have to do something now," he told the skeptics. He felt Moderna had a once-in-a-lifetime opportunity to save lives, and prove its technology worked.

Either way, the stopwatch was running.

1

Changing the Fate

AS A KID, DERRICK ROSSI WANTED TO BE A VETERINARIAN. His house in suburban Toronto was always full of animals, and his older brother was always bringing more home—snakes, raccoons, owls, squirrels. Rossi was never scared; he felt connected to them.

But something shifted in the eleventh grade. His biology teacher, a recent college graduate, introduced him to the inner working of cells, and Rossi was captivated. He loved the idea that tiny molecules could be so sophisticated that their machinations determined what made a snake's skin look and feel different from an owl's plumage. He was awestruck by the notion that cells controlled all life on Earth.

Rossi took his newfound passion to the University of Toronto, where he studied molecular genetics, first as an undergrad and then as a graduate student. In the early 1990s, he left for Paris to study at the Institut Curie, which was seeking someone as excited about cells as Rossi was.

In Paris, he fell in with a group of expats, all in their twenties, all free spirits from Norway, the Netherlands, and other countries. He partied hard, slept little, and did his best to emulate the rock-and-roll lifestyle of his musical idol, David Bowie. For eighteen months, long-haired, sporting a soul patch, and wearing thrift-store bell-bottoms and shirts, he tore up Paris and strayed from his PhD work. He never finished and had to leave. A brief research stint in Texas got him back on track and soon enough he earned a PhD from the University of Helsinki in Finland, where his research involved manipulating the genetic makeup of mice.

PhD in hand, he started a postdoctoral fellowship at Stanford University, where he focused on stem cells—the all-purpose, immature cells in animals that divide to form more mature cells with specialized roles as an animal grows. Some of Rossi's early work at Stanford compared the blood-making stem cells in young and old mice and found age-related alterations in the cells that contributed to loss of immune function and the development of blood cancer. This finding added to the scientific understanding of why the immune system declines as animals, including humans, get older.

Nearly fifteen years after his Paris adventure, in 2007 Rossi landed a job on the prestigious faculty of Harvard Medical School in Boston, running a lab at the Harvard-affiliated Immune Disease Institute (IDI). There, he'd continue his research into stem cells, and, almost by accident, make a key discovery about messenger RNA.

The timing of Rossi's discovery of his love for cells in high school was fortuitous. This was the eighties, about four decades into a massively productive era for molecular biology, which had yielded multiple Nobel Prizes.[1]

The field jump-started in the 1950s with the discovery of the structure of deoxyribonucleic acid, or DNA. The identification of the unique double helix in the 1950s was one of the most important discoveries of the twentieth century.

DNA is the starting point, the part of our genetic makeup that stores the codes of life. It is a molecule that's present in all organisms. A mix of sugars and phosphates and base compounds, it largely resides in the nucleus of cells and holds the recipes for the proteins and other material that make an animal grow and stay alive. It contains the hereditary information that determines eye color and may cause your aunts and uncles on opposite sides of the family to argue over whether you look more like this grandfather or that grandmother.

Discovering DNA and what it looked like was sort of like finding a strange new power station. You can see it, and you can tell that it supplies power to a city, but you have no idea how it is transmitting power from the station to the places that need power. So, while scientists could see the double helix, they now needed to figure out *how* it got its information out to the body.

It didn't take long for scientists to learn that DNA itself doesn't really act on the important information it possesses. They homed in on another naturally occurring molecule that appeared to be serving as an intermediary between DNA and the actions it stored in its code: ribonucleic acid, or RNA. RNA shared much in common with DNA, including three of its four basic building blocks. But it also had a different fourth building block and, crucially, was found in single strands, not double helixes. There also seemed to be more than one type of RNA.

In 1961, scientists answered the question of how DNA got its instructions out. Several scientific papers published that year identified "messenger RNA," or mRNA, as the transport for copies of genetic information from the DNA in a cell nucleus to the outer portion of a cell.[2] Once transported, the mRNA causes the production of certain proteins.

Proteins, in turn, do the work. They handle innumerable essential biological tasks like digesting food, forming muscles—or, when they're in a virus, helping the pathogen get inside a human cell to replicate.

Derrick Rossi calls it the "trifecta of life" and sums it up simply: "DNA makes mRNA makes protein makes life."

These discoveries about DNA and RNA were valuable on their own, and they have become textbook teachings in biology. But scientists in recent decades also began to think about how this knowledge of the codes of life could be used to treat and prevent disease. There were a few primary ways people thought you could do this. One was to identify the genetic mutations that cause disease, then find drugs that could block or mitigate the mutations. One of the biggest advances in cancer in recent decades was the introduction in the 1990s of the drug Herceptin, which does exactly that. Herceptin interferes with a gene called HER2's ability to cause the growth of cancer cells. It has helped women with breast cancer live longer, especially among those who undergo surgery and take Herceptin to prevent the recurrence of tumors.[3]

Another approach is gene therapy, which delivers a "correct" copy of a gene—DNA—to a patient to replace a disease-causing, defective gene. This therapy has yielded new advances in treating hereditary vision loss and certain cancers.[4]

But a few researchers saw a third, more radical approach, which was to use RNA, or a synthetic version of it, as the treatment.

Sporadically researchers poked at this concept, trying to turn mRNA into medicine. In the 1980s scientists, including Douglas Melton at Harvard, synthesized mRNA and conducted small-animal experiments.[5] Another key advance came in the 1980s at the University of Wisconsin. Jon Wolff engineered some DNA and RNA that would trigger the production of luciferase—a common substance used in lab tests because of its luminescence. It's the stuff that makes fireflies glow. It's harmless on its own and provides no health benefits. All Wolff wanted to do was see if injecting the genetic material into a mouse's body triggered the production of the glowing enzyme.

It did. The muscles of Wolff's mice glowed, suggesting that you could give people new genetic material to spur production of new proteins. They published their findings in 1990 hoping to spur follow up studies.[6]

But not much happened for several years. Among few notable follow-ups was research published five years later describing a study in which David Curiel and colleagues at the University of Alabama at Birmingham showed that injecting mRNA into mice induced immune responses to a protein linked to cancer. But the work did not advance to testing in humans.

In 1997, an immunologist named Drew Weissman signed on at the University of Pennsylvania with a stacked résumé. Undergraduate and graduate degrees in biochemistry and enzymology at Brandeis University, followed by an MD and PhD in immunology and microbiology at Boston University, followed by seven years at NIAID, where he explored

HIV and the intricacies of how that deadly virus caused disease, under Director Anthony Fauci.

At Penn, Weissman focused on dendritic cells, immune cells that serve as a kind of gatekeeper. They help detect foreign intruders like viruses and shepherd the invaders to other parts of the immune system that work to destroy the infiltration.[7]

In those days, science was decidedly analog. Weissman kept up with cutting-edge research by taking scientific and medical journals from his department library to a copy machine near his lab, where he would make copies of the articles to read later when he had time.

At the copy machine he frequently ran into another Penn scientist, Katalin Karikó. Initially, they fought over who could print out their copies first, Weissman recalls. Soon curiosity took over and they got to talking about what they were working on.

Karikó was a molecular biologist who had been working on RNA for years. A native of Hungary, she earned a PhD in biochemistry there in the early 1980s when it was still part of the Soviet-dominated Eastern Bloc. Karikó came to Philadelphia in 1985 for a postdoctoral fellowship at Temple University before landing on the faculty across town at Penn.[8]

Karikó's journey to Penn was emblematic of a key ingredient in the ecosystem that has made the United States such a dominant player in science and the biotechnology industry. It attracts a healthy share of immigrant strivers, drawn to US universities, biotech companies, government labs, and venture capital (VC) firms. For example, scientists from Canada, the Sudan, and Hungary made key discoveries in American labs that paved the way for one company's founding. Engineers born in Lebanon and France would help cofound and lead the company. As it grew, immigrants from Israel, Spain, and Morocco would play key roles in its growth, along with American-born scientists, doctors, and financial pros with degrees from top US universities. That company is Moderna.

Karikó continued her mRNA work at Penn, but, as she most certainly told Weissman, it was a tough sell to her superiors. She was even demoted in the mid-1990s for failing to attract sufficient funding for her work. This was when Wolff's Wisconsin paper about glowing mice muscles was making zero waves, and the attitude among Karikó's administrators helps to explain why. They viewed mRNA as an obscure field with few practical applications.

Despite the setbacks, she persisted, convinced there was value in her research.

Karikó told Weissman at the copier that she was experimenting with mRNA by injecting it into cancer cells in the lab to see if those cells produced certain proteins to fight the cancer. Weissman was intrigued. He thought it would be worth trying the same thing with his dendritic cells. Karikó gave him some mRNA.

The results were "off the wall," Weissman recalls. The dendritic cells produced the proteins he wanted them to, often either luciferase or other glowing proteins.

A collaboration between Weissman and Karikó emerged. Both saw potential to deliver something more than just glowing enzymes into organisms—things like disease treatments. mRNA seemed to have a lot going for it: it wouldn't hang around for long after it did its job, and it wouldn't alter a person's genome and cause unintended side effects, as some other gene-based therapies did. One gene-based therapy had been found in a study in France to cause leukemia-type illnesses. mRNA also didn't need to be spliced into a virus-based delivery vector like other gene treatments, which often meant working with biohazards in tightly controlled biosafety facilities.

But as always happens in science, problems emerged. Weissman and Karikó found that delivering mRNA inside cells—in petri dishes at first, later in animals—would trigger inflammation, which could lead to serious side effects if it were ever deployed as a treatment. The immune system viewed the outside RNA as a foreign threat. And in later testing, high doses of RNA would kill mice. To some it seemed to validate the years of skepticism following the Wisconsin study and even seemed to thwart the possibility that RNA could be used as a drug or a vaccine.

Not to Weissman and Karikó. They modified the mRNA and found that making a tweak to the composition of a nucleoside—a building block of RNA—helped mRNA sidestep the immune reaction that would cause inflammation, while still allowing the RNA to get into cells to deliver instructions to start producing a desired protein. Essentially, their modification put the RNA into stealth mode, helping it sneak past a cell's antiviral defense to deliver its protein-making genetic information.

Weissman and Karikó published their findings in 2005 in the journal *Immunity*. They concluded that their findings could help scientists better understand certain diseases and "give future directions into the design of therapeutic RNAs." Though their lab experiments were far from achieving it, they believed that their modifications to RNA could one day help combat human disease.[9]

Penn took out patents based on their work, naming Karikó and Weissman as inventors, with the thought that the patents could be of use to a new or existing company. Universities and some scientists were becoming increasingly aware of the importance (and value) of their research and the need to patent it if they wanted the work to be translated into a commercial enterprise.

But this was a two-edged sword for Karikó and Weissman. Their early effort to create a company, called RNARx, never gained traction. Penn owned the right to their work and RNARx wasn't able to secure a license for the patents. Penn later licensed the technology to another company, CellScript, which had a different plan. They only used the patents to make kits that help others make mRNA for clinical research.[10]

Penn also issued a press release about the research in 2005. It received little outside attention.[11]

"The whole way was roadblocks," Weissman recalls. "The world wasn't really interested in mRNA."

A few years after Karikó and Weissman published their pivotal research Derrick Rossi was at Harvard working on his stem cells. An ambitious faculty member in his early forties, he still sported a soul patch and thick, wavy hair. But instead of tearing up France, Rossi was leading a lab of about ten scientists, and he was eager to make his mark.

The promise of stem cells is that they can generate healthy cells to replace damaged cells in people, and potentially treat difficult diseases like type 1 diabetes, or injuries like spinal cord damage. One tantalizing line of stem cell research has been the study of stem cells taken from human embryos, which are promising because they can become almost any other type of cell. But this research creates deep ethical divides because the cells come from eggs that were fertilized at in-vitro clinics, but which were never implanted in a woman. Harvesting the stem cells destroys the embryo.

To sidestep this controversy, scientists began to explore ways to reprogram adult stem cells so that they approached the same all-purpose status as embryonic stem cells.

Rossi knew that a Japanese scientist named Shinya Yamanaka found he could reprogram mature mouse cells by splicing in certain genes, causing them to revert to immature cells, known as pluripotent stem cells. Once they reverted, they could be guided to become other types of cells such as nerve, heart, or gut cells. This finding raised the prospect that scientists could take a person's cells from skin or blood and turn them into other types to treat disease. In molecular biology, this was known as changing the fate of a cell.

The four special genes that enabled the transformation—the genes that kept embryonic stem cells immature—came to be known as Yamanaka factors—and earned Yamanaka and others the Nobel Prize in 2012.[12]

Rossi was inspired when he read the publication of Yamanaka's key findings in the journal Cell in 2006.[13] He also saw its limitations. Yamanaka used a type of virus, a retrovirus, to serve as a sort of courier to carry DNA into the adult mouse cells to trigger their transformation into immature cells. Viruses are very good at getting inside cells, and so a virus engineered to carry the four genes—the Yamanaka factors—was an understandable approach. But a limitation was that this transformation permanently altered the DNA in the cells, which could cause unintended side effects and new diseases. What's more, the method wasn't terribly efficient—many of the targeted cells never turned into pluripotent stem cells.

Rossi wondered how he might solve these problems, eventually considering messenger RNA as a solution. If the mRNA were coded for the Yamanaka factors, it would get inside a cell to start the cell's transformation without altering the cell's DNA.

It was an intriguing idea, but he gave it long odds. RNA degrades much more easily than DNA; the body's own defenses could easily break it down before it was able to do its job.

Still, Rossi decided to give it a shot. He was aware of the similar research that was already done elsewhere, but he wanted to make sure that he and his colleagues could reliably deliver synthetic mRNA that would cause protein production in cells. He wouldn't start with Yamanaka factors; first he wanted to see if mRNA was up to the task of delivering anything to the body. Rossi and his team tried a simple experiment. They used mRNA that was coded for GFP, or green fluorescent protein, which glows green under certain wavelengths of light. GFP was first isolated from a jellyfish. GFP has no health benefits and was harmless enough to use for testing.

The researchers placed the mRNA in petri dishes full of cells and turned the special lamp emitting the right wavelength on the dish.

Rossi saw a lot of green cells, which meant the mRNA successfully caused some cells to produce GFP. But he also saw a lot of dead cells. The results were mixed.

"We thought, 'Geez, what's going on here? Why are we killing all these cells?'" Rossi recalled. More work helped the team realize that when synthetic mRNA entered cells, the cells interpreted it as a viral infection and mustered their natural defenses to destroy the RNA, which also often destroyed the cells themselves, like destroying a house with water damage when putting out a fire.

The long odds seemed right, and in that moment Rossi might well have decided to move on from mRNA in search of another way to get Yamanaka factors into the body. But some of the cells did turn green. Rossi decided not to give up.

A breakthrough came, as they often do, by accident. Some of Rossi's lab workers were chatting about their work with colleagues from another lab, one of whom happened to know about a paper from a couple of Penn researchers that came out a few years before. They should look it up.

It was Weissman and Karikó's paper on stealth mRNA. Rossi couldn't believe it. This might be the answer and it was just sitting there. "Nobody paid attention to it," Rossi recalls. "We dug it up."

That's all Rossi needed. His lab just wanted to fix the problem that caused mRNA to kill as many or more cells as it made glow. If he could do that, he might be able to convert stem cells.

Rossi and his lab workers put the Penn research to work in their lab, running centrifuges to separate various molecules by spinning them, polymerase chain reaction machines to amplify and analyze tiny bits of genetic material, and incubators to warm cell cultures. They used proteins that glowed green in the mice, which came from a colony kept in the lab, and which were anesthetized so they would stay still under ultrasensitive cameras that could detect green glowing proteins.

In his lab in 2008 and 2009, by tweaking the composition of a nucleoside as Weissman and Karikó had done, Rossi and his team succeeded in using mRNA to produce Yamanaka factors to turn mature cells into immature stem cells. They transformed skin cells into muscle cells without killing the cells. They had changed the fate.

The results were later published in the journal *Cell Stem Cell* in 2010. "In light of these considerations, we believe that our approach has the potential to become a major enabling technology for cell-based therapies and regenerative medicine," the researchers wrote.[14]

Now it was Rossi's turn to think about turning his academic research into a company.

At academic medical centers, doctors and scientists tend to carry multiple affiliations and titles. Rossi, for example, wore three hats: he was an associate professor in the department of stem cell and regenerative biology at Harvard Medical School, a principal faculty member at the Harvard Stem Cell Institute, and an investigator at the Immune Disease Institute.[15]

At the IDI, professors had a custom of meeting for lunch every other Thursday. Nothing fancy, just a casual gathering in a windowless room on the Harvard Medical School campus. At each lunch, a professor would get a turn to informally present what they were up to in their lab.

In early 2010, it was Rossi's turn to present at the faculty lunch. He described his work on using modified mRNA to turn mature cells into immature stem cells, noting that they had indeed changed the fate of cells.

After lunch, one colleague approached Rossi and said to him: "Did you ever just make your career."

Ryan Dietz thought so too. He was also at the lunch, a lawyer working for the "tech transfer" office at IDI. His job was to scout for promising research that could be patented, and to look for opportunities to sell the rights to big drug companies, or to help arrange startup companies based on the research. Tech transfer had become a core function at many academic medical centers after the passing of the Bayh-Dole Act of 1980, legislation that allowed universities to hold ownership of patents for research conducted at the universities that was funded by the federal government.[16] Tech transfer is designed to help researchers, of course, but also to ensure that the institutions sponsoring the research got a cut of the profits. It's what got Weissman and Karikó's research into CellScript. Under tech transfer, the number of startups launched from university research surpassed six hundred in 2010, triple what it had been in 1996.[17]

Dietz was scouting up to fifteen new technologies from the IDI's labs each year, exploring all avenues of commercializing their research. Even so, many never went anywhere.

Still, Dietz thought Rossi's research would be a good bet. It could spur a whole new way of making drugs. For that reason, he thought, rightly, that Rossi should go the startup route, since it was less likely that a Big Pharma company would take a chance on something so fundamentally different (and frankly, disruptive) to what they did. What's more, Dietz liked Rossi, whom he found personable, honest, and smart, and, to his great relief, showed little of the pretentious attitude he encountered in many successful scientists and entrepreneurs.

Not long after the lunch Dietz and Rossi went networking. Throughout the spring and summer of 2010, Dietz introduced Rossi to players with strong scientific credentials or fat wallets, or both. They hopped from Harvard and MIT to venture capital offices in downtown Boston, to Cambridge restaurants like Legal Sea Foods and famed Henrietta's Table in the Charles Hotel in Harvard Square, the site of many deals.

"Go meet Tim," Dietz told Rossi in the spring of 2010. He meant Timothy Springer, a biochemist on the faculty of Harvard Medical School since the 1970s, who had made key discoveries that led to new treatments for the skin disorder plaque psoriasis. Springer started his own company, LeukoSite, and made $100 million when it merged with Millennium Pharmaceuticals in 1999.[18]

With his earnings, Springer began to invest in other biotech startups and developed a reputation as a connected, savvy investor. He still stayed in academia, but was also active in biotech, venture capital and, eventually, philanthropy.

The two met at Springer's Harvard office in late April 2010. Rossi shared his lunch presentation. It was a choppy encounter at first. Rossi wasn't able to speak for long without Springer interrupting him with questions. Springer took lots of notes.

"He was being really aggressive towards me," Rossi recalls. "It was a very odd meeting. He was challenging me on anything, in a way that was weirdly uncomfortable." Springer asked Rossi if he was certain that using mRNA wouldn't alter the genome of cells. Rossi said yes, that was the case. He asked if he really converted mature cells into pluripotent stem cells. Rossi answered yes. Did he have patents? Application filed, Rossi said. As the meeting went on and the questions piled up, Rossi could feel a rejection coming.

When Rossi finished, Springer said, "This is great. I want to invest."

The aggressive questioning was interest, not skepticism. Springer recalls the tenor of the meeting but for him it was unremarkable. "I'm known for giving careful scrutiny to people who present."

Stunned, relieved, and excited, Rossi had cleared his first hurdle. A seasoned biotech investor with the best connections to other investors was on board to help get his new company off the ground.

Springer, a solo investor, was eager to write a check but he wanted others to get on board so they had enough funds for office space and more resources than Springer alone could afford. So, they went looking for a venture capital firm to get involved. Dietz and Rossi first visited Third Rock Ventures, a relatively new VC firm in Boston that was one of a cluster that had set up shop to focus on biotech startups in a region with some of the best hospitals and best research universities.

At the time, 2010, the market for IPOs—a common pathway for VCs to making their initial investments pay off—was iffy, still reeling from the Great Recession. But it wasn't dead. A drug company called Ironwood Pharmaceuticals raised nearly $190 million in an IPO that year that valued the company at more than $1 billion.[19] That was good for Rossi. If he could start a new company and eventually approach those numbers, it would be a success.

But Third Rock wasn't interested in taking the gamble. All of Rossi's data was generated from manipulating cells in petri dishes, they told him. He had no evidence of his concept working in animals, much less humans, making this a bigger risk than other potential investments in the soft market. What's more, Rossi was still a junior faculty member at Harvard, and an unknown entity to the VC firm.

Rossi needed an injection of credibility, so Springer called Robert Langer, a longtime professor at MIT.

Langer was a giant in biotech, known as "the Edison of medicine."[20] He was trained as a chemical engineer, studying first at Cornell and then at MIT in the early 1970s. Many of his chemical-engineering friends used their degrees to get jobs with oil companies, looking to capitalize on the rising gas prices in that inflationary decade. Langer wasn't interested. He wanted to focus on drug-delivery technology. He believed he could build better ways to control the delivery of active ingredients in medicine so that they got to the part of the body they were supposed to when they were supposed to. Langer ran into early resistance. He was rejected for research grants. He struggled to find faculty positions, until MIT took him on as a biochemical engineer. They would get the last laugh. At MIT, Langer would rack up fourteen hundred issued and pending patents which would be licensed or sublicensed to more than four hundred drug and medical-device companies. He earned the Queen Elizabeth Prize for Engineering, handed to him by Her Majesty in a 2015 ceremony. He helped found multiple biotech startups and served on many company boards of directors, such as Wyeth, the drug giant that was swallowed up by Pfizer in 2009.

Springer thought getting Langer involved would give the venture the credibility that Third Rock felt was lacking with Rossi fronting it. Soon after his Third Rock rejection, Rossi paid a visit to Langer's office at MIT and made his pitch surrounded by the plaques and awards that covered Langer's walls.

Unlike Springer, Langer was mostly quiet during the presentation. Rossi remembers only a few interjections from Langer, along the lines of "Oh wow." "Cool." "Neat."

Langer recalls that his mind went to using induced pluripotent stem cells to repair damaged tissue or organs. "But as I was listening to it," Langer says, "to me the exciting thing was maybe you could make new drugs. My thinking was, 'Boy, this could be great.'"

It was a different meeting than the one with Springer, but it ended the same way: "This is terrific," Langer said to Rossi. "What can I do to help?"

Rossi invited Langer to be a company cofounder because of Langer's experience in biotech and his expertise in drug-delivery technology which was going to be important if they were to sneak mRNA into human cells to do their job. Langer accepted Rossi's invitation. "I remember going home and telling my wife, 'This is going to be a really big deal,'" he recalls.

So now whatever shortcomings Rossi felt at being a junior faculty member were compensated for with a deep-pocketed individual investor in Tim Springer, and an influential biotech veteran in Bob Langer who would be a cofounder and board member.

But Rossi wasn't an MD, and neither was Langer. The team still needed a doctor with clinical training and deeper understanding of disease to further assuage the skepticism of the VCs.

Rossi happened to attend a colleague's wedding that spring, where he met Kenneth Chien, a Harvard Medical School faculty member who specialized in heart research. Chien was a third-generation Harvard grad who got his medical degree and doctorate from Temple in Philadelphia. He had advised biotech and pharma companies like Genentech, Roche, and GlaxoSmithKline on drug development and had led cardiovascular research at the Harvard-affiliated Massachusetts General Hospital. Like Rossi, Chien made some discoveries in stem cell research, including identifying a master cardiac stem cell capable of changing into various cell types in hearts.

The wedding meeting was brief and informal, but enough to spur a more formal introduction from their newly married colleague afterward, who connected them by email, and mentioned both Langer and the mRNA idea. "We've played around with it, and I think it is going to be transformative," the colleague wrote. "It works better and faster than other methods and leaves the genome completely unmarked. This technology can also be used more generally for delivering almost any gene to any cell. . . . I hope you guys get together and make some hay."

Chien agreed to be a cofounder. The medical credibility was in place.

Rossi was at the same time working another of Springer's and Langer's contacts, the VC firm Flagship Ventures. Langer suggested Rossi speak to Flagship's leader, Noubar Afeyan.

Afeyan was born to Armenian parents in Lebanon in the early 1960s. They fled to Canada after the outbreak of Lebanon's civil war when he was thirteen. He went to high school in Montreal and studied chemical engineering at McGill University. He took summer jobs with Union

Carbide and DuPont. He won a grant from a Canadian science foundation to go to the United States and continue chemical engineering at MIT, where he studied why certain bacteria were able to ingest a plant material called cellulose and produce ethanol as a by-product—a potential alternative source of energy. Afeyan earned his PhD at the age of twenty-four, successfully defending his thesis in front of a committee that included Bob Langer.

Afeyan could have set up a comfortable life in academia, but he didn't—in part because of a chance encounter in 1985 with a giant of American business: David Packard, Hewlett's partner, and one of the early great tech titans of Silicon Valley.

They met at a conference, where a young Afeyan sat next to Packard, then in his seventies, at lunch and soaked up everything Packard said about how to start and run a business. Packard told Afeyan to focus on the needs of the customer, not solely on the technology itself. "It was more important to understand what the need was, versus what the technology was," Afeyan recalls Packard saying. "It was much harder as an engineer to figure out what it is people need and want." Packard was neither aloof nor arrogant. He spoke about these things in a human, relatable way, leaving a deep impression on Afeyan. He decided starting companies was what he wanted to do.

Afeyan's first venture was an effort to improve upon the laboratory equipment and instruments he had used during his research. He knew what the customer needed because he had been that customer. He cofounded and led PerSeptive Biosystems Inc., a maker of lab instruments for biotech companies and other research organizations.

He liked to push the envelope. In the 1990s, the company gained a reputation for aggressive sales tactics, including delivering expensive equipment to customers and letting them try it for free. If they didn't like it, they could return it. Afeyan told the *Wall Street Journal* in 1994 it was part of a strategy to "seed the market" with equipment. Once in place, that equipment needed disposable cartridges to operate. The more machines he could get into the market, the more cartridges PerSeptive could sell. It's a classic business tactic honed by Gillette, among others. You don't make money on the razors; you make it on the blades.[21]

He was perhaps too aggressive. After acknowledging that it had improperly recorded sales and made other accounting errors that inflated reported sales and profits, PerSeptive had to restate two years' worth of earnings.[22] Later, the Securities and Exchange Commission alleged that a PerSeptive sales and marketing executive booked sales that weren't finalized, among other improper practices. The executive later reached a settlement with the SEC without admitting or denying the allegations.[23]

At the time, Afeyan said the company's growth "outgrew its internal control systems."

The business practices didn't sink the company, which corrected itself and still posted strong sales growth. In 1998 PerSeptive was acquired by PerkinElmer, another large maker of lab instruments, for about $360 million.[24] Afeyan, who had already begun to help start other companies, took his windfall and moved into venture capital.

He founded Newcogen, which a few years later combined with other VC firms to become Flagship Ventures and then Flagship Pioneering. Over time, Flagship moved from investing in other companies to focus exclusively on incubating: creating companies in-house and running them for a few years before bringing in new investors. Flagship has founded more than one hundred companies. Since 2013, twenty-five have had initial public offerings.[25]

At Flagship, Rossi, with IDI lawyer Dietz along, first met with a partner named Doug Cole in late May 2010. Rossi showed Cole a presentation: "Reprogramming to Pluripotency and Directed Differentiation Using Synthetic mRNA." The presentation ran through all the science, from the stem cell work by Yamanaka, to the glowing cells, to the potential of changing the fate of cells with modified mRNA.

Then it set the market potential. Rossi proposed three revenue models for his research. One would be to market it as a research tool, to help other scientists reprogram cells. He projected this market at $1.4 billion by 2013, from under $1 billion in 2008—a modest rate of growth for a startup opportunity.

The second model was customized work for drug companies, such as generating cells for drug screening and testing drugs for toxicity. This market, Rossi suggested, would be $8.5 billion by 2016. Better.

Rossi saved his most lucrative market for last: therapeutics. He envisioned his research being used to directly treat disease. This work could be done by partnering with other drug companies to develop drugs or by going it alone and making proprietary drugs in-house. Rossi's slide deck put the value of this market at $15 to $20 billion by 2025.[26]

The presentation included some other details to iron out, too: the Immune Disease Institute owned the intellectual property on his work, which is why Dietz was there, but the institute would license it to Rossi's company in exchange for up-front payments and royalties on future product sales. And GlaxoSmithKline, a large UK pharmaceutical company, had a deal in place to get a first look at many of the new inventions at the Immune Disease Institute.[27]

Cole showed interest and said he'd consult with the other partners. They must have been interested too, because a month later the team scored a meeting with Flagship founder Afeyan. Afeyan remembers that the Edison of Medicine, Langer, asked him to come to MIT to see the presentation. Rossi knew that Langer would impress Flagship. Afeyan brought Cole with him for the meeting.

Afeyan seemed interested and was excited about exploring the potential of mRNA, but not so much in Rossi's core area, the stem cell application. "I did not think Derrick's work and desire to develop products based on stem cells was exciting," Afeyan recalled.

Afeyan was most enamored of the idea of using mRNA as a treatment. Afeyan asked Langer if anyone had used mRNA as a drug, stem cells aside, and Langer said no. Afeyan says he started calling around and asking if other drug companies had tried mRNA as a drug. He couldn't find any examples of companies significantly advancing the technology, likely because of the issue of cells mounting an antiviral defense against outside mRNA. Flagship's website in 2021 claimed Afeyan envisioned "a different use" of engineered mRNA as a new kind of medicine—not Rossi's use of mRNA to reprogram cells into stem cells—though how this is a different use than what Rossi suggested with the third revenue stream in his slide presentation is unclear.[28]

When Rossi had pitched Langer, Langer asked him how he might help. Afeyan and Cole simply told him how they would help: Flagship was prepared to become a cofounder of the company. Rossi agreed.

That finalized the slate of four cofounders: Derrick Rossi, the junior faculty member eager to make his mark who had the idea and the research; Bob Langer, the Edison of Medicine who brought deep connections in biotech; Ken Chien, the doctor Rossi bumped into at a wedding and who, like Rossi, researched stem cells and brought medical credibility; and Flagship Ventures, the deep pockets who knew how to start and grow companies. Tim Springer was not a cofounder, but he also chipped in some of his own money for an ownership stake. Flagship also got an ownership stake as did the Immune Disease Institute. The initial funding from Flagship and Springer was relatively small by VC standards, just a couple million dollars; memories differ over exact amounts. The individual scientific cofounders—Rossi, Langer and Chien—were granted minority ownership stakes. They would continue to work in academia but advise the company via consulting contracts and they'd serve on either the board of directors or the board of scientific advisers. Afeyan at Flagship would be chairman of the board.

Ryan Dietz, the tech-transfer lawyer who helped Rossi get going, wasn't allowed to invest as an employee of the IDI. He was still less than a decade out of law school, but he recognized something special. "At that point in my career, it felt like this was the biggest thing I had done. It turns out it's the biggest thing I'll ever do."

The overlapping of scientists, entrepreneurs, VC, and doctors and their attendant cultures isn't an easy thing to get right, Dietz says. "The interests only rarely align. There are so many competing views, knowledge bases, different expectations. To get something truly translatable and bring it to a startup company, that's a pretty rare occurrence."

There was one more matter to deal with: What to call this new company? In those early days, Rossi and the others used the placeholder "NewCo," a common term for an unnamed startup. Flagship contributed to the venture what was essentially a shell company it had incorporated in Delaware in 2009, which it called "Newco LS18 Inc."—the eighteenth life sciences company Flagship helped start.[29] Rossi first thought he wanted the name to allude to "messenger" because of his use of messenger RNA. But he thought "Messenger Therapeutics" was boring. He also considered "Harbinger," but rejected it as too sinister after learning that its original meaning in medieval times was someone who went ahead to find quarters for a roving army.

Then Rossi remembered that in the lab, he and his colleagues used "mod-RNA" as shorthand when taking notes about the modified messenger RNA they were using. He liked it, but wasn't sure about the use of the hyphen, so he swapped in the letter *e* for the dash to form the portmanteau ModeRNA. He liked that it included *modified* and *RNA*, but also that you could kind of see the word *modern*, too. He mentioned it to his wife one night, who agreed it was good.

All he had to do was an online search to see if he was too late to stake a claim. He found a furniture outlet in the Netherlands using that name. No worries there. "Moderna Designs" was the name of a fictional high-tech appliance maker in the 1980s fantasy movie *Time Bandits*, which he had forgotten, although he knew the film since it was directed by one of his favorite filmmakers, Terry Gilliam. Still, not an issue. And there was a Mexican conglomerate called Empresas La Moderna SA, commonly abbreviated to Moderna, whose products included cigarettes.

None of this seemed to interfere with his project, so he went with it. Initially, a press release issued by Children's Hospital Boston (now Boston Children's Hospital) in September 2010 that touted the publication of Rossi's research noted that Rossi had formed a company called ModeRNA Therapeutics.[30] The name would later lose the capitalization of the *RNA* part. The word *therapeutics* would stick for years but was ultimately dropped just before the company went public.

Tucked in a press release, the company description signaled great ambition, which Rossi elaborated on in a video interview from about the same time: "In terms of therapeutics, any genetic disease that involves a mutation of a gene that doesn't make a certain protein, we can now approach that with this technology to reintroduce that protein into those cells and re-establish proper function to those cells," he said. "So we think that this is going to be really important for many avenues, therapeutic avenues in addition to basic questions of biology."[31]

Though it's jargony to most of us, Rossi was describing something quite profound. ModeRNA Therapeutics wouldn't just be a one-trick pony biotech startup, betting big on a single new drug. Instead, it could be a "platform" company whose new way of making drugs could yield dozens—or even hundreds—of new drugs. It would be a new kind of biotech, something so different and so revolutionary that it would allow this startup to disrupt an industry of behemoths.

Afeyan looks back on the time with wonder. "It was really just a whim, if you will, or a leap of faith that says, 'Can this even be done, and why has no one done this before?'"

2

If This Is True

FLAGSHIP VENTURES SUBLEASED SOME SPACE FROM A biotech firm in Cambridge for a "clean room"—an area designed to keep out contaminants so experiments wouldn't be tainted. It was in a basement, through double air-locked doors. You had to close the first doors before opening the second, to keep the dirty air from the hallway out of the clean room. A pressurized ventilation system filtered out whatever air did get in. Through the second doors was a modest-sized windowless room. When Jason Schrum arrived there in the fall of 2010 it was completely empty, save for one ventilation hood, a brawnier, more sophisticated version of the hood you'd find over a kitchen stove.

That summer, Schrum, then in his late twenties and resembling the actor Neil Patrick Harris, had become a Flagship entrepreneurial fellow, a program for young scientists who wanted a taste of the startup life in biotech. He had a PhD in biological chemistry and molecular pharmacology from across town at Harvard. He also had a desire to get out of academia to develop drugs—and maybe companies.

Flagship sent him to the basement clean room to work on mRNA. For several months he worked there, alone.

He must have impressed, because his fellowship was followed by a consulting gig and when that ended, Flagship hired him as Moderna employee number one in November 2010. Company operations had commenced. And then Schrum . . . kept doing what he had been doing. Mostly his job was to find ways to improve upon the performance of mRNA. He likened it to a balancing act: he needed to make it more stable, holding together long enough to do its job, but not so long that it caused complications. For months he ran experiments, alone in the basement.

It was tough on him. "I didn't feel like I had a whole lot of support," he said. "It felt a little isolating. I was there working all the time. At night. I felt like I almost lived there."

One of the few people to visit Schrum in these early months was one of Flagship's patent attorneys. The lawyer wanted to know when any discovery was made that Moderna should try to patent. Already Moderna had patents on some of Rossi's earlier work, but a startup needs to build a portfolio of them to protect its research and help raise money. Investors follow the inventions. They want to see intellectual property that will allow exclusive selling of drugs and block competition, competition that would be trying to do the same. Even at this early stage, Moderna's founders knew they had competition. A German company, CureVac, also was trying to develop mRNA.[1]

Eventually Schrum and the lawyer put together what would become a series of patent applications covering claimed inventions in the arcane world of biotechnology, like modifications to nucleosides and engineering of nucleic acids.

(The same patent attorney also visited Drew Weissman and Katalin Karikó at Penn to inquire about licensing the Penn patents based on their work, Weissman recalled. But Penn had licensed them to another company and the lawyer couldn't reach an agreement to sublicense the patents. In their final meeting, the lawyer said Flagship and its new venture would find a way to "get around" Penn's patents and "left in a huff," Weissman said.)

But even with occasional visits from the patent lawyer, Schrum's was soul-crushing, solitary work. Befitting his basement setting, Schrum felt left in the dark for months, with no idea what his lab work would lead to. "I felt like it was me a lot of the time showing, here's all this stuff I did. I just wasn't entirely clear on where this was going as a company. How am

I fitting into all of this?" One of the reasons he had taken the fellowship at Flagship in the first place, and then agreed to become the first employee of Moderna, was to learn what it takes to build a new company. "That was very important to me. What wasn't important was being in a lab all the time by myself."

During these early months, Flagship was overseeing Moderna until it could find a permanent CEO and walk on its own two feet. It was a fine setup so long as it was temporary. Flagship eventually needed its people raising money for new funds, overseeing investments in other startups, and exiting other investments through acquisition and IPO.

From the start, Flagship's chief Noubar Afeyan had someone in mind to become Moderna's permanent CEO, a director with whom he served on another company's board: Stéphane Bancel. At the time, Bancel's day job was CEO of bioMerieux, a family-owned diagnostics equipment maker based in France with operations in many countries.

It would surprise most who grew up with him in Marseille in the south of France that Bancel would one day run a health care company. At school, he earned C's and D's in biology to the disappointment of his mother, a physician. His dyslexia made the class difficult for him, but he did excel in other subjects he loved, like math and physics. He also loved tinkering with computers, which were just emerging as he came of age in the late seventies and early eighties. Around age ten, Bancel got an early Texas Instruments computer for Christmas, and he quickly learned programming languages. Eventually he would decide to study engineering. He would be following in the footsteps of his engineer father, though Bancel doesn't see that as what drove him toward it. Rather, he says, it was the fact that he did well in math and physics that led to his decision. (His brother, Christophe, also would study engineering, and later founded and led a medical-device company in France.)

Bancel attended École Central Paris, a school devoted to science and engineering with highly selective admissions.[2] Gustave Eiffel was one of its early graduates. Bancel specialized in chemical and biomolecular engineering and would receive both undergraduate and master's degrees in engineering from the French school. While there, he also took up Japanese and developed a love for the language.

At the time, France still had a compulsory military service requirement for young men, but engineers could defer military service if they went to work for a French company overseas. Bancel looked up all the French companies with subsidiaries in Japan. He wrote to more than a dozen such companies. Only three replied. One was bioMerieux, which gave Bancel a summer internship in Tokyo. That led to a full-time job, starting after Bancel got a master's degree in engineering at the University of Minnesota in 1995—his second master's.[3]

Bancel started sales teams in Japan, Korea, China, and Australia. He worked his way up at bioMerieux to become head of the industrial microbiology business for its Asia-Pacific region. He continued taking classes in Japanese in Tokyo.

Every career decision he made was part of a calculated approach to reach a goal he set for himself early on. If he had his way, he would land a CEO job. He liked the idea of making things happen, combining all the elements of a company to make it work as a whole, even across continents.

"One day, somebody will have to make a decision about me getting a CEO job," Bancel described his thinking later. "Most probably, you're going to have a lot of candidates you can choose from, because the world is a competitive place, and there are a lot of smart people out there. And how do I make sure I'm not the bridesmaid? How do I make sure that I'm not the person that is almost selected but doesn't get the role?" He told himself he was playing the long game. Chess, not checkers. He knew that, even if he planned meticulously and everything went right, a CEO job might be twenty years away.[4]

Bancel, a trained engineer, ran the bioMerieux business unit in Asia on instinct and common sense. But he knew that to reach his goal, he needed a more formal business education, so he returned to the United States in 1999 to get an MBA at Harvard Business School. He was drawn to its famed case-study method of teaching, which he much preferred over listening to lectures. At HBS he was something of an outlier. It was near the peak of the dot-com bubble and many of his classmates were dropping out to join startups. Most who stayed leaned toward investment-banking jobs. Bancel did neither. He stayed, got his degree, and sought out another role in health care, inspired as he still was by some of the genetics and, yes, biology classes he'd taken as an undergraduate some years before, atoning for his poor performance in high school.

HBS led to work for Eli Lilly, first at the drugmaker's Indianapolis headquarters and then at its United Kingdom and Belgium outposts. He helped run Lilly's supply chain and manufacturing strategy. He married an American woman, an advertising agency worker-turned-photographer named Brenda, whom he first met when she was living in Paris, and he was still a Harvard Business School student. Their two daughters were born while they were living in Indianapolis.

In 2006, Bancel was offered the job of running Lilly's Japan business, and he began to prepare for the move, he later recalled. But before he left, the chairman of bioMerieux, his first employer, reached out to him: he was looking to groom someone as a new CEO.

Bancel jumped at the opportunity—first taking a high-ranking job that would prep him for the top job. In 2007, he was elevated to CEO. He had achieved his goal. The long game wasn't so long after all. He was thirty-four.

He ran the company from its Lyon, France, headquarters for two years. Sales and profits increased. But he found that he was spending a lot of time in the United States to scout for innovative new diagnostics businesses for bioMerieux to acquire. So he opened a bioMerieux office in Cambridge, Massachusetts, and in 2008 moved with his family to Boston, every day making the short commute across the Charles River. He flew back to France to check in at bioMerieux's headquarters about once a month.

Like Bancel, Noubar Afeyan was ambitious and an immigrant, trained as an engineer, and working in Cambridge. "We had talked on and off of his taking on a more entrepreneurial role in life," Afeyan said of Bancel. "I saw in him a level of intensity, curiosity, impatience." Bancel also seemed to harbor what Afeyan called a "paranoid optimism." Bancel questioned assumptions all the time but didn't let his habit of probing become stony cynicism. He simply wanted to leave no stone unturned.

Bancel's curiosity came through in his speech, infused with a thick French accent when he spoke English. He had a habit of using the phrase "the piece" when others might say "thing" or "aspect." as if his mind always saw everything as pieces of a puzzle to be solved. He'd say, "The piece that people misunderstand about Moderna is that it's creating a whole new drug platform, not just one new drug."

Bancel, in his late thirties by 2011, had dark hair and a dimpled chin and was in good shape. He sometimes wore a suit and tie but was as likely to don stylish gray turtleneck sweaters with high-end jeans and a Hermes belt, with its distinctive H-shaped buckle.

Afeyan had tried several times in the past to persuade Bancel to join Flagship-backed startups. "I politely declined a few times," Bancel recalled. He had become comfortable remaining at the helm of a genuinely global company operating in more than forty countries with a market cap of $5 billion.

But by the time he had settled into Boston, Bancel had gotten restless, as a fault line opened between him and bioMerieux's board. They had balked at some proposed acquisitions. Philosophically, the sides were drifting apart. He began to look around. For someone in his position, it doesn't take long for opportunities to show themselves. He went through the initial screening process for an open CEO job at Hospira, a Chicago-based drug company, but the job went to someone else.

He had begun to sour on the idea of taking over another large, established company. Clarity came when his wife asked him flat out what he wanted to do instead. "The only thing I've always dreamt of doing is starting something from scratch," he told her. "That's the one thing that's always been in the back of my mind." Refocused, he reached out to VC firms about leading new companies.

Nothing panned out initially. Then Afeyan called him one day, which wasn't that unusual. "Hey, you need to come see this," Afeyan said, asking Bancel to come to his office the same night. That was a little more unusual.

Bancel went, and Afeyan unveiled to him data from research that showed how mRNA could be used to spur the production of red blood cells in mice.

Bancel was dismissive. "This is impossible," he said in his thick French accent. "Thank you very much for wasting my evening, I'm going to go home and have dinner with my wife and kids now."

Afeyan could have put a hard sell on and pressed Bancel on the veracity of the science, scaring up more facts and data, but he didn't. Instead, he played it coy. Afeyan asked Bancel, "But if this *is* true, what does it mean to you?"

"If this is true, even though I think this is impossible, you could make hundreds or thousands of molecules that no one else can make in the world," Bancel responded, effectively doing Afeyan's bidding and speaking out loud the potential of the opportunity before them.

Afeyan suggested that Bancel could come be CEO of this startup, Moderna. If he didn't want to be CEO, he could be a board member, Afeyan told him. Or he could choose not to get involved at all, Afeyan tacked on, making sure Bancel felt the weight of that choice.

"If this is true, how are you going to feel if you say no to this?" Afeyan asked him. In some ways, this reflection is at the heart of all decisions to join a startup. *If this is true . . .* Well they know what it means *if this is true*, but of course, there's a healthy chance it's not true at all. Bancel knew Moderna's technology looked promising, maybe even revolutionary. Then again, it might not work. But what if he said no, and it did work?

"I think this could be the next Genentech," Afeyan told Bancel, pressing slightly harder. Genentech was a pioneer of biotech whose idea turned out to be true, and thus operated with little competition in its early years, a blue ocean of options for which disease targets it would pursue with its protein-based drug technology. Afeyan saw the same fair seas for Moderna. Later, he recalled, "I thought in the mRNA field, we could be the company that basically laid the map and decided what to go after."

Bancel hedged, and left Afeyan's office without giving an answer. He walked home across the Longfellow Bridge over the Charles to his home in Boston's posh Beacon Hill neighborhood. "My head was spinning," he said. Mostly, he thought that it looked too good to be true.

He floated the prospect to his wife. Could he leave a steady CEO post with an established global health care company to take a chance on a new company that would probably take years to turn an unproven technology into a single product, if ever? She asked him for data. Just how risky was it? Bancel knew most startups eventually fail. In biotech, biological complexity can undermine good ideas. And in Moderna's case, there was zero precedent. No mRNA-based drug or vaccine had ever been developed, never mind sold.

He told her he thought that mRNA had about a 2 percent to 5 percent chance of working. It was a "totally crazy idea," he said.

Bancel also spent time speaking with Moderna cofounders—Rossi, Langer, and Chien—looking for more evidence. He had thought so much about the risks. The flip side, though, of mRNA being an unproven technology was that if it worked in producing one medicine, there was a good chance it would yield many more. And this would help many people recover from disease or avoid it altogether. And it would give Bancel a chance to orchestrate the whole thing. This possibility excited him more than being the steward of a family-owned business created before he was born.

Still, he thought, it probably wouldn't work. It couldn't, could it? "Do I do it or do I not do it?" he agonized. "If I say no, and this works, I'm going to hate myself for the rest of my life."

Finally, over a bottle of wine with his wife, Bancel heard the words he was quietly hoping someone would say to him. "You have to do it," she said. He could make it work, she said, "because you are so stubborn you will go through brick walls. This has to work, so you have to go to make it work. This could change the world."

Afeyan made it official in February 2011. He gave Bancel a base salary of $400,000 a year, with potential annual performance bonuses of up to 35 percent if he hit board-defined targets. In addition, Moderna would grant Bancel about 10 percent of the company's common stock, to vest over four years.[5]

Bancel joined Moderna's board of directors in March 2011. He became executive chairman in July, when bioMerieux announced he would step down as CEO. Various bureaucratic delays in getting his green card (he had been on a work visa prior to this) meant he didn't officially become CEO of Moderna until later in 2011, but he had already started running the company before that.

While Afeyan was cajoling Bancel, Jason Schrum was filling up his clean room with more and more biotech materiel—tissue-culture incubators, microscopes, centrifuges, and pipettes. He bought some off-the-shelf nucleosides—the stuff used to build mRNA—through special catalogs. He also ordered up some custom-made ones.

It was complicated research. Schrum engineered mRNA so that once it was delivered into cells it would produce proteins known as granulo-cyte colony-stimulating factors, or GCSF. This is the same protein that is used as a drug to prevent infections in cancer patients undergoing che-motherapy. Schrum wasn't trying to prevent infection, though. He just used it as a proof of concept, to show the mRNA could order the produc-tion of the protein.

He hit on something with one of his custom modified nucleosides— known as a pseudouridine. It minimized inflammatory responses in the cells and caused high protein production, while extending the mRNA half-life to about a week to nine days, much longer than the two or so days other tests had managed. These were positive early results.

"What did surprise me was it worked as well as it did," Schrum recalled.

He reported the results back to Moderna's cofounders. "There was a lot of excitement. This was the first significant and meaningful improve-ment" on what had come before, he said.

Success meant Schrum got some company. Moderna hired enough

new scientists that by spring 2011, it could open a new lab. It was in the same office complex as Schrum's monastic basement clean room, but this one was on the third floor, with windows. The company held a wine-and-cheese reception to celebrate.

Many of Schrum's new colleagues were researchers from other biotechs and area hospitals. (And many were, like Afeyan, Rossi, and Bancel, immigrants.)

Alnylam, a Cambridge biotech also working with RNA but in a different way, proved to be fertile ground for recruitment. There, Moderna found Sayda Elbashir, who was born in the Sudan to parents who couldn't write their own names. Her father died when she was young, leaving her mother to raise nine children. Though she had little schooling herself, Elbashir's mother prized education and did all she could to make sure her children excelled in school. Elbashir recalls her mother telling her and her siblings, "I can't help you with the homework, but I can stay helping you just to give you positive energy, serve you tea and coffee and snacks."

Elbashir studied hard and earned postgraduate degrees in Germany in microbiology and vaccine development, followed by a PhD and postdoctoral fellowship at the Max Planck Institute in Goettingen, Germany. There, she worked in the lab of a biochemist who studied RNA interference, the science behind the founding of Alnylam. Alnylam's cofounders took notice and recruited her to start working at the new company in Cambridge in 2002. Nine years later, Bancel convinced her to come over to Moderna. She was drawn to the idea of working for an even younger startup than Alnylam, and the chance for a new way to approach RNA.

Another immigrant and former Alnylam researcher, Tony de Fougerolles, also joined at this time in 2011 to take the top R&D post, chief scientific officer. De Fougerolles, a Canadian, would bring expertise on how to protect RNA on its journey into cells so it didn't break down before it could do its job.

Schrum, de Fougerolles, Elbashir, and a handful of other Moderna scientists spent those early days running countless tests in everything from cell cultures to mice, rats, and monkeys. They tested different routes of administration: injecting into muscle, injecting under the skin, intravenous infusion, through the nose. Every modification they made was in search of fewer side effects and better, more stable delivery—anything to arrive at the best possible use of mRNA.

Progress was painstakingly slow. They suffered setbacks, unsuccessfully trying to make a formulation of mRNA that could be applied to skin and mRNA that had particularly long genetic sequences. They changed tack. Then changed tack again. All of them, to some extent or another, had been lured by the prospect of what Moderna was trying to do. Elbashir recalled thinking in those days "The technology worked. But can you make it a drug?" They had been drawn in by that idea that you could make it a drug. It would work. And if this is true . . .

3

Kendall Square

CAMBRIDGE, MASSACHUSETTS, IS THE FLAT NORTHERN
bank of the Charles River, facing Boston to the south. Its prominence
in American letters and science is belied by its size: just seven square
miles and home to about 118,000 people.[1] It's shaped something like a
high-heeled shoe. The stem of the shoe, to the southwest, is mostly Cambridge Cemetery and a small part of Mount Auburn Cemetery. The rest
of the city is thirteen neighborhoods. Some have directional names, like
West Cambridge and North Cambridge, both found near the heel. Others' names point to once-present features, like Strawberry Hill. A couple
of the neighborhoods have economical, dismissive names: Neighborhood Nine in the middle, for example. And at the front sole, that steps
on one of the widest parts of the Charles River, sits Area 2, home to MIT.

Most people who don't live there identify Cambridge by its five
squares, moving roughly west to east: Porter, Harvard, Central, Inman,
and Kendall. In typical Cantabrigian fashion, none of these squares is a
square. They are just areas surrounding a main intersection with vaguely
defined boundaries, sort of neighborhoods within the neighborhood.

Kendall Square, at the eastern end of the city, at the toe of the shoe, is
where Moderna set up shop in 2010.

Kendall for a long time was the industrial section of town, literally
and figuratively miles from leafy Harvard out in West Cambridge. A

sprawling water-hose factory was among the manufacturers in Kendall Square. The industrial businesses of course died, and the neighborhood died with it. NASA came in the 1960s intent on building a massive electronics research center, but fewer than half of the planned buildings were constructed before NASA abandoned the project. That left some empty buildings and acres of cleared land prepped for building, land that was cheap by the area's standards.[2]

The land also happened to be just northeast of MIT, where Philip Sharp, one of the founders of a small but growing biotechnology firm, was a professor. The firm decided to take advantage of the cheap land near campus, breaking ground on a 63,000-square-foot facility on Binney Street in the heart of Kendall Square in 1982.[3]

John Maraganore arrived in Kendall Square as part of that firm—Biogen—in 1987. He remembers that even then, five years after the company moved there, "it was a bit of a wasteland." Vacant lots and empty warehouses still dominated the reasonably bleak toe of the city. If you wanted to grab lunch with a colleague, about the only place you would find nearby was a Legal Sea Foods. MIT professors, biotech workers, and the occasional venture capitalist all flocked there.

Maraganore is still in Kendall Square, well known to many and easy to spot in his thick-framed glasses and often wearing a sweater. He's now a seasoned veteran of the Cambridge biotech scene who led Alnylam Pharmaceuticals—a block-and-a-half down from the original Biogen building—from Alnylam's founding until he stepped down at the end of 2021.

Only now, it's not a wasteland. Kendall Square has become the beating heart of the biotech industry, unrecognizable to someone who left in the late 1980s. Other biotech companies followed Biogen, including Genzyme, which made pioneering advances in the treatment of rare diseases caused by enzyme deficiencies and would later be acquired by French drug giant Sanofi; and Vertex Pharmaceuticals, which would develop drugs for hepatitis C and cystic fibrosis.

"It's hard to walk down the street in Kendall Square without running into someone from biotech or pharma," Maraganore says. "It's rare to see such a concentration of biomedical innovation within a couple square miles at most. It does make it a very rich place for company formation."

Office rents soared, eventually reaching $100 a square foot. Dozens more biotech firms rushed in and the ones that hit it big have built glassy headquarters and R&D labs in the neighborhood. They commingle with old industrial buildings that serve as the retrofitted outposts for tech firms like Google and Microsoft. The money followed too. Venture capital firms like Noubar Afeyan's Flagship Ventures, Atlas Venture, Polaris Partners, Third Rock, and MPM Capital all hung shingles nearby. Hotels dot the neighborhood. Trendy condos and lofts attract young talent, and with them, gyms, hip takeout places, and nice restaurants used as spaces to broker deals. Bicyclists abound, riding the bike lanes painted on most streets and hitching up to requisite bike racks outside their offices. Some complexes surround grassy plazas, where workers lounge at lunch in Adirondack chairs. Construction cranes still dot the landscape, and workers in hard hats take breaks in cafés next to hipster millennials from the biotechs.

Kendall came to dominate biotech in large part because of MIT. The university took a more ambitious approach to translating research from its labs into startups than many universities, including crosstown Harvard. And once established, early pioneers like Bob Langer, who would later help form Moderna, and Philip Sharp, the Nobel Prize–winning cofounder of Biogen, continued to champion the neighborhood by, among other things, supporting the addition of research institutes to the neighborhood.

Over the years, governors of several states, hungry to emulate Kendall Square's transformation, have asked Bob Langer the secret to creating such a dynamic neighborhood around the biotech industry. "I usually say it starts with the academics," he says. "Having an MIT or a Stanford."

Langer had MIT. Then, he says, young scientists began to flock to labs like his at MIT (and at Harvard) with the thought that, if their research looked promising, they could start a business. They had all the financial and scientific infrastructure for their startup right there, including alums of their labs and the VC types, many of whom were just a short walk away and who probably knew someone they knew. It's a virtuous circle that you didn't find in many places and maybe couldn't replicate, either.

James Crowe, an infectious-disease and vaccine specialist at Vanderbilt University in Nashville who has collaborated on research with Moderna, recalls coming to Cambridge several years ago to attend a board meeting for another biotech startup. During a break, another board member, a Cambridge VC investor, asked Crowe what he was working on in his lab. Crowe told him about his work on isolating and cloning immune-system antibodies from blood samples.

The VC asked Crowe, "If I gave you $10 million, can you do something with it?"

Crowe didn't take him up on his offer, but he remembers the exchange signaling that Kendall Square was different. Even though he later founded a biotech near Vanderbilt, he says, "People aren't walking around with money in their pockets to invest in biotech in Nashville."

When Moderna moved Jason Schrum into the basement clean room, in late 2010, biotech companies were proliferating and Kendall Square was booming. At the same time, Big Pharma companies were closing out their "lost decade" as one industry CEO described it.[4]

For almost a century, large pharmaceutical companies had dominated the medicine-making industry. Johnson & Johnson, Eli Lilly, Pfizer, Bayer, Merck, and others created medicine like aspirin, insulin, penicillin, and the measles vaccine. By the 1990s, many were among the most profitable companies on the planet. Anti-cholesterol and blood-pressure medicines, and yes, Viagra, too, generated multibillion-dollar annual sales and high profit margins. The companies used some of those massive profits to fund research and development aimed at churning out future blockbuster drugs. Merck in particular invested heavily in R&D, attracting top scientists and giving them the leeway to follow their ideas no matter what diseases their discoveries targeted. Its culture and success made Merck a mainstay on *Fortune* magazine's annual list of most admired companies. By 2000, most of the top-selling prescription drugs were pills for conditions like heartburn, cholesterol, and depression. And most were developed by Big Pharma using the industry's tried-and-true methods.[5]

But between 1999 and 2010 applications to the FDA to market new prescription drugs—those with an ingredient never marketed before—plummeted, and FDA approvals of what they did submit dropped, too, about 40 percent. The industry averaged fewer than twenty-five new drug approvals a year, compared with more than thirty a year in the previous decade.[6]

To compound the pain, many Big Pharma companies were approaching a "patent cliff" when their exclusive rights to market drugs they had developed would expire, opening the door to competing generic versions of their drugs—often sold at 90 percent discounts. Pfizer fell off one of the biggest patent cliffs when its cholesterol-lowering medicine Lipitor lost patent protection in 2011. Some $5 billion in sales of the original brand vanished in the first year after the expiration.[7]

At the same time, regulators, including the Food and Drug Administration, were taking a tough stance on new and existing drugs, rejecting several companies' requests to sell new products, including proposed diet pills, over concerns about their safety or effectiveness. Federal prosecutors were scrutinizing drug companies' marketing tactics, investigating allegations that sales reps were promoting drugs for uses that weren't cleared by the FDA, and paying kickbacks to doctors.[8]

The triple whammy of low R&D output, patent expirations, and increased scrutiny caught Big Pharma flat-footed. Many companies, under pressure from shareholders to shore up the near-term bottom line, responded with cuts. The same month that Bancel took the Moderna job, once-mighty Merck announced plans to cut thirteen thousand jobs from its workforce as it lost patents for its biggest drugs.[9]

Others also slashed costs, laid off tens of thousands, and closed factories and R&D labs. Some drugmakers struggled to uphold manufacturing-quality standards, issuing recalls of contaminated medicines. Johnson & Johnson warned it had a shortage of a cancer drug because of problems at a contract manufacturer.[10] Prices went up. Some chased growth through mergers and acquisitions, industry heavyweights conceding to a new reality. Pfizer and Wyeth merged, as did Merck and Schering-Plough.[11] Others blew up their strategies. Pfizer said it would consider spinning off its animal-drug and nutrition divisions, a sign of a significant shift away from diversified business models that had long been a hallmark of the industry.

The industry's reputation dimmed. Built on bold bets and big break-throughs, pharma got downright conservative. Once a company like Merck would hire scientists and set them free to find potential drugs, no matter where it took them. Now, many pharma companies wouldn't even advance an experimental drug if its market potential wasn't abundantly clear and chances of success extremely high.

Big Pharma may not have fully realized it at the time, but its risk-averse turn and its patent cliffs were accompanied by another force that was putting downward pressure on it: biotech.

The lost decade for companies like Merck was not so bad a time for Kendall Square and the increasing number of biotech firms landing there, in large part because these firms were doing what pharma companies weren't willing or able to do: finding new ways to develop drugs.

Early biotech research was nurtured in academic, government, and startup labs in the 1970s and 80s and enjoyed a few early breakthroughs, like the life-saving stroke treatment tPA made by biotech pioneer Genentech, which combined DNA from two different organisms to create the drug that treated the disease. Another early pioneer, Amgen, cloned a gene to make a groundbreaking treatment for anemia. These were very different ways of making drugs than what most Big Pharma companies had been doing for decades.

From the outset these companies looked and acted different than traditional pharma companies. They were smaller and nimbler. They seemed more willing to take risks on new technologies. Even their names reflected the different approach they took. The older generation of companies were typically named after a founder. These companies were named for the science, the new approaches they were taking to making drugs. Genetic engineering technology became Genentech. Applied molecular genetics turned into Amgen.

Those two companies helped create biotech hubs in the Bay Area and Southern California. Venture capital firms began to take notice and invest in more biotech startups in the hopes that this new science would produce additional lucrative breakthroughs. Biogen was one such startup, and the one that created the hub in Kendall Square.

Traditional pharma, behaving like many industries do when they're being disrupted, was slow to embrace these new technologies. Many had a bias toward their own in-house research, suffering from "not invented here" syndrome. This behavior had the knock-on effect of a talent drain as many young scientists opted to find work at smaller biotechs—or to start one on their own, which in part explains the massive drop in drug approvals in the 2000s.

Much of early-stage drug R&D migrated away from the Big Pharma firms and into hip, fast-moving biotech startups. Big Pharma companies increasingly were relegated to the back end of the process. They'd help carry someone else's idea across the finish line through license deals or acquisitions, and they served as experts on the labyrinthine processes around clinical trials or submitting drugs to the FDA for approval, which is a massive bureaucratic undertaking startups didn't yet have the heft or know-how to do.

This was the new reality as the aughts gave way to the 2010s.

Even when Big Pharma finally saw what was happening, it wasn't easy to adapt effectively. Their large sizes sometimes got in the way. Merck's CEO at the time, Ken Frazier, said in an interview in 2016 that "companies become hierarchical. They become bureaucratic. They become slow. They become risk averse. And those are the cultural challenges that we face every day inside our company."[12]

Unable to beat the biotechs, many pharma companies joined them, literally, in Kendall Square. That way, they could be closer to early-stage research and hire talent away from the growing biotech workforce, talent that might not be willing to move to pharma companies' locations in suburban New Jersey or the Midwest. Novartis, the Swiss drug giant, was one of the first to move in, opening a drug discovery center in Kendall Square that brought hundreds of scientists to town. Nearly every other Big Pharma company, including Pfizer and Eli Lilly, followed suit, opening labs and offices. Some, in cost-cutting mode, consolidated R&D in

Kendall Square. Pfizer, for example, moved its neuroscience and cardio-vascular research divisions to Cambridge from Groton, Connecticut.[13]

Ryan Dietz, the tech-transfer lawyer who worked with Derrick Rossi, says it's not really optional for pharma companies anymore: "Every pharma company now has a presence here in Boston. They didn't before. They need to be here to access the expertise of the individuals, in addition to the partnering opportunities."

By the middle of the 2010s, Kendall Square had become a global hub of both pharma and biotech. While there's something to be said for the two sectors packing themselves into a couple of square miles, it creates challenges, too. It creates a war for talent in which everyone can recruit from everyone else. Success at a startup often meant those companies would lose the best and brightest, who would get rich and go off and do their own project. And, if you were out to lunch in Kendall Square, you had to be careful what you said about your company's proprietary research, because you never knew if someone from a rival company might be sitting at the next table over.

And even though they now occupied the same space, the cultures of the two types of companies still didn't always mesh. Recalling Novartis's early move into the neighborhood, Flagship's Noubar Afeyan says, "It brought hundreds of professionals of the sort we never had here before." Some were scientists with twenty years' experience in industrial-level drug discovery, not the freshly minted PhDs who were joining Kendall Square biotechs right out of academia. It was an injection of experience that many in the emerging biotech community didn't have, and that was sometimes helpful—especially if a biotech could poach a veteran. But Big Pharma newcomers sometimes brought their old-school caution with them, a reluctance to advance the riskier drug projects, Afeyan said.

Maybe the best example of the juxtaposition comes from John Maraganore, who started at Biogen but eventually took over as CEO of Alnylam, in 2002. The company was a mirror of what Moderna would be, trying to use RNA not to spur the creation of proteins but to stop cells from producing proteins that caused disease. They called it RNA interference, or RNAi.

It took Alnylam more than fifteen years to get a product to market, but it finally did in 2018, and that drug, used to treat a rare genetic disorder, generated $306 million in revenue by 2020. The company has produced two more marketed RNAi drugs since.[14]

Back in 2006 Merck decided to try to take on Alnylam when it bought a competitor, Sirna Therapeutics, for $1.1 billion, double the company's value at the time. For nearly eight years, as Alnylam started studies on nine potential RNAi drugs, Merck never advanced any products based on the technology into clinical trials. In 2014, Merck bailed on the effort and sold Sirna's assets to Alnylam for $175 million, less than a fifth of what it had paid for them.[15]

To Maraganore, the contrast between Alnylam and Merck's handling of RNAi technology was clear, and emblematic of the difference between the pharma and biotech companies sharing the same space in Cambridge, but not the same mindset. "It is without a doubt true that the innovation needed to advance a cutting-edge technology like RNAi is best done in the hands of an entrepreneurial company," he says. "It's not like Alnylam is smarter than Merck. But what Alnylam had was the culture needed to take early technology like that and persevere through challenges to make products a reality. That culture really comes down to a paranoia of death. If you don't succeed as a small company with your technology, then you're not going to survive as a company."

This is not to say things were entirely rosy for biotech in 2010, when Moderna set up shop, first with Schrum's lab, and soon after with headquarters a few blocks over in the southwestern corner of Kendall, just above Main Street, which roughly divides the neighborhood from MIT (though the two have bled into each other in recent years).

Other firms in the neighborhood, like Genzyme and Biogen, were under pressure from activist shareholders itching for better performance. Investors also were growing impatient with Alnylam. Though it eventually did succeed, its momentum had stalled in 2010 when two Big Pharma companies, Roche and Novartis, ended development partnerships with the biotech at a time when Alnylam still had no products. (Perhaps not surprisingly, then, some of Alnylam's talent would soon emigrate to Moderna.)

That was biotech's fundamental challenge: time. If you started a biotech company in 2010 (or maybe even more importantly, if you *invested* in one) you knew that its first product wouldn't reach the market for years. Maybe not until 2015 or even 2020. Or maybe it never would. Everyone in Kendall Square knew about the timelines, about drugs like the multiple-sclerosis treatment Gilenya, which was cleared by the FDA in 2010, but had been in development since the 1990s, when researchers derived it from Chinese caterpillar fungus cells. No doubt those scientists were as excited in the 1990s as Moderna's were now in 2010.[16]

Moderna's odds in some ways were even longer than your average biotech because it was setting out not only to make new drugs, but to make them in a new way that would turn a person's own body into a protein factory.

As much as biotech had disrupted pharma, its model had its weaknesses, too. High-risk, high-reward startups are exciting, right up until people stop believing in them and the capital dries up. Startups can't bankroll long-term research from product sales because they have none. False starts and failure come at a cost that's hard to absorb. Drug development startups in particular face deep uncertainty. The money starts running out the moment you open for business. The early stage is largely a race to do enough good work to secure more funding before what you have runs out, and then do enough more good work to not run out again.

As an example of someone coming from old pharma into biotech, Stéphane Bancel understood all of this. He had come from a billion-dollar global company with six thousand employees. At Moderna, he led ten people in Cambridge with an idea no one was sure would ever work, and six months of cash. When Bancel moved into his new office, he and his wife brought their own vacuum cleaner in to clean up over a weekend, to save time.

From the start Bancel focused on speed. He wanted the scientists to work as quickly as possible to advance mRNA tech beyond lab tests and

mouse tests to other animals, including monkeys, which are closer prox-
ies for how a drug will perform in humans. This way, Moderna could
generate enough data about the safety of mRNA to file what's called an
"investigational new drug" (IND) application to the Food and Drug Administration. The FDA must approve an IND before human clinical trials can start. An IND is a bright beacon to investors to send more money.

To get to an IND, Bancel knew he needed more scientists to move
as fast as he wanted to, but even in the optimistic world of startups,
Moderna was a hard sell.

"I had so many 'No's' at the beginning," he recalled later. "When you
go after a scientific idea that most people tell you will never work, and
you tell them you have six months of cash, it's hard to recruit."

Bancel did manage to scrape together a few staff to join Jason Schrum,
but not as many as he'd like. So he found another way to battle the clock:
get those he did have to do more and do it faster.

From the start, Bancel set a culture of hard-charging, unsparing de-
mands that wasn't perceived by all as team oriented or collaborative.
Some former employees described it as a punishing place to be, with
Bancel using all sticks and no carrots to motivate people.

Bancel was blunt. He wanted results. Fast. Scientists were asked to
generate new data on experiments at speeds they had never operated at
before. If the pace of, say, clinical-trial enrollment didn't meet his expectations, Bancel would demand "Why can't we move faster? I don't understand why you can't get this done more effectively!" a former employee
recalled.

Bancel would admonish subordinates in front of others in meetings.
"He was very dominating. If he didn't like somebody, he could be tough
on them," said one person close to the company at the time. People who
didn't perform slowed things down. "He would not suffer fools. He tells
people what to do. He won't take no for an answer. He puts extreme
pressure on people."

While this approach seemed to spur some to do their best work, for
others it created paralyzing fear. Many people felt they couldn't stand up
to Bancel, a fear that dampened the healthy back-and-forth needed for
good decision-making in a scientific endeavor. It left some workers with

the sense that nothing they did was good enough. Certainly it wasn't fast enough.

"When expectations were so bold and aggressive, people could hardly ever exceed expectations," one former employee said. In addition to feeling underappreciated, many employees were stressed and exhausted. Some broke down in tears after particularly bad meetings. One employee worked until two in the morning and passed out in the shower while getting ready to come in the next day. Another employee went to the emergency room after falling from exhaustion and hitting his face on a table. Bancel gave some early scientists a hard time about coming in late or leaving early, not recognizing the extra hours they put in on other days. "He hired people and made their life hell," one former scientist said.

It also didn't help that Bancel established a pattern of what he called "upgrading" the workforce, but what others saw as a cold demoralizing judgment on their effort and value. Bancel didn't hesitate to find people with more experience than his current staff and, if he could land them, replace the people he had—no matter how extraordinarily hard they had worked for him. Borrowing language from the high-tech world, Bancel would openly describe early Moderna as "Moderna 1.0" and say that he needed to upgrade the workforce to make it "Moderna 2.0." Better people would mean Moderna could get better results. Faster.

Some saw this as ultimately true but poorly conveyed. "When you're building a company, you can get better and better people as time goes on," the person close to Moderna said. "Stéphane knew that, and he was rebuilding the company. I think it just could have been explained better."

Bancel didn't feel the need to explain much, and in fact he valued a culture of secrecy. He even advised new hires not to update their LinkedIn profiles to show they were working at Moderna, according to one former employee. "We wanted to be stealth," Bancel recalled.

Mostly, he didn't want early-stage research published, lest competitors get ahold of it. Publishing research is what cofounder Derrick Rossi did for a living so to him it seemed like Bancel didn't want him around at all. Rossi continued to work on mRNA in his lab at the Immune Disease Institute on the campus of Harvard Medical School, while serving on Moderna's board of directors and as a consultant to the company.

In August 2011, Rossi wanted to submit a paper to a journal called *Nature Protocols* that described synthesizing and using modified mRNA to reprogram mature cells into pluripotent stem cells. As part of his consulting agreement with Moderna, he first had to send the manuscript to the company to sign off on the plan.

Bancel told Rossi he had serious concerns about publishing a protocol paper because it might reveal know-how that Bancel regarded as a critical Moderna asset that could help a rival, such as the German competitor CureVac. Worse, it could entice a well-funded Big Pharma company to jump into the field.

Rossi was peeved by Bancel's objections. It seemed to him that Bancel was trying to dictate what Rossi could and couldn't publish from his own lab work at Harvard Medical. This annoyance was compounded by the fact that while Bancel didn't want the world to know what Rossi was doing, he himself demanded to know what Rossi was working on in his lab, according to Rossi. Rossi said he tried to explain that there was a firewall. Any intellectual property arising from his academic lab research belonged to the Immune Disease Institute, not to Moderna. If Moderna wanted to license it, it was free to send a lawyer (perhaps the one that ventured down into Jason Schrum's basement) to negotiate a deal with the institute. Rossi recalled: "He would say to me, 'You have to tell us,' and I would say 'No.' That really pissed him off. I don't care if it pissed him off, it was the right thing to do."

Ultimately, Rossi published the protocols paper.[17] Bancel wasn't happy. "Derrick was creating problems for the company," he recalled.

The tension continued through 2012, when Bancel invited Rossi to his office one day, according to Rossi, and said he wanted to end Rossi's consulting contract with Moderna. Rossi reminded Bancel that the contract wasn't up for renewal for another year or more. No matter, Bancel said, he wanted to terminate it now.

Rossi knew that not only would he, the cofounder whose science the company was built on, lose his company, he would also lose some of his Moderna shares before they fully vested.

"If you do that, I will sue you," Rossi told Bancel.

According to Rossi, Bancel responded by noting that would be bad for Moderna's shareholders and pointed out that Rossi still owned Moderna shares.

"I don't give a fuck!" Rossi yelled, loud enough, he recalls, that others in Moderna's office surely heard him. According to Rossi, Bancel turned white at the outburst, unprepared for Rossi's anger. According to Rossi, Bancel backed off from the idea of terminating the contract.

But the experience left Rossi disturbed. "It upset me. I lost sleep over it. It used to keep me up at night. You don't want to work with people that are just somehow scheming and doing bad shit. It's just not my style at all."

For his part, Bancel found Rossi difficult to work with, Bancel recalled later. He said Rossi wasn't a great listener and didn't have experience in drug development or running a business.

Besides the early press release about Moderna's founding in fall 2010, the company didn't release much more information publicly until December 2012, when it raised additional money and came out of "stealth mode"—a period in a startup's early stage when it quietly builds its foundations without much public attention.

For a while, before it tested anything in humans, Moderna publicly disclosed virtually nothing more about the results of its mRNA work. "For eighteen months, no website, no press release, no nothing, just focus on the science," Bancel later explained in a public presentation in late 2013. "Make this science work."[18]

The secrecy may have pleased Bancel, but it also fueled the skepticism about Moderna among scientists, industry players, and investors.

In fact, Moderna's whole mode of operation and Bancel's brusque management seemed to create twin effects. In one way, it worked. Bancel's public rhetoric and promises strewn with buzzwords you might get from a Silicon Valley CEO were enticing enough that the company grew. It notched more funding, buying itself more time. But at the same time, he was grinding employees to dust to get the work done that would deliver on his promises. Employees started to vote with their feet. Many left the company. Schrum, who had toiled alone in the basement in hopes of learning the ropes of startups, exited in 2012. He said he was looking for companies with shorter times-to-market than Moderna appeared to have.

More high-level executives and scientists followed—getting prized jobs at the startup only to leave after remarkably short stays. Bancel had poached Joseph Bolen from Millennium Pharmaceuticals in 2013 to serve as Moderna's chief scientific officer, a coup that was noticed in biotech, as was his abrupt departure not two years later.[19]

In such tight quarters as Kendall Square, people talk. Moderna had earned such a poor reputation and built up so much skepticism about its prospects that it eventually garnered news coverage in industry journals and newspapers. Biotech journalists wrote up the buzz. The influential journal *Nature* published an article in 2015 calling Moderna "something of a mystery" because virtually no studies of its mRNA technology had been published at the time, with details only appearing in patent filings, eighteen months after their submission. That sounds neutral enough, but the message was clear: there might be no there there.[20]

The following year, in 2016, the health care news site STAT published a deeply reported, scathing article on Moderna, describing a "caustic work environment" that drove away top talent and suggested Bancel prized the company's rising valuation over its science.[21] The hard-hitting STAT coverage stuck in the craw of Moderna's leaders—some would still bring it up with bitterness in conversations years later. Bob Langer, speaking five years after the story ran, hadn't forgotten and said STAT "criticized Moderna from the beginning."

As often happens, the backlash against Moderna brought out a backlash to the backlash. Some employees noted that the company did make efforts to keep workers happy. The bosses allowed a foosball table. They held happy hours and rented out pubs and bowling alleys for parties.

And some defended Bancel's management, saying that if you were smart and did good work, you were OK. Defenders said the company culture wasn't for everyone. It might not suit people who need more structure, or people who can't handle the intensity. Years later, even people who didn't love working there would point to Bancel's hard-charging style as one of the reasons Moderna was positioned to deliver a Covid-19 vaccine in 2020.

"I think what's not tolerable is to do sloppy science," said Marcello Damiani, a native of Lebanon who served briefly under Bancel at bioMerieux and joined Moderna to oversee its technology in 2015. "Stéphane is very rigorous and he's very demanding. You cannot come and present the outcome of your studies without knowing the details and making sure they're all lined up and correct. . . . If the work has been sloppy, his reaction will be, 'Well, first of all we need to rebuild the whole experiment. It's not acceptable.'" And if such sloppy work happens more than once, it's time to rebuild the team.

Some newcomers said Bancel and other Moderna leaders were receptive to change. Tracey Franklin left a human resources job at Merck to become chief human resources officer at Moderna in 2019. Early on, based on employee feedback, she suggested to Bancel that Moderna let individual employees decide the mix of options and stock they receive. Bancel agreed and told her to act on the plan as soon as possible. She implemented the change in about eight months; probably about half the time it would have taken at a large company, she said.

"I have not met the Stéphane that's depicted in a lot of these articles," she said. "I do understand he was probably like that in the earlier days. He is hard-driving. He has a high performance standard. . . . He wants to do great things. But I think he's evolved as a leader over time."

Bancel also would later point out that Moderna's location in the biotech hotbed of Kendall Square made higher turnover more likely. Moderna employees could walk out the door and find plenty of other jobs within a few blocks. Many, like Sayda Elbashir, didn't do that. They stayed.

Still the problems were bad enough that people did periodically try to intervene. Derrick Rossi once approached Bancel, asking him to lighten up on the workload. That didn't go over well. Some of Bancel's deputies brought the concerns of lower-level employees to him. In pressuring employees to speed things up, they told him, he risked crossing a line that would have the opposite effect and cause people to shut down or leave.

Even before the scathing STAT story was published, Bancel had begun to work on softening his edges. "He checked himself," one former employee said. Which meant that instead of berating someone in front of their peers, he would schedule a follow-up meeting to explore why someone wasn't moving as quickly as he would like. The STAT story noted that he had traveled to Silicon Valley to talk with top companies there about talent retention.

Bancel later looked back and explained that he himself felt pressure, which contributed to what others saw as a harsh management style. Bancel pressed his scientists to advance mRNA to the point where Moderna could test an experimental mRNA drug or vaccine in people as quickly as possible, and the science was hard. "I would come home sometimes and say 'Geez, it might never work,'" Bancel recalls. "We would be trying to make something work and we'd be at it for two, three, four months, and making no progress."

He knew the company was working on unproven technology, with tight resources, and making planning decisions with limited information. And there is always the money winding down, every day, and the need to get more. "You're trying not to die," he said. "You're trying to not kill the company because you have this burden, which is, you know, if you can find a path, and the company fails because of you, you will shortchange a lot of patients."

If he were to apologize for anything, it seems, it would not be the hard-driving culture he created, but rather his failure to communicate to people that that's what the culture would be. In hindsight, he says he wished he had been more up-front with new hires about how hard the work would be. "The intensity of the company and the mission-driven [culture] that we have always had as a company," he later said, "that is the type of thing I would want to be more explicit about."

One thing that saved Moderna from imploding under Bancel's pressure was a key hire in late 2012. Stephen Hoge had an MD from the University of California, San Francisco, and spent a few years as a resident physician in New York before joining the health care practice of the McKinsey & Company consulting firm in 2006. A few years later, the brand-new Moderna hired McKinsey to analyze its portfolio of potential drugs and vaccines and help identify what to focus on. McKinsey was also brought in to help Moderna craft a message about its technology that might entice a Big Pharma company—many of which are McKinsey clients—to form a partnership with Moderna. Hoge was a partner in McKinsey's health care practice and liked what he saw after spending a few months on the Moderna project. Moderna enticed him to come on board. He was named senior vice president of corporate development and new drug concepts. He would become president in 2015. He eventually took over much of the R&D function at Moderna and would often serve as the public face of Moderna.

The youthful-looking Hoge, with short, sandy brown hair parted to the side and often wearing stylish, black-rimmed glasses, brought a calming effect to Moderna, and over time he became a buffer between Bancel and many employees. He also was one of the few who could argue with Bancel successfully, or who even dared to. "If I say black, he will say white," Bancel later said. Hoge, the diplomat, says: "We have different strengths, and we balance each other really well."

Bancel, the "paranoid optimist," liked that Hoge didn't fear failure. "In my previous life, what I've seen is when something fails, people run away," Bancel said. "Stephen thrived on negative information."

Hoge saw negative information as just more information. He liked to say that "there is no black magic." If an experiment failed, there must be a scientific reason for it, not some inexplicable force. Hoge wanted to methodically hunt down the reason, and to learn from it. Moderna made sure at least one wall of every room in its offices had whiteboard paint and erasable markers on hand. In meetings, Hoge would get up and start writing on the walls all the possible reasons something didn't work and stir up discussion among company leaders and scientists to try to narrow it down.

Hoge also did something Bancel wasn't known for. He tried to goad Moderna's scientists to visualize future success, which must have shocked many of them who had lived in perpetual fear of failure and being told they weren't moving fast enough. In meetings and conversation, Hoge would drop the phrase "anticipatory nostalgia." He wanted Moderna's hard-working employees, if they were feeling burned-out, to look forward to the day when they could look back on the present as something they had to endure to get to success. Stephen Kelsey, who led Moderna's cancer-drug division from 2014 to 2017, remembered Hoge's encouragement working with the scientists. "They were looking forward to the day when they could look back and say, 'We finally cracked it,'" he recalled. "'We finally did something useful with mRNA.'"

At the time Hoge came in, Moderna was focused mainly on improving the design of its mRNA to maximize its ability to produce proteins, while minimizing inflammatory immune responses. This goal was made more complex by the fact that mRNA itself is unstable. So even if the scientists could improve the design, they also had to find a way to get the mRNA inside the body and inside cells without the material breaking down first. Without a good delivery mechanism, the mRNA wouldn't get inside human cells in sufficient numbers to make a difference.

Initially, researchers working with mRNA in lab tests and small-animal tests used a courier known as a transfection reagent—substances that combined with mRNA to create a certain electrical charge that facilitated its entry into cells. It worked well for cells in petri dishes and small-animal tests but was proving less viable for larger-animal tests because the reagents could be toxic and weren't terribly efficient.

Tony de Fougerolles, Moderna's first chief scientific officer, who joined in 2011, had a different idea for delivering the mRNA, something his previous employer Alnylam had been playing with: lipid nanoparticles. A lipid is a naturally occurring substance, a fat. Many people recognize the term from common blood tests measuring various types of lipids, including cholesterol and triglycerides. A lipid nanoparticle is just an engineered version of the material and formed into a tiny sphere that creates a protective shell around RNA: bubble wrap for a package's delivery.

In 2012, with Bancel pushing hard on the team, de Fougerolles and some Moderna colleagues decided to test mRNA encased in lipid nano-particles in monkeys. A contract laboratory in Montreal would inject it into about eighteen monkeys. Some would be given mRNA coded to produce erythropoietin—EPO—while others would be given mRNA coded to produce granulocyte-colony stimulating factor, or GCSF. If the results were positive, the monkeys that got EPO would increase pro-duction of red blood cells, and the ones that got GCSF would increase production of infection-fighting neutrophils.

De Fougerolles could have let the contract lab do all the work and ship blood samples back to Moderna in Cambridge to test the results. But he didn't want to risk the samples getting lost or held up by paperwork. He was also eager to see if his theory was right, so he and two colleagues traveled to Montreal to do the work with the lab techs in Montreal. It was a two-day process, a lot of complex lab work that came down to a bunch of people in a lab waiting to see if a liquid in test tubes lined up in a well would change from clear to blue, which would indicate success.

The result: blue. In science, there is so much trial and error that when something works like you envisioned, it can produce a fair bit of elation. It was validation on another level, too: it worked in a higher species than rodents. He and his colleagues exchanged high fives.

De Fougerolles immediately called Stéphane Bancel, who took the call at a Boston Red Sox baseball game. "He was ecstatic," de Fougerolles recalled—for the science working probably, but equally important to Bancel, it meant he had more positive data to get more funding.

Rossi and Chien, the scientific cofounders at Harvard Medical School, were at the same time making progress in their labs. They had moved on from using mRNA to make mice glow, to more complex tests. With funding from National Institutes of Health grants, they began to explore using mRNA to instruct animal cells to make a protein known as vas-cular endothelial growth factor, or VEGF, which causes the growth of new blood vessels. A groundbreaking cancer drug, Avastin, *blocks* VEGF around certain tumors and deprives tumors of the blood vessels they rely on to grow. Chien thought that a therapy to *boost* VEGF could help repair damaged hearts.

It had been tried before by developing VEGF proteins in a lab and then injecting them into the patient. That process didn't get the VEGF to the heart in sufficient numbers to provide a benefit, and it caused a side effect of lowering blood pressure.

Rossi and Chien thought that instead they could inject mRNA, coded to instruct a person's own cells to *make* the VEGF protein where it was needed. So scientists from their labs injected VEGF-coded mRNA directly into the hearts of mice that previously were induced to have heart attacks.

The injected mRNA caused the formation of new blood vessels and reduced the size of damaged heart tissue in mice, helping them recover.

These were tantalizing results, and Rossi and Chien submitted them for publication in the prestigious journal *Nature*, but even after revisions, one of the peer reviewers didn't think the data were ready for prime time, Chien recalled. It was another frustrating reminder of the scientific skepticism that still greeted mRNA. Even with promising lab results, it was hard for people to envision it because it just hadn't been done before. "People had been trying for decades to get VEGF to become a drug," Chien said. "We come along with an entirely new technology, mRNA, and could achieve the thing they could not."

Fundraising was still a constant necessity for Moderna. The expense of developing new drugs and vaccines, never mind new ways to make them, is extraordinary. Specialized lab instruments can cost hundreds of thousands of dollars. Hiring outside contractors to test mRNA in monkeys in Montreal—just the one test, for example—could run upwards of $500,000.

But with the promising successes in Montreal and across Cambridge in Rossi's and Chien's labs in hand, Moderna raised more money. Flagship, the VC firm, invested more, as did Tim Springer, the Harvard professor. By December 2012, Moderna had raised a total of $40 million.

The time was right to come out of stealth mode and announce itself to the world, which the company did in its first official press release in December 2012, two years after its founding.[22] The release noted at a high level that, on the research front, Moderna had conducted various "proof-of-concept studies" in animals, including monkeys, which showed that injecting or infusing mRNA could induce production of proteins in the animals. The release noted that the company had filed more than eighty patent applications. Some of the patent applications listed Stéphane Bancel and Noubar Afeyan as inventors, in addition to the scientists working in labs at Moderna and in academia. Moderna identified four areas that it would focus on for products: cancer, inherited genetic disorders, the blood disorder hemophilia, and diabetes. Infectious diseases and vaccines weren't mentioned.

The company was getting more comfortable talking about itself publicly, because it had more evidence that could spur investment. The $40 million was impressive, but Bancel and Afeyan wanted more, which they thought they could get from a partnership with a Big Pharma company. This was smack in the middle of pharma's disruption and transition to a role as the money and distribution channels for products invented at nimble startup biotechs.

For Moderna, doing a deal with a Big Pharma company could provide several advantages. For one, it could give Moderna a cash infusion without significantly diluting the ownership stakes of existing shareholders. And even though it meant giving up full sales and profits for resulting products, it would allow Moderna to tap into the expertise and resources of a Big Pharma company that was accustomed to running huge clinical trials and filing the voluminous paperwork to get regulatory approval.

Most important, it would provide much needed public validation for Moderna's technology—which still faced a phalanx of skeptics—and that new credibility in turn could ease the way for additional fundraising. As much as the biotechs had upended the pharma companies' business, they were still cash-burning startups that welcomed—needed—the old guard to survive.

Moderna used the Montreal data and the data from Rossi and Chien as Bancel sought interest from a bigger drug company to acquire the rights to codevelop and commercialize drugs. Bancel and others flew to Indianapolis to hold discussions with drugmaker Eli Lilly—Bancel's old employer. They flew to Basel, Switzerland, to visit Roche Holding (which by this time had acquired biotech pioneer Genentech). Neither was interested. The new results were good, yes, but there were no INDs. The increasingly risk-averse pharma companies noted that Moderna still hadn't started any tests of an experimental drug in humans. It was still early.

Moderna kept searching as it burned through its cash. Chien had a side gig advising Anglo-Swedish pharmaceutical company AstraZeneca (AZ) on its cardiovascular drug research. He flew once a month to an AZ research site in Maryland. He said that he introduced Bancel to AstraZeneca executives he knew from this gig. Eventually, Bancel connected with Pascal Soriot, the new CEO of AstraZeneca and a fellow Frenchman. Soriot, who has a degree in veterinary medicine and an MBA from HEC Paris, previously held various top roles at Roche, including leading Genentech while Roche was integrating it as a fully owned division.

AstraZeneca lured Soriot from Roche in the wake of its lost decade, when AstraZeneca was facing big losses from patent expirations, including its big-selling anti-cholesterol medicine Crestor, along with setbacks in its R&D pipeline that led to the departure of the prior CEO. Soriot's job was to turn AstraZeneca around and stock up its R&D pipeline with future home runs.

Bancel put the hard sell on Soriot and stayed ready to pounce at any time. At one point, Soriot's schedule opened up for a breakfast meeting in Gaithersburg, Maryland, on extremely short notice. Bancel's assistant could only find a room for the Moderna CEO in a Motel 6 the night before the meeting. At breakfast the next morning, the two Frenchmen bonded, and Bancel made the pitch.

"I saw in his eye he got it," Bancel would say later.

Negotiations intensified. In early 2013 came "due diligence," when AstraZeneca sent a team of about fifteen R&D scientists to investigate Moderna's operation and make sure its claims during courtship checked out.

"We wanted to impress AZ," chief scientist Tony de Fougerolles re-called, and Stephen Hoge's McKinsey experience helped refine Moderna's message to that end, de Fougerolles said.

De Fougerolles and several other Moderna employees prepped for the arrival of the AstraZeneca scientists for about two weeks, some nights getting only two hours of sleep. They prepped reports on experiments. Created presentations. They needed to print voluminous copies of the patent applications Moderna had filed to that point—enough binders stuffed with technical data to fill the trunk of one employee's car. Before the meeting, they lined up the binders neatly on a table in a conference room.

When the AZ team finally did arrive, they proved unsparing. They were detailed and thorough, asking deep questions about mRNA chemistry, delivery, and all the results to date of animal testing of mRNA, including the Montreal experiments and Rossi's and Chien's VEGF experiments.

To the AstraZeneca scientists, the science largely checked out. Moderna was onto something. But they were also impressed by something else: Moderna's self-confidence, which was driven in part by Hoge's messaging and his anticipatory nostalgia. "Many biotech companies would have been less sure of themselves," recalled David Blakey, one of the AstraZeneca scientists who visited. "They were confident this technology was going to work. Stephen Hoge and the others really showed a strong story, backed up by data, that convinced us it was worth the bet." Hoge, in particular, "gave the insights that made you realize what the potential of the technology was."

It worked. After months of courting Big Pharma companies Moderna had found a partner. AstraZeneca would pay $240 million upfront to Moderna, gaining exclusive rights to dozens of potential mRNA-based drugs for heart health, metabolic and kidney diseases, as well as cancer. AstraZeneca also would pay royalties to Moderna on the sale of any resulting products.[23]

The deal also called for potential future payments of an additional $180 million if the companies' collaboration hit certain milestones, but in biotech parlance this amount was known as "biobucks," not quite hard currency because it might never be paid. Companies often used biobucks to inflate the total value of a deal, much the way sports agents use incentive clauses that might never be reached to inflate an athlete's contract size.

The details of the final deal shocked the industry when they were announced in March 2013. It was one of the biggest upfront payments to license potential drugs ever made, for a technology that hadn't even reached human testing. It was a lot of money to shell out for something that might never work. But Pascal Soriot needed to make big bets to reverse AstraZeneca's dimmed fortunes.

On the same day the Moderna deal was announced, AstraZeneca said it would cut twenty-three hundred jobs from its sales and marketing operations, on top of the sixteen hundred R&D jobs the company had just recently said it would cut.[24] This was Big Pharma's new reality: investing in others' cutting-edge research while cutting back on in-house R&D and on marketing its own drugs. The future looked different.

Still, AstraZeneca's executives continued to heap praise on its new partner. Even a year after the deal was signed, an AZ research executive told analysts and investors: "If anyone had asked me, five, ten years ago, would anyone be able to create a stabilized messenger RNA that you can express in the cell and actually produce other interesting protein, a trans membrane protein or secretive protein, I would have said, 'You're nuts.' No one will be able to crack that. But what the Moderna guys have done is actually generate a chemistry platform or chemistry technology that really stabilizes the messenger RNA, enables you to transfect it into cells, and express whatever protein fusion, protein antibody, vaccine that you want. It's incredibly powerful." For most of us, this is nearly impenetrable language. In places like Kendall Square, this is almost immeasurable fawning.

For Moderna, the AstraZeneca deal was "totally transformative," Bancel said. "That changed the company forever." Just before the deal, the company was down to $20 million in the bank. Nearly overnight, it had thirteen times that, $260 million. It was enough to hire one hundred to two hundred more scientists and buy the time needed to fail, learn, retry, and repeat until all the failing and learning would lead to a breakthrough. "To do that type of high-quality science, we need capital,"

Bancel said. "And you need a runway. Because you need time. If you are running for your life and have six months of cash, you cannot do it."

Bancel was in a celebratory mood and wanted to show his gratitude to Ken Chien, the cofounder who used his connections with AstraZeneca to help broker the deal. Bancel remembered how, in some of the pitch meetings to pharma companies, Chien, an American scientist less accustomed to haute couture, had teased Bancel about his chic Hermes belt with the H-shaped buckle. He wondered if it was a good luck charm. Shortly after the AstraZeneca deal was signed, Chien received his own Hermes belt as a gift from Bancel. "That was the first token I had gotten, the first kind of material reward that I got from Moderna," Chien recalled.

For Derrick Rossi, the mood was different. According to Rossi, Bancel told him that the terms of the collaboration with AstraZeneca included a provision that anyone doing separate research on mRNA could not serve on Moderna's board of directors. AstraZeneca's lawyers asked that Rossi be removed from the board because of concerns he could use insights from his involvement with Moderna to advance mRNA research in his own academic lab, Bancel recalled. It seemed to Rossi that Bancel was doing anything he could to force Rossi out of Moderna. He was displeased about the news and probably could have fought it. But he had had enough. Rossi stepped down from the board. The following year, he let his term on Moderna's scientific advisory board expire as well. He had fully cleaved himself from Kendall Square. He no longer had any say in what Moderna would do either scientifically or strategically. The man whose science got Moderna off the ground was now just an investor.

"I walked away from Moderna at that point," Rossi said. "I kind of felt like my baby had turned into some crazy monster."

4

Feeding the Beast

LORENCE KIM IS A SON OF KOREAN IMMIGRANTS WHO GREW up in Pittsburgh, went to Harvard, and studied biochemistry in the lab of Tim Springer, the future Moderna investor. He went on to medical school at Penn and, along with an MD, tacked on a Wharton MBA, which proved valuable when investment bank Goldman Sachs recruited him. Instead of practicing medicine, Kim went to work orchestrating deals for biotech companies. One of his biggest deals was the sale of Maryland biotech MedImmune to AstraZeneca (AZ) for $15 billion in 2007—at the time one of the biggest ever for a US biotech company.

In 2013, Kim was trying to close another deal between AZ and a small drug company called Omthera, but right in the middle of negotiations, AstraZeneca's M&A chief went incommunicado. Calls and emails went unanswered for weeks. "What's going on?" Kim wondered.

The announcement of the Moderna deal explained the silence. The due diligence and contract negotiations between Moderna and AZ had pushed aside everything else. Eventually Kim closed the Omthera deal, but in the meantime he also became intrigued by Moderna, a company he had never heard of before this.

His interest grew later that year when Kim got a call from a head-hunter, who said, "Lorence, I don't pitch you on anything, but you need to hear this story. Come have breakfast with me." They met in

Manhattan, where the headhunter teed up the position of chief financial officer at the Cambridge startup.

The baby-faced Kim, who wore obligatory banker's suits but usually opted for the value variety at high-end stores, visited Bancel at Moderna's headquarters the week before Christmas in 2013, and Bancel gave him the scientific rundown. In lab and animal tests, Moderna's researchers had caused the production of hundreds of proteins. Still no human trials, but they were working toward it. Bancel showed him a sketch of what he called "the Beast," a machine the size of a limousine that Moderna was planning to build to make mRNA itself in-house.

To build all this would require a lot of money. "That's why we want you to come join us," Bancel told Kim.

In trying to persuade Kim, Bancel again turned to a tech analogy. "In software you invest a bunch of money upfront to figure out how to make this stuff work," Bancel told him. "Once you figure out how to make mRNA and build an infrastructure around it, every subsequent time you make a product, it's going to be faster, cheaper, and less risky." And this could help Moderna develop many medicines, targeting many diseases.

Stephen Hoge put the hard sell on, too, reminding Kim that he could apply all the pieces of his past to the job of CFO of Moderna—his biochemistry training, his MD, his Wharton MBA, and his Goldman Sachs banking experience.

In a scene that mirrored what Bancel went through when Noubar Afeyan recruited him, Kim spent the Christmas holidays thinking it over, unable to sleep at night, weighing risks and experiencing that fear of missing out. "What if this works?" he thought. "It's going to be an enormous company." He told his wife: "I have to do this thing. And if I don't, I'm going to kick myself. Can you imagine if this pans out, and I passed it up?"

Then again, it was a gamble. It might not work. And while working at Goldman was demanding, it was lucrative. To become Moderna's CFO meant taking a seven-figure hit to his compensation. Still, Moderna stock options would make up for some of that if it worked.

Ultimately, Kim was taken by the vision that Moderna's leaders projected. It was grander than most other biotechs he had worked with.

Some biotech startups were content to make one new drug and cash out, while Moderna wanted to make a new way to make many drugs. "To me," he recalls, "it was just a compelling opportunity that was not plain-vanilla startup territory."

Kim started in April 2014, and by the fall it was time to embark on a new round of financing for Moderna.

Already by the time Kim joined, Moderna had turned into a fundraising machine on the back of its AstraZeneca deal, which turned out to be as momentous and critical as Bancel thought it would be.

With that deal in hand, he continued his hard press for more funding in pitch after pitch. "We just manufacture information," he would say in meetings. For any new disease target—a virus, heart disease, a tumor—Moderna simply had to switch around the sequence of the genetic code and plug it into a uniform template.

His pitches worked. After landing the $240 million upfront payment from AstraZeneca in 2013, Moderna raised an additional $110 million from investors later that year. It secured a grant of up to $25 million from the august Defense Advanced Research Projects Agency, or DARPA—the agency that laid the groundwork for the internet and other common technologies. DARPA wanted Moderna to develop mRNA to make antibody-producing drugs to protect against emerging infectious diseases and engineered biological threats as part of its mission to protect service members from outbreaks when deployed overseas.

All told, by the end of 2013, Moderna had amassed more than $415 million through financing and partnerships since its inception three years earlier. The company moved its administrative offices and main R&D operations to its current home, an office complex in Kendall Square called Technology Square, part of a site that was once a soap factory.

Bancel was thrilled and a little surprised by the cash flow. In one financing round, a single investor wrote a check for $150 million. "Until I saw it, I did not believe this could be possible," Bancel told an interviewer in 2017. "I've never heard of something like this in Europe. . . . There's so much more money in the United States, that people are willing to take risks. I think it's very much in the culture. . . . People are willing to take a chance for something they think could be very big." He viewed this as an advantage over rival mRNA biotechs, CureVac and another new one, BioNTech, both based in Germany.[1]

At the same time, the company's profile was rising. While still shrouded in some mystery—this was before the reports of a difficult work environment had been published—market watchers were taking notice after the AstraZeneca and DARPA deals. In 2014, the financial news channel CNBC included Moderna on its Disruptor 50 list of the most "disruptive" private companies, behind Elon Musk's SpaceX, Warby Parker, and Etsy, and ahead of Spotify, Uber, and Dropbox. The channel ran a segment featuring Bancel, who discussed his admiration for Amazon CEO Jeff Bezos, for transforming his online bookseller into the behemoth retail powerhouse it had become.

It was time to be bold. To move to human trials as fast as Bancel was demanding, the company needed even more money to grow: to hire contractors, to make enough doses of its experimental drugs to supply the trials, to recruit patients and volunteers, to reimburse doctor's offices and other clinical testing sites for the work.

In late 2014, Moderna's board of directors discussed its fundraising strategy. Another hot biotech, cancer drug developer Juno Therapeutics, had raised an unprecedented $176 million that year, including from Amazon's Bezos.[2] Moderna set its sights on $200 million. Up to then, no privately held biotech company had raised that much in a single financing round.

Not bold enough, said one board member. It was Henri Termeer, the Dutch biotech veteran and longtime CEO of Genzyme, who had joined Moderna's board the previous year. This was surprising. Termeer's was usually a cautious voice, but not now. Kim recalls him saying: "We need to raise more. Go raise more so that we can build more."

Bancel, Hoge, and Kim had their marching orders, and the march went well. Kim remembers going into one meeting hoping for $25 million from an investment fund. Half an hour into the presentation the CEO of the fund said, "I'm in for $50 million."

Other deals followed, including another $50 million in investment from a blue-chip Big Pharma company, Merck, to collaborate on the development of mRNA-based vaccines and preventive treatments for viral diseases.[3]

Merck was trying to emerge from its lost decade as patent expirations thumped sales of older drugs, and new drug development slowed. Merck's R&D chief at the time, Roger Perlmutter, had been keeping an eye on Moderna as he tried to jump-start Merck's storied research engine.

Perlmutter, an eloquent industry veteran whose eclectic hobbies ranged from amateur airplane pilot to pianist, met Stéphane Bancel for breakfast in Boston in the fall of 2012 to discuss Moderna's work, prior to joining Merck. He was being recruited for Moderna's board, a job he ultimately wouldn't take because he ended up with the Merck job.

"My general impression was that, scientifically, I thought it was interesting," Perlmutter recalls. "But it was technology looking for the ideal application and I wasn't sure what that application was."

Still, he thought Bancel was "a very capable guy" and they stayed in touch. In 2014, Bancel called Perlmutter to discuss some developments he thought Merck might be interested in. Bancel and Hoge shuttled down to Merck's R&D labs in Rahway, New Jersey, in Big Pharma's Jersey corridor about twenty miles southwest of Manhattan. Far from Kendall Square's shiny new biotech labs, the Merck site smacked of old industry. Rahway held a cluster of brick buildings which had served for many years as Merck's headquarters. A smokestack jutted above it all with massive white block letters MERCK running down it, visible to passengers on the busy Northeast Corridor railroad.

Inside the research facility, hallways displayed molecular models, museum-style, of Merck's most important drugs, including the anticholesterol drug Mevacor, and Mectizan for river blindness.

The Moderna executives told Perlmutter that Moderna scientists were finding that engineered mRNA could trigger a favorable effect on an animal's immune system, helping to build defenses against pathogens. In short, mRNA had the potential to make powerful vaccines.

Perlmutter's ears pricked up. Merck was a vaccine powerhouse that had delivered groundbreaking vaccines over the years against measles, mumps, rubella, chickenpox, human papillomavirus, and rotavirus, among others. Yes, Merck used older, tried-and-true pharma technologies for these vaccines, but Perlmutter knew those methods didn't always pan out. Merck struggled to find vaccines against certain viruses like RSV, respiratory syncytial virus, that usually causes cold-like symptoms but can be dangerous for infants and older people. Despite years of efforts by Merck and others, no one had created an approved RSV vaccine. Maybe mRNA was the answer, he thought. Maybe this was part of Merck's way back.

Perlmutter was focused on the science, but it wasn't lost on him in the meeting that Bancel "is a gifted communicator and clearly had passion for the work and was able to recruit terrific people to work with him."

The $50 million Merck deal that resulted from this seemed like it was just adding to the coffers, but it reflected a significant strategy shift at Moderna. Initially, the company was mainly searching for ways to use mRNA to treat sick people. This meant developing drugs for cancer, heart disease, and rare diseases. The science for this approach was proving difficult. Treatment often required repeat dosing, which sometimes created complications. One was safety—it became more toxic the more you dosed it. Another was decreasing effectiveness with increased doses.

In contrast, vaccines prevent people from getting sick in the first place. Most vaccines required only one, two, or three doses, thus limiting side effects and obviating the need for ongoing protein production. While not abandoning mRNA-based drugs for sick people, Moderna tacked to see vaccines as mRNA's most immediate payoff, a low-hanging fruit. The strategy shift was reinforced around the time of the Merck deal by the formation of a new division within Moderna called Valera, focused solely on vaccines and treatments for infectious diseases.

But the move raised eyebrows among investors and even some employees. What can produce the most immediate success, scientifically, wasn't necessarily the right strategy. Brand-name prescription drugs, particularly for cancer and rare diseases, commanded high prices and produced hefty profits. Vaccines, on the other hand, rarely command more than $200 per dose and are only given once or a handful of times.

It was not enough to cast serious doubt over Moderna's prospects, but it was a reminder that, for all the promise Moderna had shown, this stuff wasn't easy. Balancing its grand vision for a new science with the reality of investor expectations would require a deft touch.

It turned out, though, that Termeer's instincts were impeccable. A few months after he pushed for more fundraising in the board meeting, Moderna had raised an absurd $500 million, including the deal with Merck, easily the largest round of financing for any private biotech to that point. The infusion valued the company at about $3 billion. Moderna was a "unicorn"—the term in finance for privately held companies with valuations above $1 billion—three times over.[4]

Raise more to build more, Termeer had said, and Moderna kept building. Another 100 scientists and support staff came on board, boosting its workforce to about 245 from 145. It advanced dozens of experimental drugs.[5]

But any notions that this newfound capital would cause Bancel to relax were errant. He continued to demand results at a breakneck pace. Now, in 2015, flush with cash, it was time for Moderna to deliver on its promise and start testing mRNA in people.

For its first test in humans, Moderna chose to target a strain of influenza called H10N8. It was rare but had the potential to cause a pandemic. It had jumped from animals to humans in China in 2013. Researchers traced the outbreak to a live poultry market. A handful of infected people died, but it did not become a widespread outbreak.[6]

Moderna had no intentions to make this a product. The experimental H10N8 vaccine would be used only as a proof-of-concept test of its mRNA technology. Scientists were eager to see if their years of tests in petri dishes and animals would translate into success in humans. Were their glowing mice predictive of a powerful new tool against human disease? Or would the glow dim when mRNA faced the complexity of human biology?

But some other employees found it perplexing that Moderna, which had raised so much money on the broad potential of mRNA, would choose a rare flu strain as the first human test. Why this, which had limited market potential? Why not try something that could become a bestselling product? And what was with this pivot to vaccines? It was as if Apple was trying to open its app store and the first app it developed was a metronome for harpsichord players.

Concerns were significant enough that Moderna's new chief medical officer Tal Zaks rented a movie theater in Cambridge for an employee town hall. Zaks, bespectacled with wavy brown hair, was only a few months into the job. He was a native of Israel and had served as a medic in the Israeli army. He spent many years doing cancer research at the National Cancer Institute and the University of Pennsylvania. But Zaks grew antsy in academia and jumped into the pharmaceutical industry, with stints at several companies, including Sanofi SA's cancer-drug division in Kendall Square, where Moderna found him.

At the movie-theater town hall, Zaks showed black-and-white images of the devastating Spanish flu pandemic of 1918 that killed 25 to 50 million, and other major flu outbreaks. Moderna, he said, had the unique technology that could be harnessed to make vaccines that would end future outbreaks, thus the focus on H10N8. Trying to convince the skeptics, Zaks used his own form of Stephen Hoge's anticipatory nostalgia, noting that Moderna might one day provide a major benefit to humanity in the form of a vaccine.

It was a lofty talk with slides with titles like: "How Moderna Can Save the World." Zaks recalled thinking that he reached some of them, while others left the theater shaking their heads.

The H10N8 flu-vaccine study went forward with about two hundred volunteers in Berlin, Germany, who received two doses of Moderna's experimental vaccine, called mRNA-1440. Some volunteers got a placebo, a fake vaccine, to serve as a control group and make sure the shot was what caused any changes in patients.

Moderna needed to know two things: Was this safe for the patients, and did the shot induce the sought-after immune response that would fight the virus, which they would find in blood samples collected about six weeks after the shots.

Initially, Moderna said frustratingly little about this milestone experiment. A few weeks after the trial started, Bancel flew to San Francisco in January 2016 for a large annual health care conference hosted by investment bank J.P. Morgan. The conference had grown to become the can't-miss event of the health care industry, a crowded affair in an old luxury hotel overlooking Union Square Park. Pharma and biotech execs flooded the neighborhood, hustling past the city's homeless in their expensive suits to hold meetings and recruit talent in cramped rooms, busy lobbies, and packed restaurants. Vigilant security guards checked badges and kept watch over protesters who accused the people inside of charging excessive prices that put life-saving drugs out of reach for many.

Bancel faced a standing-room-only crowd of analysts and investors in the hotel ballroom, eager to finally know what this mysterious company had achieved. But all Bancel gave them was that Moderna had started a Phase 1 human study in Europe for an infectious-disease vaccine, code-named mRNA-1440. He didn't reveal the specific disease it was targeting, nor did he talk much about the twelve other drugs and vaccines it was working on at the time. All he had done was signal to them that Moderna was now a "clinical-stage" company. For many, it was more of the same from the secretive unicorn.[7]

Still, the company racked up more high-profile funding during this time. The Bill & Melinda Gates Foundation committed at least $20 million to support the development of an mRNA-based antibody that could prevent HIV infections, with the potential for five times that much funding if it went well.[8]

The Biomedical Advanced Research and Development Authority, known as BARDA, pledged in 2016 to chip in up to $125 million to fund Moderna's development of a Zika vaccine, and the Dr. Anthony

Fauci–led National Institute of Allergy and Infectious Diseases (NIAID) helped conduct early testing of the vaccine.[9]

Zika is spread by mosquito bites and causes mild symptoms in many, but it could carry devastating consequences for pregnant women, whose babies were often born with severe birth defects affecting the brain. Brazil was hit with a high number of babies born with small heads and brain defects. Fauci and others called on Moderna and other companies as some Zika infections began to show up in southern parts of the United States.

Moderna's initial Zika vaccine candidate disappointed; it produced antibodies against the virus, but at suboptimal levels. Another candidate was developed but didn't progress quickly enough to make a near-term impact, as the outbreak waned in the Americas. Moderna and other drug companies turned their attention elsewhere. This was a risk in the vaccine game: you follow the outbreaks, and if those fizzle, so does demand for development and you must make tricky business decisions about slowing down or canceling development you've just ramped up. Bancel later called Moderna's early experience trying to develop a Zika vaccine "traumatizing." This technology that Bancel so believed in had yielded a suboptimal result. It was discouraging. All that hard work and no payoff made Moderna's leaders question whether they should have tried in the first place.

Even so, the work they did would convince Fauci and other NIAID and BARDA scientists that mRNA would be well suited to rapid responses to outbreaks and the partnership steadily expanded.

The H10N8 vaccine trial was underway but Bancel, of course, wanted more. He set a goal of bringing four more drugs and vaccines into human testing during the second half of 2016, an ambitious undertaking for a small biotech. But for Bancel it wasn't just about developing products faster; it was training the company to find new ways to speed up drug development, to set it up for a more efficient way of doing things in the future. And it worked, mostly. Three of the four trials started by the end of the year, and the fourth followed in early January.

"Some people bristled at it," the CFO Lorence Kim recalled of that second-half 2016 rush. "Some people weren't used to this sort of thing.

Other people responded to it." Kim himself approved of the exercise, thinking that if mRNA was truly revolutionary, what's the point of sticking to the same old industry timelines?

In addition to building its research pipeline, Moderna was bulking up on its patent portfolio. The lawyer who had failed to broker a deal with Penn to license the work of Weissman and Karikó and said he'd find a way around it evidently didn't. Moderna would eventually come back to them and ink a new license deal for Penn's mRNA patents, agreeing to pay about $75 million over a three-year period, along with royalties if certain products made it to market.[10] There was no way around this; otherwise Moderna risked patent-infringement litigation if it sold an mRNA product that relied in part on the research of Karikó and Weissman, which it probably would.

At the same time Moderna was tackling another challenge: manufacturing. Even if Moderna hit on the perfect design for a vaccine or drug, it needed the means to produce it at scale. To make some of its own mRNA, the company had built the limo-sized Beast that Lorence Kim heard about when he came on board, but that wasn't big enough for the kind of production Moderna now needed. Moderna turned to contract manufacturers to make its mRNA products for clinical testing. This, too, was challenging. The team couldn't find any US suppliers to do it, eventually landing a manufacturer in Portugal. Bancel wanted in -house capacity to support his aggressive expansion of clinical trials, and eventually, a commercial supply for anything that turned into a product.

The Beast was dismantled and in 2016, ground broke on a full-sized plant, in Norwood, Massachusetts, about fifteen miles south of Cambridge. It would cost $110 million to gut an old Polaroid camera plant and use its shell to install a state-of-the-art mRNA production line— effectively a series of much bigger, much more powerful Beasts.[11]

To oversee all this activity, Moderna poached a pharma veteran, Juan Andres, from Novartis, where he ran a global network of manufacturing plants and had done a stint at Eli Lilly with Bancel. It was another Bancel "upgrade" of the workforce, as Andres replaced a Moderna executive who at one time had juggled human resources and operations and didn't approach Andres's level of experience or expertise.

Finally, a year later at the 2017 conclave in San Francisco, investors and competitors learned more about Moderna's human trial. It was targeting the rare H10N8 flu, they discovered. Moderna also mentioned that further behind in its pipeline were vaccines against several viruses, including chikungunya, Zika, cytomegalovirus, plus a therapeutic vaccine for cancer, and a heart treatment. Still, no results from the human tests were announced.[12]

The results of the H10N8 vaccine study would come later that spring of 2017 for thirty-one of the test subjects, twenty-three of whom received the real vaccine and eight the placebo. The results were promising. Moderna said the vaccine was generally safe overall. Some subjects had mild to moderate side effects; a few had severe injection-site reactions and common cold–like symptoms. More importantly, twenty of twenty-three showed certain antibody responses, meaning their body developed defenses against the virus. Also, none of the placebo recipients showed an antibody response.

After seven years of lab tests, and seven years of skeptics constantly pointing out that all Moderna had to show for itself was lab tests in petri dishes and small animals, the company could for the first time say that its technology worked in human beings. "That we can make safe and effective vaccines with mRNA is now proven," Moderna's CEO, Stéphane Bancel, declared triumphantly to the *Wall Street Journal*.[13]

Moderna never advanced the H10N8 vaccine any further.

5

Broke Offer

AFTER ITS SHORT FLIGHT FROM NEW YORK, STEPHEN HOGE'S
plane landed at Boston's Logan Airport and taxied toward a gate on a
cold Friday in December 2018. Like virtually everyone does when a plane
lands now, he checked his phone.

"What a gut punch," he thought. "What did we do wrong?"

The night before, Hoge was in Manhattan, celebrating with the company's executive team and board members and with investment bankers
who helped prepare Moderna to go public. There was elation; it was one
of the biggest-ever initial public offerings for a biotech company, and a
moment it had taken nearly a decade to achieve. Of course, it would lock
in a fair amount of wealth for some of Moderna's employees and early
investors, as IPOs do. But Moderna's C-suite executives, investors, and
champions thought the successful deal would be validation of their long
quest to turn obscure genetic research into new medicines and vaccines.
Even now, in 2018, skeptics were legion, viewing Moderna as a go-go
startup with a difficult workplace and obsession with secrecy, just another biotech they thought would probably fail to deliver on its unusually lofty promises.

The stock market would be a good barometer of the forces amassing
on each side. On day one of trading, a company wants to see an IPO
"pop" a bit in its stock price, or at least stay flat. If it rises too much,

that means you underpriced your stock and left money on the table. A decline, though, would mean that the stock "broke offer" in Wall Street parlance. It meant investors thought the company was overvalued.

By the time an exhausted Hoge had landed in Boston and checked his phone, elation had plunged into disappointment. In its first day of trading, the price of the stock with the newly minted ticker symbol *MRNA* had dropped 19 percent.[1]

Hoge felt sick about it.

The successful human trial with the H10N8 flu vaccine helped put Moderna on its IPO path. In seven years, the company had been transformed. From a single scientist in a basement lab and six months of cash, the company now had taken in nearly $2 billion in funding from partners and investors. It still had about $1.3 billion in cash and investments. Its Norwood manufacturing plant opened in mid-2018. It was the most highly valued biotech "unicorn"—the term in finance for privately held companies with valuations above $1 billion. And, finally, it had human trials underway.

The next natural step was an IPO. Going public would raise significantly more money, give the firm greater access to capital that would be used to hire more employees, purchase more equipment, and start more clinical trials and, eventually, push its mRNA drugs and vaccines into the market.

But timing an IPO is tricky business, so Moderna's leaders had been deliberate in their planning. Stéphane Bancel worried that if Moderna went public too soon, it could be hurt by a negative surprise in one of its drug studies or a broad downturn in biotech stocks. Setbacks like these could crater Moderna shares, stunt its scientific progress, and make it an attractive target for a takeover by a Big Pharma company. That buyer might have a much smaller vision for Moderna's mRNA technology than the ambitious one Moderna's leaders harbored, and the full potential of the technology would not be realized. Bancel feared such a scenario enough that when Moderna raised the record-setting $500 million from private investors in late 2014 and early 2015, the company told the investors to be prepared to hold their shares privately for three years or more before they could sell them publicly. This was unusual; some prospective investors balked and decided not to get involved.

Bancel wasn't being overly cautious. It did take three more years until Moderna had a solid enough pipeline of experimental drugs and vaccines that Bancel and his board decided it was time to go public. The company began gauging investor interest in a time-honored Wall Street ritual, the "testing the waters" tour. Executives and investment bankers met with mutual fund and hedge fund managers, high-net-worth families, and international investors to see how receptive they would be to buying shares in a potential Moderna IPO. For all the complex intricacies of modern finance, going public is still rooted in the simple act of telling people your story, and getting them excited enough about it that they'll give you their money.

In one exhausting two-week stretch in the fall of 2018, the team, including Bancel, Hoge, Kim, and their bankers, journeyed to London, Paris, Stockholm, Geneva, Zurich, Frankfurt, Abu Dhabi, Singapore, Hong Kong, and Beijing, sometimes sleeping on red-eye flights between stops rather than staying at hotels.

At each destination, in back-to-back-to-back meetings that lasted all day, the executives told their story of where Moderna came from and sold the lofty promise of where it could go.

Some investors were receptive to the pitch: this revolutionary new drug technology, mRNA, was going to work, somehow, and the first success would likely signal many more successes to come. They explained that all mRNA medicines used the same underlying building blocks. All you had to do was rearrange the genetic sequence to generate a new product. Like using the same coding language to make a new app.

Other prospective investors were skeptical. mRNA couldn't possibly work for everything, they said. They focused on the limitations in the science, and the unknowns, all of which translate into limitations and unknowns on profits.

"A lot of people would say to us, 'I think the vaccines are going to work,'" Lorence Kim, the CFO, recalled. But making mRNA work as treatments for cancer and rare diseases? That seemed like a stretch. Moderna's leaders tried to spin this line of thinking positively: OK fine, they'd say, but vaccines alone would justify Moderna's pre-IPO market valuation of around $7 billion.[2] If Moderna were to also successfully develop drugs to treat cancer, heart disease, and more, that would make Moderna even more valuable, so why not take a chance?

Some fund managers simply doubted that mRNA would ever work, and not just in a general sense. They had done their homework and asked pointed questions about whether Moderna could keep the material from breaking down before it did its job. They wondered if the fatty chemical envelope that Moderna used to ferry mRNA through the body to where it needed to go would cause toxic side effects.

All throughout these exhaustive and exhausting pre-IPO meetings, Bancel charmed, using his tireless ability to tell compelling stories about Moderna's mission that made the science accessible and irresistible. In Paris, his native land, Bancel gathered about forty French investors for a breakfast meeting at a luxury hotel to make his pitch. He seemed relaxed, switching between English and French seamlessly. What Moderna was trying to do, he said, was to design and inject synthetic mRNA into people to turn their own cells into protein factories. These targeted proteins would help prevent or treat disease. People knew that at a high level, but it wasn't always easy to grasp. So Bancel trotted out one of his favorite analogies to explain mRNA as his audience dined: Think of your grandmother's recipe book, prized as a family heirloom, he told them. The original recipe book was the genetic material DNA. But you make a photocopy of the chocolate chip cookie recipe to bring into the kitchen because you don't want to spill chocolate and flour on the original. This photocopy was the mRNA, and it delivers the information needed to make something happen.

Bancel was "so in his element," Lorence Kim said. The French investors leaned forward in their chairs as Bancel spoke of recipes and cookies. His audience looked ready to buy in.

Moderna filed requisite paperwork with securities regulators in the fall of 2018. One of the documents explained mRNA technology in a flow chart; it didn't use a cookie recipe metaphor. It started with "DNA," pointing rightward to "mRNA," and then rightward again to "Protein." Underneath, a matching flow likened DNA to "storage," mRNA to "software" and protein to "applications," as if a cutting-edge, gene-based drug could be an app downloaded from the cloud.[3]

The document included the company's mission: "To deliver on the promise of mRNA science to create a new generation of transformative medicines for patients."

Wall Street doesn't let you stop there. You have to list risks for investors, too, and Moderna's risks were there, in plain English: "No mRNA drug has been approved [by government health regulators] in this new potential category of medicines and may never be approved as a result of efforts by others or us." Moderna, even with all the money it hoped to raise in an IPO, might never succeed in selling a single product.

Papers filed, the team took a final round of investor courtship meetings, known as the "road show." It was a whirlwind trip around the United States and to Europe. Ten meetings a day, arranged by bankers who ushered the Moderna executives out of black cars into swank board rooms and then back into black cars to get to the next one. In every board room, Moderna's executives told the same story, and every time they got almost zero meaningful feedback from the stone-faced investors playing it close to the vest. Hoge said it felt like being a standup comic performing in front of an audience being paid not to smile or laugh. Did investors want in on this IPO or not? Hoge thought so but it was hard to tell. Only later would word filter back through the bankers about whether these poker-faced investors were interested.

Bancel was dogged in his pursuit of investors. When one of Moderna's bankers asked an Australian fund manager, Bianca Ogden of Platinum Asset Management, if she wanted to buy shares in the IPO, she balked.

She liked what Moderna was doing. But she told the banker she wasn't comfortable with the projected $7.5 billion valuation of the company, which would expose investors like her to losses if the price dropped in trading.

Not long after her conversation with the banker, Ogden got a phone call. It was Bancel. "What's your problem with the valuation? Let's talk about this," she recalled him saying. He wanted her in on the deal because she had a science background and a reputation as a savvy biotech investor, Bancel recalled. They talked and she said she'd think it over. A few days later Ogden was walking into a meeting in Sydney when her phone rang. It was Bancel again, half a world away, still trying to land her as an investor. "I can't believe it's him again. He wants to talk about valuation," she thought. But his persistence helped convince her that Bancel had passion and a vision and was willing to help others understand it. Ogden was in.

Other investors weren't swayed by Bancel. Michael Caldwell, a portfolio manager at Driehaus Capital in Chicago who focused on health care stocks, had been eyeing Moderna ever since CFO Lorence Kim paid him a visit two years earlier to pitch the company and answer questions. Caldwell was particularly intrigued by the prospect of turning mRNA into cancer treatments, and he was impressed that the company had so many drug and vaccine candidates in its R&D pipeline. But Caldwell noticed that Moderna's IPO pitch prioritized vaccines for infectious diseases. To Caldwell, this didn't seem like the most promising business because it was already dominated by large pharmaceutical companies.

"We wanted to see more progress and de-risking of the platform to understand where they could go with it," Caldwell recalled. "We were worried that the development timelines would just be long, and it would be expensive to continue funding."

By early December 2018, Moderna was ready to go. But a few hiccups emerged. First, Moderna made a last-minute decision to drop a bank, Bryan, Garnier & Co., from its underwriting team because the bank made an unauthorized communication about the offering. Banks aren't supposed to publicly communicate anything about an IPO outside of the official documents filed with securities regulators and circulated among prospective investors.[4]

Moderna still had a team of top-notch banks to underwrite the IPO, so the absence of Bryan, Garnier wasn't likely to be too damaging. But then another bump hit when Moderna and its bankers decided they wanted to move up the IPO a day or two because investor interest appeared strong, and they wanted to strike when people are feeling excited. This would have worked except the stock markets had a rare mid-week closing on Wednesday, December 5, in honor of former president George H. W. Bush, who had died a few days before.[5] The frenzy over timing led to nothing but a bit of confusion. The company stuck with the original plan to price the IPO after the market closed on Thursday, December 6, with trading to start the next morning.

The obstacles were small but significant enough to create questions and a little bit of uncertainty on the road show—something no company wants. The last stretch to the IPO is like getting a plane off the ground— you want everything to be smooth and routine. The bank's exit and the timing confusion put some on edge. "It put this gap in the middle of our road show," Lorence Kim, the CFO, recalled. "It was this weird air pocket in this typical IPO process. You're trying to build momentum into that last day." It made Kim nervous.

Thursday, December 6, was a turbulent day on the market, with fears of a United States–China trade war escalating.[6] No matter, Moderna was ready. The bankers had taken orders from investors to determine what an appropriate opening price would be. Moderna's executives and some members of its board gathered in a conference room in the Times Square office of one of Moderna's lead bankers, Morgan Stanley, with sweeping views of the Hudson River. Other board members and bankers phoned in. The board approved a price of $23 per share, smack in the middle of the $22–$24 range they had envisioned.

But the bankers and Moderna decided to increase the total number of shares being sold in the IPO, allowing Moderna to raise $604 million, more than the expected proceeds. The transaction—selling 7 percent of Moderna's shares publicly—gave Moderna a market capitalization of about $7.5 billion, impressive for a company with no products, no profits, and still possibly years away from having either. It looked solid.[7]

"On the night of the pricing everything looked really outstanding," Kim said.

Bancel, Hoge, and Kim went to a hotel bar to toast the IPO. They didn't stay out late, though. They were exhausted from the road show, getting only three hours of sleep some nights. And they wanted to rest up for what they hoped would be more celebration the next day, when trading would begin.

By most measures, the IPO itself—the pricing and the proceeds—was a resounding success. At the time, Moderna had raised more money than any other biotech going public for the first time. Its $604 million easily topped the $324 million raised two months earlier by Allogene Therapeutics, a Bay Area company developing new cancer treatments. And Moderna's market cap of $7.5 billion was within striking distance of some older, more-established drug companies that already had products on the market. On top of all that, Moderna managed to raise more than it had initially planned to.

Bancel had his own reason to celebrate. He owned about 9 percent of Moderna shares, which were now worth more than $700 million. Flagship Ventures, the venture capital firm that helped form Moderna and whose leader was Moderna's chairman, owned about 18 percent of the company, now worth more than $1.3 billion. It was a home run for a VC firm, one that would help make up for the losses from investments in less successful startups. Other Moderna executives, cofounders and early investors also saw windfalls with their valuable ownership stakes.[8]

Eyes popped later when Bancel's compensation was revealed to hit $58.6 million that year. This was a huge number. For comparison, in 2018, the total compensation for the CEO of the biggest health care company in the world, Johnson & Johnson, was valued at $20.1 million, one-third of Bancel's.[9]

All but $2.7 million of Bancel's pay was stock-option awards granted as Moderna finalized the IPO. In its securities filing, Moderna's board of directors said it granted this tranche of options "to recognize Mr. Bancel's continuing leadership of the Company in its mission to create a new category of transformative medicines based on mRNA."[10]

The morning that trading was to start, the executives and some family members joined longtime Moderna employees and others who won an in-house lottery to attend a breakfast celebration at Nasdaq's Times Square office. In what has become a tradition at the exchange, the group gathered behind a dais, the Moderna corporate logo hung behind them to ring the ceremonial opening bell, clapping and cheering for the cameras of financial news channel CNBC, airing the event live. A smiling Bancel and a few other top executives did the honors by placing their hands together to press the button that would activate the bell and start trading. Confetti rained down from above.[11]

The pomp was followed by not much. It takes a couple hours after the start of regular trading for traders to sort buy and sell orders for a newly listed stock following its IPO. It wasn't until 11:40 a.m. that the Nasdaq ticker showed Moderna shares open for trading. The opening price: $22 a share, a dollar less than where the shares were initially priced the night before.

Not a great start, but it was still early.

Then, more trades came in and the price dropped more: $21. Then $20. Then lower. The executives' smiles faded.

Stephen Hoge couldn't bear to watch. He was still sleep-deprived from the IPO road show. And now, for all that effort, the stock market was delivering its verdict: Moderna was overvalued. It didn't help that the broader stock market was down that day, but that could only account for some of the drop Moderna was experiencing.

Hoge turned to his wife, who had joined him at the Nasdaq offices for what they hoped would be a celebration. "Can we go home to see our kids now?" he said. They hopped on a shuttle flight from LaGuardia Airport to Logan in Boston. When they landed at Logan Airport, Hoge checked his phone. MRNA closed at $18.60, down 19 percent. It was one of the worst trading debuts for an IPO that year. In the span of about six and a half hours of trading, Moderna's value had dropped from $7.5 billion to about $6 billion.[12] Over the course of the trading day, Moderna's value dropped $64,000 per second.

Moderna's leaders were perplexed. They thought they had checked all the boxes. What transpired seemed so at odds with what they'd anticipated. "It stood in contrast from what we had seen in the weeks and months leading up to it," Lorence Kim recalled. "We thought we had the support of all these great institutions, all these great investors lining up globally to support the company." But in the end, "the buying power wasn't there."

The weak trading debut cast a pall over Moderna's much-hyped image, showing to the world that some investors didn't have as much confidence in mRNA technology as the company did. Certainly, the stock price might rise in the future. But the broke offering at the IPO could dampen enthusiasm for future, secondary stock offerings that are routine money-raising events for companies.

Bancel worried about what the IPO investors would think, the ones he had recruited so aggressively, like Bianca Ogden, who paid $23 per share only to find it was worth $4 less after a day. "Anybody who just did an IPO would rather people who just invested feel good about their investment," Bancel recalled later. He and CFO Lorence Kim divvied up a list of the top twenty-five investors and spent the weekend calling them. They wanted to acknowledge any disappointment, and to show that they were making themselves available for questions. "It's not like we had anything new to say to people," Kim said. "It was really about, 'We're not going to hide. We know it's disappointing. Obviously, no one's happy.'" There was a little carping among the investors about the bankers who managed the deal, but the outreach by Moderna disarmed most investors.

From the devastating opening day, things only got worse. By the end of 2018, Moderna shares were down to about $15. The share price recovered the next spring, in 2019, to more than $25, but plummeted again to below $13 that summer, and by the end of 2019, after a year on the market, MRNA was still under $20. Short sellers—investors who bet on a stock price's decline—bought into the shares.[13]

All this time, the perception that dogged Moderna was that it talked a big game but that's all. A year after its IPO and now nine years into its existence, it still hadn't gotten a single drug or vaccine approved by health regulators. Investors remained concerned that Moderna's potential was limited to the less lucrative field of vaccines. Skeptical investors added up the sales potential for each of the known drugs and vaccines in Moderna's R&D pipeline and didn't see enough to justify a big stock valuation. The most promising near-term product was a vaccine against a common virus, the cytomegalovirus, but it was still a few years away from reaching the market.

Perhaps Moderna was just another overhyped unicorn, strong on salesmanship, weak on execution. Maybe its earned reputation of secrecy and a hard-charging culture were just ways to hold up the facade, to hide the fact that the emperor is indeed naked. The thing about reputations is they're hard to shake in the absence of evidence to the contrary. And, to some investors, Moderna produced little evidence at this point that it was anything but a flop. Without products, the company obviously wasn't profitable, and it was spending more than $400 million a year on R&D and other operating expenses. Bancel had pushed so hard to get Moderna to this point, raising so much money on the backs of scientists pushed to their limit, causing some employees to flame out, enduring deeply skeptical observers and negative news coverage about a secretive and demanding culture, losing cofounder Derrick Rossi. Despite it all, he improbably got them to a successful human trial and a respectable pipeline of potential products. And still investors were saying, *Yeah, but prove it.* Still, all they wanted to know was, *Will it really work, and when will you have products?*

Stephen Hoge remembers that after the disastrous IPO, he just wanted to unplug from the world and make it to the Christmas holidays for a much-needed break. As an executive who joined the company in 2013, he still had a valuable ownership stake and compensation package. But he worried what the stock's disappointing performance meant for newer employees whom he recruited. Some had stock options that were now under water—with exercise prices higher than Moderna's newly listed market price. "I thought, look at all the people I've talked into joining. All those promises I made, and I haven't delivered."

The deep disappointment Bancel, Hoge, and others felt was understandable. To the outside world IPOs feel like singular events. It's easy to look from the outside and just accept the market's verdict. But if you've put in eight years of building and grinding, fundraising and recruiting, failures and successes, promises and pivots, all to get to this one day, that verdict might feel like a gut punch.

Despite their rattled nerves, Moderna's leaders had no intentions of accepting the verdict. The deal had raised a good chunk of money. The stock was stuck but Moderna soldiered on. By 2019, it had more than twenty different drugs or vaccines in various stages of research and development, and several of them were in human trials. In talks with analysts, Bancel highlighted a few that he said could be blockbusters. The biggest, and potentially the first that Moderna could bring to market, was a vaccine against cytomegalovirus, or CMV, a common virus that can be harmful to people with weakened immune systems and to babies whose mothers were infected during pregnancy. Bancel called it a "company builder," potentially generating up to $5 billion in annual sales. Early testing looked promising. The next step would be a large, late-stage clinical trial to generate enough evidence to secure regulatory approval.[14]

Bancel left for Cannes for the holiday break in late 2019 focused on the CMV vaccine, which he believed would be its first approved product, hopefully within a few years.

Then came 2020.

6

No Boundaries

DURING THOSE FIRST THREE MONTHS OF 2020, BANCEL jumped from Davos to Washington to Cambridge, trying to marshal support (and dollars) for developing a vaccine against the new Disease X. He met with Dr. Anthony Fauci and others at the government's infectious-disease research institute, who signaled they were ready to partner, using Disease X as the "stopwatch drill" for rapid vaccine development they had previously planned to do anyway with the Nipah virus.

He also met with his own board of directors and executive team, who were less certain. It would be a significant pivot for the company and carried opportunity costs vis à vis other projects in the pipeline. All of them remembered the last time Moderna tried to do this, with the Zika virus, which initially didn't work and ultimately wasn't needed urgently when cases dropped. Moderna's stock was still stuck under water.

Ultimately, Bancel convinced his board and his company to proceed with the project. But it was a unique situation. The scientists were concerned enough about the rapidly rising number of cases that they didn't wait to get started, even as others hedged and debated. Even before Moderna had fully committed to the vaccine, some of its scientists and their counterparts at NIAID were plowing forward, trying to learn what Disease X actually was and how they might attack it.

First, they would need to know more about the virus. What family of virus did it belong to? What part of the virus would be the best to target with a vaccine?

Early in the process, when Bancel was still in Cannes with his family on vacation, he emailed Barney Graham, the veteran vaccine researcher at NIAID, to ask if he and his colleagues had learned the genetic sequence of the virus. This knowledge would allow the design of the right sequence of messenger RNA that could be used in a vaccine to trigger the right immune response.

Graham said his team was on it. "If it's a SARS-like CoV we know what to do and have proven that mRNA is effective at a very low dose . . . this would be a great time to run the drill for how quickly can you have a scalable vaccine," Graham wrote back to Bancel.

"Let us know in real time," Bancel wrote to Graham. "I will get the team aware of it and ready to run when you give us a sequence."[1]

They got the DNA sequence within days, when Chinese researchers analyzed specimens taken from people with the mystery illness. No cases of the new virus had been reported in the United States or Europe yet. Only a few dozen infections were known at the time, most of which were in people living in Wuhan, China, or who had been there recently and returned to a handful of other Asian countries.

The Chinese researchers, Graham and Bancel learned, found that it was a new strain of coronavirus, as Graham suspected, similar to the one that caused the SARS outbreak in 2003.

The Chinese researchers, working with scientists in Australia, posted six initial sequences from the new virus online on January 10, 2020, on virological.org. "Please feel free to download, share, use, and analyze this data," the researchers wrote in their post. This surprised some American scientists, accustomed to more secrecy from China. If Chinese scientists were releasing the sequence, it must be serious, some thought.[2]

Kizzmekia Corbett, from NIAID's vaccine research center (VRC), had set up Google alerts on her phone for any news about the virus in China. She woke up the morning of Saturday, January 11, to find alerts that genetic sequences from the new virus were posted on GenBank, an on-line database of all publicly available genetic sequences operated by the National Institutes of Health.

The posting on GenBank included text that looks random to most of us—what might happen if a young child started tapping on a computer keyboard. Random letters in long chains with no apparent pattern. Included among these were rows of combinations of the letters A, C, G and T, which corresponded to the four nucleic-acid bases found in DNA. Here's a sample of the sequence, which includes hundreds of lines that look like this:[3]

2701	cttcacactc	aaaggcggtg	caccaacaaa	ggttactttt	ggtgatgaca	ctgtgataga
2761	agtgcaaggt	tacaagagtg	tgaatatcac	ttttgaactt	gatgaaagga	ttgataaagt
2821	acttaatgag	aagtgctctg	cctatacagt	tgaactcggt	acagaagtaa	atgagttcgc
2881	ctgtgttgtg	gcagatgctg	tcataaaaac	tttgcaacca	gtatctgaat	tacttacacc

For trained scientists like Corbett, these sequences spell out essential clues to fighting the virus. She rushed to Building 40 on the sprawling NIH campus in Bethesda, Maryland, that Saturday morning and met another scientist in the lab to comb over the sequences.

Corbett, thirty-three years old, had already spent six years at the VRC as a senior research fellow. She had made similar analyses of other coronaviruses like SARS and MERS. Even though outbreaks of those other viruses were limited, Corbett saw them as a potential recurring threat, and it was important to study their structures to find vulnerabilities that a drug or vaccine could target.

Corbett noticed quickly that this new virus had a fair amount of genetic overlap with the older coronaviruses, including a hallmark spike protein. The spike protein is the stem-like structure that juts out from the surface of the coronavirus. In artists' portrayals of the virus, it's usually shown as a red blob, contrasted against a lighter-colored surface. Moderna president Stephen Hoge described the spike as a "sort of weird digit sticking out" and "mushroomy."

Functionally, the spike protein is like a piton that a rock climber drives into a cliff wall as an anchor. It helps the virus lock on to human cells, allowing the virus to pass inside of those cells, where it can replicate. Enough replication causes infection and, depending on the ultimate viral load, disease and possibly death.

To Corbett, a strategy targeting the spike protein was the most promising path to dealing with this new virus.

At the same time Kizzmekia Corbett sprang to action in Bethesda, Moderna's own researchers downloaded the sequence of the new virus to their computers and compared it to sequences for other viruses. One way to do this was to "BLAST," a technique that's short for "basic local alignment search tool," an online service from the NIH that helps researchers find similarities between genetic sequences of various organisms and pathogens. The Moderna researchers also used 3-D software to examine the structure of the protein.

Work was done wherever and whenever. Researchers at Moderna's Kendall Square headquarters communicated with others at home, working into the night from their couches. Phone calls and emails were shared between Moderna and NIAID, mostly focused on what portion of the spike protein to target with a vaccine.

From the perspective of vaccine hunters, who are always on the lookout for ways to trick the body's immune system, introducing a copy of some part of this spike protein by itself to the human immune system could generate an immune response that fought off the spike without the risk of infection by the whole virus. You basically teach the body to deal with these spikes at a time when the spikes can't cause harm, thereby theoretically stopping the virus from getting inside human cells in the first place, thwarting its replication.

One of the key insights by Corbett and her colleagues in the years leading up to the Covid-19 pandemic was that you couldn't just clone a real-world spike protein and drop it or its genetic code "as is" in a vaccine. During the process of the virus binding to a cell and then getting into it, the spike protein changes its shape. A spike protein introduced as part of vaccination would do the same and could mute the immune response to the virus. Corbett and others found that making modifications to the design of the spike protein could lock its "pre-fusion" structure into place—even after it locks on it can't change shape. The modification is known as a "2P substitution," referring to the two prolines—types of amino acids—that are swapped out. Doing this would make a better target for the immune system, and lead to a stronger immune response. In other words, it wouldn't do to use any old piton as the target—it had to have just the right length and sharpness. In theory.[4]

One way to get a spike protein-based vaccine working would be to make cloned copies of the protein itself and inject them into the body in sufficient numbers to induce the immune system to learn to fight them off. Some companies and researchers eventually used this approach for Covid-19 vaccines, with varying degrees of success. One drawback is that it takes a long time to manufacture enough of the proteins in huge, stainless steel tanks.

The mRNA approach—and this is the beauty of it—cleverly turns the body into the spike protein factory. The vaccine carries the genetic code of the spike protein into human cells and instructs them to produce the pre-fusion spike protein. The immune system would detect the spikes as invaders and react appropriately, generating antibodies and other cells. These would remain on alert so that if a person later became exposed to the real virus, the immune system would recognize it and fight it off.

mRNA was also preferable to doing this with another option, DNA, because DNA has to get into the nucleus of cells, which can be difficult to do. Some experimental DNA vaccines, for example, required the use of an electrical device that delivers a mild shock to a person after injection to cajole the DNA into cells' nuclei. While the shock isn't particularly painful, it's not feasible for a mass vaccination campaign.

mRNA on the other hand only has to get into a cell's cytoplasm, the space between its outer wall and its nucleus. This is easier to accomplish.

It was a productive weekend. By Monday, January 13, three days after the sequence was posted, Corbett and the VRC researchers had landed on what they felt was the best sequence of the spike protein to use in a vaccine, and the Moderna scientists agreed with their assessment.

They had agreed on a vaccine design within three days, and now they would set a general plan for testing. Moderna would manufacture initial batches of a vaccine and send them to NIAID, where Corbett and colleagues would test them in animals. More importantly, Moderna would also make a batch for human testing quickly enough for NIAID to start the first clinical study in humans within ninety days—which would be a record for a new vaccine against an emerging infectious disease. Typically with new vaccines, just the animal testing phase took six to twelve months.

The stopwatch drill—a proof of concept that mRNA vaccines could be designed and manufactured quickly—was turning into a necessary race against an infection showing signs of frightening virulence.

It created another level of anxiety and second-guessing for many involved.

Barney Graham, the deputy director of NIAID's vaccine research center, felt reasonably confident about the design of the new vaccine targeting the spike protein that resembled the spike proteins of other coronaviruses like MERS. In this way, researchers were fortunate that the new pathogen in early 2020 was a coronavirus and not another type of less well-understood virus. It made the new coronavirus a more manageable target for a vaccine.

But there are many different sections of that spike to target. Once you pick one, you can only hope you've picked the right one. If it were wrong, researchers would have to start all over. Valuable time would be lost. Despite at first feeling confident about their approach, doubt crept into Graham's mind. His team had made most decisions on the spike-protein sequence by consensus, but they didn't agree on one key feature, leaving it to Graham to make the final decision. That weighed on him after he made the call.

"Knowing there's probably dozens of different changes you could make, I had a little bit of a panic attack," Graham recalled. With colleagues, he concealed it well, but at home he was more distracted, pensive, and restless than usual. His wife, a psychiatrist, helped calm him, he says.

In Boston, Moderna's chief medical officer, Tal Zaks, had a similar moment of panic soon after Moderna and NIAID agreed on a vaccine design. One night his wife, a biochemist-turned-artist, nudged him awake. "You guys put this into production, but how do you know you have the right sequence?" she asked her husband, referring to the spike protein sequence. How did Moderna know whether the sequence posted online by Chinese researchers was right?

"Shit, you're right, I didn't ask that question," Zaks responded and got up from bed. He sent emails that night to his Moderna colleagues, relaying his wife's question.

He said the next morning he received assurances that it was the best sequence for a vaccine, based on past research of other types of corona-viruses. He and Graham had some reassurances but would have to wait for results to completely overcome these doubts.

With a design in hand, it was time to manufacture doses of the vaccine for animal and human trials. The decision a few years earlier to dismantle the Beast and spend more than $100 million to open the Norwood manufacturing plant was looking prescient. Moderna didn't have to waste precious hours searching for a contract manufacturer to make doses of the new vaccine and then manage that contractor.

In the plant, employees wearing white lab gowns, hairnets, and safety goggles worked amid lab hoods, robots, and steel tanks to produce drugs and vaccines for clinical trials. In some areas, machine operators wore sensors so that manufacturing leaders could later analyze movements to investigate why problems emerged, or to look for ways to make the process more efficient.

To save time, Moderna's manufacturing leaders also realized that they could repurpose some of the specialized robots they had already installed for another cancer vaccine project rather than wait to install new equipment.

As many as one hundred manufacturing and quality-control employees were involved in the new vaccine effort, many working nights and weekends.

By late January, even as executives continued to debate the merits of diving into the project, Moderna made about twelve vials of vaccines, to send to NIAID for testing in mice. Kizzmekia Corbett, the viral immunologist, injected the vaccine into hundreds of mice in early February.

About two weeks later, Corbett and colleagues crowded around a lab bench to examine blood samples from the mice. The blood was run through a "colormetric" solution that would change to yellow if the mouse blood contained antibodies to the coronavirus.

"We all stood around and watched it develop this bright color yellow," Corbett said. "We were very excited."

Meanwhile, Moderna finished manufacturing about five hundred more vials of vaccine meant for human testing, on February 7, a Friday. Normally, the company would have taken the weekend off and started quality-control tests on Monday. Instead, about a dozen workers spent the weekend testing samples for potency and other features. The batch cleared most tests that weekend, but it still took about two more weeks to complete sterility testing. Moderna stored the supply in freezers set to –70°C—the temperature needed to keep the vaccine potent. It also monitored a sample of the vials to make sure no bacteria or other toxins were present. The company also sampled the mRNA in the manufactured batch, running it through a special machine to make sure its genetic sequence matched the original design.

Moderna, as was typical for the company, said little publicly about its coronavirus vaccine efforts at first. But on the same day that Moderna finished making the vials for human testing, February 7, at a news conference in Washington, NIAID's Tony Fauci walked through the entire process to that point, including the positive results in mice and plans for human testing. He said: "I'm happy to tell you that there have been no glitches so far. . . . And in fact, all of those have now been successfully implemented, and now there have been no, thus far, glitches. And I think there will likely not be, but you never know. If that occurs, we will be in people in a Phase 1 trial within the next two and a half months."[5]

A few days later, Moderna gave a brief update in a securities filing that was part of its preparations to sell more shares to the public, only noting that the first batch for human testing was complete as of February 7 and was undergoing analytical testing prior to release.[6] This latest stock of-fering raised about $478 million, but priced the shares at $19 apiece, still $4 less than the IPO price.[7] Selling shares at a lower price than a previous round was rare for Moderna. Investors were still skeptical, which partly explained the ambivalence and spirited debate about pursuing a coro-navirus vaccine among executives. Even in February 2020, even when investors knew Moderna had started work on a coronavirus vaccine, the company was no wunderkind.

Next came waiting. During much of February 2020, Moderna had to wait for the manufactured doses to pass sterility testing. And NIAID had to wait for the FDA to approve the first clinical trial in humans.

While they waited, I met with Bancel in his sixth-floor office at Moderna's headquarters in Kendall Square, which commanded views of MIT's campus out the window. I was there to learn more about the com-pany and its vaccine project, for a planned article in *The Wall Street Jour-nal*. A painting of a monkey and a photo of a coastline hung on one wall. Pictures of his daughters were perched on his desk. A bookcase covered the wall opposite Bancel's desk. One shelf held a row of clear rectangular paperweights, with tiny vials encased in the glass. Each contained the name of a potential Moderna product and the date it started human test-ing. Moderna had established a tradition of giving every employee these paperweights when human trials started. On that February afternoon, Bancel's shelf held sixteen paperweights, markers of Moderna's progress, and reminders of as-yet-unfulfilled potential: none of the drugs and vac-cines represented on the shelf had yet to receive approval to become a product. Bancel was hoping to add another paperweight to commemo-rate the start of human testing of a Covid-19 vaccine soon.

He wore a gray turtleneck sweater and stylish framed glasses and dis-cussed the basics of mRNA using his favorite analogies, including the recipe book. He outlined Moderna's progress from the beginning. That early work, he explained, had enabled Moderna to make the first batch of a new coronavirus vaccine about twenty-five days after selecting the genetic sequence—an astonishing feat. Bancel was typically grandiose. "If we can make this technology into a coronavirus product," he said, "you could do so much for mankind."

But he was also mindful of the uncertainties that the team's strategists had been debating fiercely. "Nobody really knows what this virus is going to become a year from now," he said. And by proceeding with a coronavirus vaccine, he acknowledged, Moderna was taking manpower away from its other projects. And of course, he had no idea whether the vaccine would work.

"It is possible it's going to work, but we have to wait and see," Bancel said, knocking on his wooden desk.

While Moderna waited during February for sterility testing of its vaccine to finish, the virus didn't wait. In China, a doctor who warned about the dangers of the virus, and was arrested for speaking out, died from an infection. Global case counts soared. In just a couple of weeks, confirmed cases had risen from a few thousand to 31,000 confirmed. Deaths topped 630—nearly all still found in China.[8] Two weeks later, the death count topped 2,200 and the case count ballooned to more than 76,000.[9] Most of the cases were still in China, but the virus was showing signs of spreading elsewhere, including the United States, where there were about 15 confirmed cases in Washington State, California, Texas, and a few other spots.[10] American authorities began quarantines of anyone returning from China, some at military bases—for two weeks.[11] The *Diamond Princess* cruise ship, with 3,500 passengers and crew members, docked in a Japanese port after the virus was found on board. Hundreds of American passengers, some infected, were evacuated and brought back to the United States.[12]

All Moderna and NIAID could do was wait for approvals. In mid-February, a week after visiting Bancel in Cambridge, I met Tony Fauci at his office at the NIH campus outside Washington to discuss the emerging coronavirus vaccine efforts. We shook hands, which was completely unremarkable at the time.

Fauci at the time was neither a household name nor a political lightning rod. He was well-known and well-regarded in infectious-disease circles as a leading researcher on HIV and AIDS, and as the director of NIAID since 1984, when the AIDS crisis was exploding.

The Brooklyn-born Fauci, seventy-nine at the time, had worked at the NIH for most of his career. He had advised at least seven presidents on infectious-disease issues. He was a savvy communicator, seasoned at translating complex medical topics into plain language for journalists, the public and the lawmakers who decided on the NIH budget. Now, as leader of NIAID, he was also serving on the White House coronavirus task force established in late January 2020. This role involved daily meetings by phone or at the White House situation room with other government officials, including the Secretary of Health and Human Services, Alex Azar (Vice President Mike Pence would be named chairman of the task force later in February). At the time, they were focusing on concrete, immediate decisions, like what to do with the American passengers on the *Diamond Princess* cruise ship. Should they bring the sick ones back to the United States? And if they did, could they be transported in special compartments on planes?

Indicative of the complexity and confusion surrounding this outbreak early on, the virus didn't have an official name until this time, when it was already a severe crisis in China. Fauci and others commonly referred to it as either the "novel" or "new" coronavirus. On February 11, the International Committee on Taxonomy of Viruses officially named the virus "SARS-CoV-2," short for severe acute respiratory syndrome coronavirus 2, to distinguish it from the SARS that emerged in 2003. The World Health Organization (WHO) named the disease that SARS-CoV-2 causes "Covid-19," meaning coronavirus disease-19, the "19" referring to the year the disease was first detected in humans.[13]

Fauci discussed the emerging response to the virus in a small boardroom adjoining his office. A wooden bookcase on one wall held books with titles such as *Cured: The People Who Defeated HIV, AIDS in Nigeria,* and *Bioterrorism.* On the opposite wall were the markers of his distinguished career: plaques with various honors such as an honorary degree from Wake Forest, and photos of Fauci shaking hands with the likes of former president Bill Clinton.

Sitting at the head of the conference table, Fauci said he was convinced a vaccine was needed against the new coronavirus. "Classically and historically, the only way you can completely suppress an outbreak by intervention, as opposed to waiting until it dies down, is with a vaccine," he said. "We've eradicated smallpox. We've eliminated polio in most of the world for the people who take the vaccine. Measles is a disease that should not be around. The only reason it's around is because mothers are not vaccinating their kids." That was a reference to measles outbreaks that were popping up in the United States as resistance to vaccines grew among a small portion of parents (fathers, too, not just mothers). In 2019, there were 1,282 cases of measles, most of which were in unvaccinated children, the most in twenty-seven years.

Fauci was convinced that the US government should lead the charge on a coronavirus vaccine, whether the virus spread widely in the Unites States or not. "We live in a global community and my institute is the National Institute of Allergy and Infectious Diseases. Infectious disease has no boundaries. So, when there's an outbreak of Zika in South America, Ebola in Africa, chikungunya in the Caribbean, AIDS throughout the world, and now coronavirus . . . we're so interconnected," he said.

Under Fauci's leadership, NIAID had collaborated years earlier with GlaxoSmithKline to develop an Ebola vaccine and ran clinical trials with Moderna on a Zika vaccine, both of which were certainly threats to the United States, but for which the vast majority of victims were in other countries.

"It's important because we are a world leader in public health and in research," Fauci continued. "But also because we have to protect our own citizens. It's a combination of a responsibility as a rich nation to be a leader in the development of countermeasures of outbreaks that may never get to us, as well as ones that might actually get to us."

Fauci was enthusiastic about NIAID's collaboration with Moderna, but with some caveats. mRNA "really transformed vaccinology" he said. It meant rapid response. It would be possible, he promised, to start the first human study of Moderna's new coronavirus vaccine within three months, by the end of April. He said this "is unquestionably the world indoor record" for developing a vaccine. In contrast, using older technologies would probably take eighteen months to two years just to start the first human trial, he said. "We partnered with Moderna because of the real potential of the messenger RNA platform," he said.

Still, that didn't mean most people would start getting a vaccine in three months. Even on the rapid timetable that mRNA permitted, additional human studies would be needed to get a vaccine ready for wider use—and he felt the minimum was likely eighteen months. Optimistically, he thought, that meant a widely available vaccine by mid-2021.

Fauci acknowledged mRNA wasn't fully proven as a technology, but it was worth a bet. "It isn't as time-honored" as older vaccine technologies, "but the ability to rapidly get into the trial and rapidly scale up is really quite promising," he said. "If you really want to make a vaccine, for the last six or seven decades, we've been growing it in eggs." Some flu vaccines, for example, were created this way. "Sure, give me two billion eggs and we'll grow it up, and it'll take five times as long, but I guarantee we'll get a vaccine from it. Whereas if you want to really get it quickly, you're using technologies that are not as time-honored as the standard, what I call antiquated, way of doing it."

Fauci also spoke of the uncertainty of animal testing. People shouldn't read too much into successes at that stage. "Often, you get fooled by mice," he said. "The mice tend to do very well and make your experiments look really good. It's only when you get into a non-human primate that's more akin to a human do you see that it doesn't necessarily always work."

Even if Moderna's coronavirus vaccine proved to work safely in clinical studies, it wasn't clear in February 2020 how it would be deployed. If the ultimate spread of the virus was limited, a successful vaccine might only be given to health care workers and first responders, Fauci said. If it was more widespread, everyone should get the vaccine, Fauci said, though distributed to higher-risk groups first, such as the elderly and people with chronic health conditions.

But at the time, as concerning as the China numbers were, none of that seemed likely, much less certain, as Fauci sat arms-length from me, maskless.

"We wouldn't vaccinate anybody right now here in the United States, unless it started to proliferate here," he said.

Fauci was mindful of the first SARS outbreak in 2003, for which NIAID had started a clinical study of an experimental vaccine, some twenty months after learning the genetic sequence of the virus. In the meantime, public health measures suppressed the epidemic, so there was no way to test whether the vaccine was actually preventing infections or illness. The suppression also discouraged pharmaceutical companies from investing heavily in developing a vaccine against the original SARS.

Still, this new SARS virus was different and drug companies seemed more interested in developing vaccines against the new virus "because this does not look like it's going to go away," Fauci said. The rate of transmission might slow, but even if that happened, Fauci foresaw the virus coming back the following winter. "And if it comes back again next winter, then you're really going to want a vaccine. Because if this turns into something that's seasonal, the way influenza is, then just like you have influenza vaccine you're going to want a coronavirus vaccine. I would imagine that even if this virus starts to taper down in the summer, I think the commitment to continue its full development into a usable vaccine will not go away. I think people are enough concerned about this being really a global health threat and global health hazard, that I'm fairly confident that the money's going to get invested to push it through over the finish line."

The first human study of Moderna's vaccine, he said, would recruit healthy adult volunteers. NIAID would inject them with the vaccine, then later take blood samples to see if the vaccine caused the body's immune system to produce antibodies against the coronavirus. And researchers would monitor the volunteers for any side effects and safety issues.

If the first study showed the vaccine was safe and induced the desired immune response, subsequent larger studies would need to be conducted in areas where the virus was spreading, to see if the vaccine prevented infections or disease, in places like Thailand, Japan, Hong Kong, and Singapore.

At that time, he didn't envision the United States as a large-scale proving ground for Moderna's vaccine. But his tone suggested this view was colored more by hope than by virology. A large-scale vaccine study would have to be conducted "where there are infections. And we don't anticipate there will be infections in the United States. Hopefully there won't be. If there are, you can do the entire trial in the United States.

"I hope it doesn't come to that."

7

mRNA-1273

NEAL BROWNING, A FORTY-SIX-YEAR-OLD NETWORK ENGI-
neer at Microsoft with close-cropped brown hair that came to a point
in the front, always told his young daughters that they had to get their
childhood vaccines and seasonal flu shots even though they hated needles. Now, in March 2020, he was going to subject himself to an injection, not with a proven flu shot but an unproven vaccine for an emerging
disease. If his daughters were worried, he reassured them, telling them
there was a trusted system of testing vaccines to make sure they're safe
and effective before they're jabbed into the arms of millions of people.

Browning was hoping to model good behavior for his girls and show
them that if you have an opportunity to make a positive change in the
world, you should step up and do it. It's why he volunteered to become
one of the first people injected with Moderna's experimental coronavirus
vaccine, which had been designed just two months earlier—an astonishing timeline by vaccine-development standards.

At the time, the coronavirus threat felt closer to the Browning family than it did to much of America. Washington State bore the first significant cluster of cases in the United States, with nine deaths among
twenty-seven cases of Covid-19 reported by early March.[1] Browning lived
just a few miles from a nursing home where an outbreak killed several

elderly residents.² Government officials in Washington State began closing schools before most of the country.

Browning was becoming increasingly concerned about the news, and
he wanted to do his part to help end the epidemic, so Browning would
participate in one of the staples of medical research: the clinical trial.
This was the proving ground for potential new drugs, vaccines, or medical devices, testing whether they are safe and effective enough to earn
the blessing of government regulators and be sold widely. Drug companies and doctors ask patients with diseases—or healthy volunteers like
Browning—to take a chance by trying a new or experimental approach.

Most drugs and vaccines need to pass three phases of clinical trials before they can be deemed safe. In Phase 1, a small number of people,
perhaps one hundred, get various dose levels of the treatment, and researchers focus on whether it causes any safety problems. This usually
takes several months. They may also look for early signs of whether the
treatment is working as intended. If the treatment passes the first phase,
it goes onto a Phase 2 study, which settles on one dose level and enrolls
more people, usually several hundred. This phase, which often takes up
to two years, is intended to continue to monitor safety and identify more
evidence of efficacy.

Experimental drugs and vaccines don't always work, and the chances
of advancement predictably decrease with each phase. About 70 percent
of drugs that enter Phase 1 testing move onto Phase 2. But only 33 percent of drugs move from Phase 2 to Phase 3, the most important phase
and usually the final phase before a treatment becomes commercially
available.³

Phase 3 trials enroll thousands, can last several years, and usually
determine whether a drug or vaccine will be approved by regulators.
These trials nearly always have the critical "control group." Some study
participants are given the experimental treatment, while others get either a placebo or an established treatment. Doctors and researchers then

closely track the outcomes among study subjects to see if those receiving the experimental approach fare better than the control group.

In cancer trials, for example, researchers track whether patients receiving a new therapy live longer than those who don't get the therapy. In cardiovascular disease, they track whether people receiving an experimental cholesterol medicine have fewer heart attacks and strokes.

Nearly all new drugs and vaccines go through this battery of clinical trials. The FDA, which is responsible for final approval, rarely conducts the trials. Instead, the agency's experts analyze the results of studies that are submitted by the drug companies or medical organizations that fund and run the studies.

Most big drugmakers have decades of experience running clinical trials. Merck, for instance, tested its human papillomavirus (HPV) vaccine Gardasil in more than twenty-seven thousand girls and women in dozens of countries, finding that it significantly reduced the incidence of the precancerous lesions that can lead to cervical cancer. The FDA cleared the shot in 2006, nine years after the first human study started.[4]

Big pharmaceutical companies also have the resources to spend the hundreds of millions of dollars it takes to run the series of clinical trials—and to absorb that spending as a loss if the trials fail. In 2006, Pfizer shocked the industry by halting research on an innovative heart disease treatment, torcetrapib, which the company thought would become a blockbuster medicine. But a Phase 3 study of fifteen thousand patients failed disastrously—the treatment increased the risk of heart attacks and deaths because of an unintended consequence that wasn't detected in earlier studies. Pfizer had sunk $800 million into research and development of a drug that never made it to market.[5]

Before 2020, just over fifteen hundred people had enrolled in early-stage studies testing safety and various dose levels of Moderna's drugs and vaccines, some of which, like the H10N8 vaccine, were simply proof-of-concept trials to show its basic technology could work. And most of those studies were only testing safety and immune responses, as measured by the detection of antibodies in blood samples taken after study participants were vaccinated.[6] An immune system response is not the same as proven protection from disease. It's more just a signal that the body is doing the things you'd expect it to do to fight the disease.

In the case of H10N8, the virus didn't circulate widely, and so the people who participated in the study in Germany were highly unlikely to become exposed to it in their everyday lives. That meant there was virtually no chance of proving the ultimate benefit of a vaccine—the ability to prevent or reduce the risk of disease. It was theoretically possible that the type of immune responses induced by the experimental vaccine would turn out to be insufficient for protection from actual disease.

When it started its clinical trials on a Covid-19 vaccine, Moderna was largely leaning on these limited results, showing its experimental mRNA vaccines could produce an immune response in people, without any direct evidence that mRNA vaccines protected people from disease.

The batch of five hundred vials of vaccine produced in Moderna's Norwood factory in February 2020 were code-named mRNA-1273, and they passed sterility testing, finally, on February 24. Moderna shipped the doses to a NIAID contractor's facility in Maryland, where they were stored at –70°C to keep the mRNA stable. The facility would ship the doses to a handful of sites where the study would be conducted within a few weeks.

The *Wall Street Journal* broke the news of the shipment of doses for human testing, and the news sent Moderna shares surging 28 percent, finally climbing back above the $23 IPO price.[7]

The market wasn't as cautious as the scientists, who knew it was still early. "You're never sure what you have until you're at the end," said Bruce Gellin, president of global immunization at the Sabin Vaccine Institute. "The sequence of testing is designed to sort out what works from what doesn't. That's why it's important to try as many things as possible that seem feasible, because not all horses will finish the race."

At the same time the vials were shipped out, health authorities were sounding louder alarms about the virus itself. The World Health Organization warned that it might not be possible to stop the spread of the virus globally. A US Centers for Disease Control and Prevention (CDC) official warned that the virus would spread in the United States and could cause severe disruptions to everyday life such as school closings— news met with a mélange of fear, skepticism, and confusion. In turn, the stock market plummeted, turning in its worst week since the financial crisis of 2008.[8]

President Trump, in a reelection year, tried to dampen growing concerns. Just a couple of weeks earlier, when the first case was reported, he had said the situation was under control. Now he was saying at a news conference that there were only fifteen confirmed cases and that the number "within a couple of days is going to be down to close to zero."[9]

That didn't happen. Trump soon changed tacks, focusing instead on the burgeoning efforts to find a vaccine, to send a signal that help was on the way. A photo op at the White House offered a preview of what would turn into a massive federal effort to find a Covid-19 vaccine.

In early March, the White House invited executives from several drug companies that were developing vaccines or treatments for Covid-19 to brief the president on their efforts. Stéphane Bancel received his invitation a few days in advance and provided the requisite personal information to get a security clearance to get into the White House. On the day of the meeting, he flew to DC early and paid another visit to BARDA to continue his pursuit of more federal funding for his vaccine project.

When he got to the White House, the security guard said Bancel didn't have clearance to enter. He had to step aside and wave hello to his counterparts from GlaxoSmithKline, CureVac, Johnson & Johnson, and others who were getting in with no problems. Bancel didn't know exactly why he was told he couldn't go in but thought it might have had to do with an error in the Social Security number he provided. The France-born Bancel wasn't a US citizen but as a green card holder, he had a Social Security number.

Finally, Bancel was allowed in about five minutes before the scheduled meeting. He was ushered into the White House Cabinet Room, adjoining the Oval Office. He took a seat in one of the leather chairs surrounding a long, oval mahogany conference table. Busts of George Washington and Ben Franklin flanked a fireplace along one wall. Natural light came through the curtain-framed French doors behind the president's seat.

Bancel sat across the conference table from the president. Anthony Fauci sat three chairs to Trump's left. Each invited executive took a turn introducing their company and how they were trying to fight the virus. The main topics were money, research, and time. The CEO of Inovio Pharmaceuticals said the company needed federal help to expand its vaccine manufacturing capacity. The CEO of Novavax said the company needed money, and it would help if FDA sped up its approval process for the start of new clinical trials.[10]

When it was his turn, Bancel told the president Moderna was working with Fauci's team and had already delivered a batch of the vaccine they codesigned, and now was waiting for the first study to start. He said the company was moving fast because of its collaboration with NIAID, which had started several years before. "And so we're able to move very, very fast from a few phone calls to getting a vaccine made, ready for clinic," Bancel said.

Trump began to grill Bancel on just how fast. "What is your timing then, what would you say?" Trump, sitting with his arms crossed, said in a low voice.

Bancel, mindful of Moderna's collaboration with NIAID, looked across the table at Fauci as he responded. "So we're hoping to get the Phase 1 start very soon now. We're just waiting for a green light." He waved his right hand toward Fauci as he said, "The product is at the NIH." Once the Phase 1 study started, it would take a few months to get results. Then, Moderna could choose the best dose and start a second study, Phase 2, Bancel told Trump.

"So you're talking over the next few months, you think you could have a vaccine?" Trump said.

"Correct," Bancel said, but quickly added that he meant the start of a Phase 2 study would be in a few months.

Fauci quickly raised a hand and interjected: "You won't have a vaccine. You'll have a vaccine to go into testing." There was a difference between a vaccine being ready for the next phase of testing and being ready for widespread use. Fauci was trying to make sure Trump understood the difference. Trump leaned forward and listened to Fauci as he spoke.

"And how long will that take?" Trump said.

"The Phase 2 will take a few months before we can go into a Phase 3," Bancel said.

"All right, so you're talking within a year," Trump said, waving his hands to indicate a rough approximation.

Fauci interjected again: "A year to a year-and-a-half."

After some more back-and-forth, Trump leaned back, folded his arms, and said: "I mean, I like the sound of a couple of months better, I must be honest with you."

It was a confounding statement. Bancel had no way of knowing whether that meant Trump was prepared to spend to speed things up. Ultimately, Trump said he didn't think the drug companies needed federal funding, saying some were "so rich they could actually loan money to the federal government." Instead, what they needed were officials like Fauci to shepherd the companies through the process as quickly as possible.

NIAID had the infrastructure to get the first study of Moderna's vaccine off the ground. It oversaw a network of vaccine clinical sites that had run hundreds of trials over five decades to prove the benefits of flu vaccines and an emergency vaccine against smallpox. It was accustomed to the kind of public-private coordination required to do this right. Drug companies often needed to work with clinics typically located in large academic medical centers with the equipment and staff to execute.

Initially, the plan was to design and produce a vaccine for human trials in three months, implying a start date of April. Ultimately, they decided to start even sooner, in March, running human tests in parallel to the "challenge" testing in monkeys in which they vaccinate the animals and then infect them to see if their immune systems fight the disease.

Running in parallel was unusual, but it would allow the researchers to cut months from the development timeline, which seemed necessary given the mounting crisis.

The challenge tests of the vaccine in rhesus macaques that did take place were promising. Among sixteen vaccinated monkeys, only two showed detectable levels of virus RNA in their lungs, whereas all eight unvaccinated monkeys had detectable viral loads in their lungs. And five of sixteen vaccinated monkeys had detectable virus in their noses, versus six of eight unvaccinated monkeys. What's more, of the monkeys vaccinated with the same 100-microgram dose of the vaccine that would be tested in humans in a large Phase 3 trial, there was no detectable virus in their noses two days after being exposed to the virus.[11]

Kizzmekia Corbett, the NIAID researcher who helped design the vaccine, would write later with coauthors in the *New England Journal of Medicine* that the results suggested that the vaccine might not only protect against Covid-19 illnesses, but could also help prevent or limit transmission of the virus. But these results weren't known at the time of the start of the Phase 1 trial in people.

Even with the first study starting a month early, Fauci was preaching caution on timing. He still thought in March that it would take at least a year to eighteen months to generate enough evidence to support the use of a safe and effective Covid-19 vaccine. That meant it would be mid-to-late 2021 before the world could start to inoculate itself.

The plan for the Phase 1 study was to administer various doses in a staggered fashion, thereby minimizing the number of people exposed to the vaccine if safety problems emerged. Initially, just four people would get the lowest dose, followed by four people getting a medium dose. If no serious side effects were seen, more people would get those low and medium dose levels. And if no serious side effects were seen in that bigger group, the highest dose level would be given to a new group of volunteers.

A 182-page NIH document laid out the details of how the study would be run. The rationale for the study: "There is currently no vaccine against the 2019-novel Coronavirus (2019-nCoV). Therefore, there is an urgent public health need for rapid development of novel interventions."

The protocol also cautioned: "There is no direct benefit to the subjects. There is potential benefit to society resulting from insights gained from participation in this study due to the emerging threat of the 2019-nCoV outbreak. Vaccination using mRNA-1273 may or may not provide protection against infection by 2019-nCoV. The duration of any such protection is currently unknown."[12]

Kaiser Permanente is a large health care system, mostly in Western states, which operates hospitals and health care facilities, as well as health insurance plans. One of its offices, Kaiser Permanente Washington Health Research Institute in Seattle, managed the Phase 1 trial from its offices near downtown Seattle, in a building that also houses a Starbucks and a WeWork shared office space. NIAID chose the Kaiser institute—one of the clinics in its network—to start the first study of Moderna's vaccine because of its experience running such trials, including one on a compressed time frame in 2009 during the H1N1 "swine flu" pandemic. The fact that Seattle was an early hot spot for Covid-19 cases lent more urgency as the study got underway.

Dr. Lisa Jackson was Kaiser's primary vaccine study investigator. Trained in internal medicine and with a master's degree in public health, she had long played a critical, behind-the-scenes role in the hunt for vaccines. At the Kaiser institute, she ran studies of vaccines against pneumococcal disease, influenza, and diphtheria. She helped run the fast-moving clinical trials that contributed to approved vaccines against the swine flu, but that pandemic fizzled out before many people could get the shots. Still, it helped prepare her, at least a little, for what was to come this time around in terms of speed.

Dr. Jackson and her colleagues would need to find about forty-five healthy adults between the ages of eighteen and fifty-five in the Seattle area willing to take a chance on the vaccine. The age group targeted was the most likely to have an immune response to a vaccine and to be able to endure any side effects. If there was no immune response in this group, there would be no point in expanding testing to older or younger people. The volunteers had to be willing to get two injections, four weeks apart, and come to the Kaiser clinic for regular visits, to give blood samples and have vitals checked. They planned to call volunteers on the phone several times to see how they were doing, monitoring subjects for twelve months after the second vaccination, though they hoped to have preliminary results on safety and immune responses much sooner.

On the one hand, the Seattle area outbreak made recruiting volunteers for the study easier. People could see firsthand the effects of the virus. The healthy people needed for the vaccine study had even more motivation to help vet a vaccine that might end the outbreak. On the other hand, the spread of the virus in the Seattle area "created an unexpected complication," according to Barney Graham of NIAID's vaccine-research center. The researchers would have to keep people safe and out of quarantine during the trial.

To recruit, Dr. Jackson and colleagues sifted through Kaiser's databases to search for people in the targeted age range and who lived close enough to make regular visits feasible and sent them letters inviting them to participate. They also looked up people who had participated in previous trials, asking them or family members if they were interested.

The institute publicized the study, noting that participants would receive $100 for each in-person study visit, totaling $1,100 for all scheduled visits.[13]

Social media helped. That's how Neal Browning, the Microsoft engineer, got involved. In early March 2020, he was scrolling through Facebook and saw that a friend had started a discussion about the coronavirus. The friend knew about the upcoming vaccine study because his wife worked at the Kaiser institute. He knew Browning was a frequent blood donor, wasn't scared of needles, and thought he might be interested in volunteering, so he forwarded the information to Browning.

But Browning had never participated in a clinical trial before.[14] So he did some research before deciding to pursue it. He googled "mRNA" and learned that the vaccine didn't contain killed or weakened virus material. He decided the mRNA technology was a "good attack vector." He enrolled.

Browning remembers signing the "informed consent" form, which described the vaccine and an exhaustive list of potential risks. The form warned that in prior studies of mRNA vaccines for other diseases, people had side effects like fever, injection-site pain, and headache after vaccination. And some had allergic reactions. Even the blood draws in the study carried risks like causing fainting and bruising.

The long list of side effects reminded him of the long list of side effects recited in the voiceover of the average prescription-drug TV commercial ("may cause tears in the stomach or intestine;" "may increase risk of death," viewers were warned in some ads). In comparison to those, the potential risks for the Covid-19 vaccine sounded manageable to him. His fiancée, a nurse, also read over the informed consent and thought it was reasonable for Browning to sign up. It wasn't a tough decision; he viewed the virus as a bigger threat. He had already seen it in Seattle.

"I knew it was basically out there and Pandora's box was open," he said.

Browning was one of the first four in the staggered Phase 1 rollout. He arrived at the Kaiser institute on a bright, chilly Monday, March 16. By this time, SARS-CoV2 was no longer just a problem in China. It had infected at least 4,500 people in the United States, and at least 88 had died. Globally, the cumulative tally was 6,600 deaths out of more than 167,000 cases.[15] The virus was starting to loom over the presidential primary elections. Washington State had held its primary election the week before (former vice president Joe Biden narrowly defeated Senator Bernie Sanders on the Democratic side), but other states were starting to postpone their primaries because of the virus.[16]

In an unremarkable patient room, a nurse drew nearly twenty vials of blood from his arm. These would be used as a baseline to compare to future blood drawn to see if there were signs of an immune response after vaccination.

Browning thought he would be the first person to get the vaccine, because he was assigned subject number 1. But another person was injected before him, so he would be the second person in the United States to receive the vaccine. About a half hour after Browning gave his twenty vials of blood, a pharmacist wearing a white lab coat and purple gloves entered the room. Browning pulled back the sleeve of his gray, collared shirt to expose his right shoulder. The pharmacist prepped Browning's skin with rubbing alcohol, then used a syringe to puncture the rubber stopper on top of the vial of mRNA-1273. He drew up the dose into the syringe.

He pushed the needle into Browning's shoulder muscle and plunged the medicine in. It was over in less than ten seconds. His neutral facial expression didn't change during the injection. Browning said it was less painful than the typical flu shot. The procedure was as routine for him as it was momentous for Moderna, and for public health in general.

Browning may have forgotten about that momentousness were it not for the presence of a photographer and videographer from the Associated Press, invited in by Kaiser to document the occasion.

After the shot, the clinic staff kept Browning for nearly an hour to make sure he didn't have any immediate reactions. He felt fine, got his parking-garage ticket validated and drove home. He worked remotely that day, helping to configure Microsoft's internal computer network to accommodate the surge of employees suddenly working from home because of the emerging pandemic. He had no way of knowing then that he would be working from home for months to come.

The next morning, Browning said he woke up with slight soreness in his shoulder, but it soon went away. He felt no other symptoms.

Word began to spread within Microsoft that Browning had been one of the first to be vaccinated in the Moderna trial. Colleagues around the world began to flood his inbox with congratulatory and supportive emails, he said. The publicity generated by the AP photo from the vaccination day would also lead to numerous media appearances for Browning. One TV interviewer hailed his "daring decision" to become a "human guinea pig." Browning's neighbors would yell to him across the street whenever they saw him on the news.

Browning returned for weekly visits to the Kaiser clinic for eight weeks to have blood drawn for the analyses of his immune response. Browning didn't assume that the vaccine gave him protection, so to be safe, he abided by social-distancing and mask guidelines as if the vaccine didn't work. He received his second dose four weeks later, in mid-April 2020. He felt fine after that one, too.

By then, pandemic restrictions were in full force. The March Madness college basketball tournament had been canceled.[17] Other sports followed and shut down. Concerts disappeared. Restaurants closed; many never reopened. Schools shut down and learning shifted to remote virtually overnight. The preliminary tally of jobs lost to the shutdowns was seven hundred thousand in March, the biggest drop since the Great Recession.[18] The full tally for April would be far worse.

The pharma and biotech industries were struggling to adapt. Pfizer, Eli Lilly, and Bristol-Myers Squibb among others had to delay starting new trials of non-Covid drugs and vaccines or pause enrollment of ongoing clinical trials because it became too complicated to get patients in.[19] The Kaiser institute suspended a study of a different respiratory virus in older adults because it wasn't feasible, given the need for social distancing. Moderna itself put off a promising experimental cancer vaccine.

Companies working on Covid drugs or vaccines had to find unusual ways to keep doing the research and manufacturing as quickly as possible, while also keeping employees safe and avoiding disruptions to the work caused by outbreaks. At Eli Lilly, one lab pathologist was sent home because of a positive Covid test, so his colleagues rigged a wheeled robot and an iPad with a live video stream that roamed the lab at his command.[20] Lilly went on to successfully develop a treatment for Covid-19, as did Gilead Sciences and Regeneron Pharmaceuticals. The industry's race for effective treatments for those already infected ran in parallel to the vaccine hunt, though often with much less fanfare.

Visits to the Kaiser clinic changed. Study volunteers like Browning were required to wear masks during visits. Nurses greeted volunteers coming off the elevators to screen them for Covid symptoms and to take temperatures before letting them into the patient rooms. They also constantly monitored staff so that an outbreak didn't threaten the trial because they didn't have enough people available to inject the vaccine or take blood samples for follow-up visits.

Some of the other doctors, nurses, and pharmacists running the study came out of retirement to help. They told volunteers their work on the trial could end up being the most important of their careers.

The different approach to conducting this trial underscored to Dr. Jackson the seriousness of the threat posed by the coronavirus. Even during her frenzied work on a swine-flu vaccine in 2009, that pathogen felt like a known entity. She refused to call the new coronavirus "influenza-like." "This is a much greater threat," she told an interviewer in April 2020. "What we know is almost uniformly extremely concerning to me." The ease of transmission and the severity of some cases led her to view the pandemic as "an unprecedented event in world history."

Not all study volunteers had as smooth an experience as Neal Browning. Ian Haydon was a twenty-nine-year-old science communications specialist at the University of Washington who learned about the Moderna vaccine trial from a coworker. He got his first dose of the Moderna vaccine at the Kaiser institute in early April 2020 and a second shot in early May.

The night after his second shot, he woke up with chills, nausea, and a severe headache. A fever developed that reached 103°F (39°C). Haydon's girlfriend called the Kaiser institute hotline for study volunteers. Dr. Jackson advised Haydon to go to an urgent-care center, where she met him. He was given intravenous fluids and Tylenol to help with his fever. Discharged from urgent care, Haydon went back home and tried to get more sleep. But the suffering wasn't over. He threw up and fainted, saved from crashing to the ground by his girlfriend. His girlfriend called Dr. Jackson again, who said Haydon could go back to urgent care. But they stayed home, and he drank sports drinks to rehydrate. Finally, later that day, the fever broke, and he soon felt better.

Haydon learned he had received the highest dose of Moderna's vaccine that was being tested, about 250 micrograms. He attributed his severe side effects to that dose level. Moderna and NIH researchers opted not to continue testing that dose level in future studies.

Haydon's story made it into news coverage of the new vaccine trial. He noticed that anti-vaxxers began to spread his story online, in a way that misconstrued his experience, he felt. He chalked up his severe symptoms to an immune response to a high dose of the vaccine, not to any inherently unsafe design flaws that would cause long-term safety problems.

Still, his side effects were a preview of a challenge for the mRNA vaccines from Moderna and Pfizer and its partner BioNTech. Publicity around similar side effects would become one of the leading factors in deterring people from getting vaccinated. Even people willing to get the vaccine—and their employers—had to make contingency plans if side effects laid them up and made them unable to work for a day or two. Hospitals had to stagger vaccinations among nurses so that entire units weren't debilitated by side effects at the same time.

The Seattle work was soon expanded to other regions. The NIH started enrolling healthy study volunteers ages eighteen to fifty-five at Emory University in Atlanta as a geographic hedge in case the outbreak in Washington State interfered with the study at the Kaiser institute.[21] The NIH also decided it was safe to expand enrollment in the study to adults over age fifty-five at both sites and at NIH's own site in Maryland. This would be an important age group to study because it was becoming clear that age was a major risk factor for severe Covid-19. People over sixty-five were at much greater risk of being hospitalized and dying from Covid-19.[22]

Carol Kelly, sixty-one, a dietician in the student-health department at Emory, read about the Moderna vaccine trial on the Nextdoor app on her phone, where someone from Emory's vaccine clinic had posted about it. She was interested, but she was intimidated.

"I was given information that this is a vaccine that had not been tried in humans," she recalled. "It was experimental." She called a nephew who is an emergency-room doctor, and he reassured her that there's inherent risk even in the safest vaccines, but the potential benefits for the population outweighed the risks. She also felt reassured when she learned that Moderna had been working with the NIH and that the new vaccine built upon several years of research on other coronaviruses.

Kelly decided to enroll, mindful that both the virus and the restrictions imposed in response to the pandemic were causing such deep human suffering. A vaccine was the best way out.

The day after her second dose, at Emory's Hope Clinic, Kelly woke up with a feeling of vertigo "and about a half a thimble full of energy." The rest of the day she felt "massive fatigue" and a headache. She took pain relievers, and the symptoms were gone by the next day, she said.

Despite getting reassurances from her nephew, Kelly couldn't help but wonder about the vaccine. "You see the sci-fi movies, scary things," she said a couple weeks after the incident. "Yeah, it's like well gosh there is that small chance that something could go awry, and is something going to pop up later? Some kind of rebound, renegade mRNA that's going to come back and do something to me?"

By this time, the virus had delivered a devastating April that strained hospital capacity in many hot spots, threatening to deplete the supply of ventilators for patients and personal-protective gear for nurses and doctors. In March, when Neal Browning got his first shot in Seattle, there were 4,500 confirmed infections in the United States, and 88 deaths. Less than seventy days later, when Carol Kelly got her second hot, the virus had infected about 1.5 million people and caused more than 90,000 deaths in the United States alone. It was clearly going to be the worst pathogen outbreak since the 1918 influenza pandemic. Thousands of family members were barred from being at the bedsides of parents, grandparents, and other loved ones who were critically ill in intensive-care units, forced to say goodbye through screens, if they could say goodbye at all. David Michael Dudley Jr. said goodbye to his sixty-one-year-old father in a Baltimore hospital on a Zoom call. He told him he loved him but felt the hollowness of not being by him. "You're not only telling me my dad is not going to recover," Dudley later told the *Wall Street Journal*, "but I can't even be there to say anything. I've got to do it in probably the most impersonal way possible."[23]

As the pandemic raged out of control, some states were loosening pandemic restrictions on activity, often under pressure from businesses and a public growing weary of the limits of quarantine. President Trump was touting an obscure antimalarial drug, hydroxychloroquine, which he said he was taking as a preventive measure against the virus, even though the evidence of its benefit for Covid-19 was thin.[24] Doctors and scientists pleaded with the public to endure, knowing that easing restrictions would lead to more sickness and death.

The appetite for any sign of hope was insatiable.

Some hope arrived on May 9, 2020. Barney Graham, deputy director of NIAID's vaccine-research center, got a phone call from researchers at Vanderbilt University in Nashville. These researchers were analyzing blood samples of the first eight study subjects to receive the second dose of Moderna's vaccine. They exposed live coronavirus to the blood in a biosafety lab to see if the antibodies in the blood would neutralize the virus. Researchers told Graham the vaccine induced the production of antibodies, and the antibodies prevented the virus from infecting cells, by blocking or interfering with the spike protein's ability to attach to and get inside cells. The potency was better than expected.[25]

For the first time, Graham knew the vaccine was likely to work. He called Moderna CEO Bancel at home that night to tell him that they were still finalizing the data, but that he was blown away by how high the antibody levels were. It was a quick call. Bancel thanked Graham for calling, hung up, and allowed himself to do something he rarely did: cry. "I don't cry easy," he later recalled.

More good news would follow. The next week, Bancel received an electronic file from NIAID containing the preliminary results of the Phase 1 vaccine study.

Positive. The vaccine induced the immune responses researchers were hoping for. "There was incredible relief," Bancel said the week after getting the news. "A lot of joy because we know how much the world is hurting right now. Some of us lost family members to Covid. We can see the economic damage."

Moderna spent a few days going over the data with NIAID.

Four days after Bancel first saw the results, Moderna announced the details in a press release. (Even though results were preliminary, it could be argued Moderna was duty bound to report them as a publicly traded company with material information for investors; of course, this is easy to do when the news is good.) In the news release, Moderna character-ized the vaccine as "generally safe and well tolerated." There was a se-rious case of redness around the injection site in one subject. And three people who received the highest dose had serious systemic symptoms—likely including Ian Haydon, the Seattle area participant whose symp-toms sent him to urgent care.

It said that all forty-five people ages eighteen to fifty-five in the study "seroconverted" after the first dose, meaning their bodies produced anti-bodies against the virus. Among these, all fifteen who received the low-est dose of the vaccine had so-called "binding" antibodies in their blood two weeks after the second dose. This was a good sign because it meant that the immune system was sending antibodies to bind to the virus. The levels of binding antibodies were comparable to those seen in people who were infected by and recovered from Covid-19.

But binding antibodies alone don't stop a virus. Success also requires the body to produce neutralizing antibodies that stop the virus from entering human cells. Detecting these requires more complex tests, for which NIAID researchers only had data from eight people in the study, four who got the lowest dose and four who got a medium dose.

Here, too, researchers found that the vaccine elicited the necessary neutralizing antibodies in all eight subjects at levels that matched or exceeded the neutralizing antibodies seen in those who were infected and recovered, Moderna said. This also was good news, albeit in a small number of people.[26]

Even more tantalizing evidence: Moderna disclosed that a study of the vaccine in mice showed that it prevented viral replication in the animals' lungs after they were exposed to a modified version of the coronavirus.

That was significant because Covid-19 often lodges itself in the lungs of humans, where it can wreak havoc.

As the company press release crossed the wires that Monday morning, an elated Bancel sent an email to what he called "real-life friends" along with journalists and business contacts.

"Today is an important day in the fight against the SARS-CoV-2 virus. One important step forward," he wrote before listing some of the bullet points of data. "I could not be happier about these data. The Moderna team has been working for many years to lead us to this place, through long-term investments in our platform science and manufacturing processes. I would like to thank all of [you] for your support and trust over the years."

Moderna was already busy manufacturing doses for a Phase 2 study that would start by the end of May and finalizing the protocol for a Phase 3 study—the large trial that would definitively prove whether the immune responses seen in the first study could actually protect people from Covid-19, which it hoped to start within a couple of months.

These were unprecedented speeds compared with historical vaccine development timelines. The company was taking days or weeks to hit vaccine-development milestones that would normally take months or years.

"The sequence of the virus was made available to the world only four months ago," Bancel said on a conference call with analysts to discuss the hopeful Phase 1 results. "It is humbling to already have this positive data and to be finalizing as we speak of Phase 3 protocol with the aim to start dosing in July."

If it all panned out, a vaccine could be ready for use in the fall, months before Dr. Fauci thought was feasible.

Moderna's stock price shot up 20 percent that day, not necessarily because it had the potential to save the world from a crippling pandemic, but because it increased the chances that the company would succeed in developing its first product approved for the market. Its shares hit $80, four times its price after its first day of trading. The broader stock market also surged, with investors hopeful that a vaccine could bring the pandemic under control and return life to normal.

In a video interview from his home office the day the results became public, Bancel, wearing a white-collared shirt with no tie, said such immune responses in a Phase 1 vaccine trial indicated a high chance that a vaccine would prove protective against disease in a Phase 3 trial. "Does it mean we're going to have 100 percent efficacy? Of course not. We don't know yet." He said even 50 percent efficacy would likely be enough to garner regulatory approval given the state of emergency. The original shingles vaccine from Merck had only 50 percent efficacy, he noted. "Of course," he added, "I would prefer 95 percent protection."

Moderna's publicity hit was unusual for a positive Phase 1 trial result. Phase 1 results typically get no public attention because the chances are low that they'll advance to market, and even if they did it would be years away. But many seized on the favorable data as a reason to be optimistic in a dire situation. "We're desperate for positive hope," Kathryn Edwards, an infectious-disease specialist at Vanderbilt, said in an interview on the day the results were announced. "I think it's an extraordinary time. If these data showed we didn't get a very good immune response, that would be pretty disheartening."

Some experts and analysts remained professionally skeptical despite Bancel's sense of triumph. The most pivotal data about the vaccine's immune response, the data about neutralizing antibodies, came from only eight people in the study. And of course, only a later, larger trial would show real proof of protection from disease. In a way, Moderna and its NIAID partners were walking a tightrope between an understandable impulse to offer hope and share the news, and the hard-earned knowledge that early success in the development of new medicines often fails to be replicated in more comprehensive testing.

Paul Offit, a veteran vaccinologist at Children's Hospital of Philadelphia, recalled thinking that Moderna's leaders appeared overly confident in media interviews when discussing these early-stage results. Offit, who helped invent a rotavirus vaccine that was more than two decades in the making, knew that problems can surface for drugs and vaccines as they move on to bigger and bigger clinical trials. "They were suffering this hubris and there would be a price to pay for that," Dr. Offit said.

Even those involved in running the study were trying to maintain their scientific caution about the vaccine's potential. Barney Graham, the veteran deputy director of NIAID's vaccine-research unit, told an interviewer that day: "This is just the very beginning of the clinical work."

"The vaccine appears to be safe, appears to be immunogenic," Dr. Carlos del Rio, who was helping run Emory's portion of the study, said soon after the preliminary data were released. "I think it's exciting news, but it's early news. The proof is in the pudding, in the Phase 3 trial. I have learned to be skeptical on research findings.

"Think about going up Mount Everest. We got to Camp One."

8

More Money

A SECOND, LESS-NOTICED PIECE OF THE NEWS CAME OUT OF Moderna on the same day it announced the positive results in its Phase 1 trial, in the middle of May 2020. That evening, the company staged another secondary offering of its shares, capitalizing on the price surge that followed the vaccine news in the morning. With this new offering at $76 per share, the company raised another $1.3 billion.[1]

For CEO Stéphane Bancel, the stock sale in May 2020 was born of necessity. It followed weeks of trying to raise money from other sources, an uncertain drama that played out in parallel to the scientific one with the human trials.

While the world looked for hope from Moderna's vaccine effort, Bancel knew, to his frustration, that he had not raised enough to support the monumental task that lay ahead.

The challenge he faced was convincing investors to fund uncertainty on a massively compressed timeline. For several weeks, Bancel was asking for money for Phase 2 and Phase 3 trials, which would involve thousands of people, when Phase 1 results weren't even in. And money for a massive manufacturing scale-up.

The plan, Bancel was saying at the time, was to accomplish in one year what normally takes ten years or more—advance a vaccine through development at breakneck speed and to begin producing a stockpile of doses to distribute to hundreds of millions of people as soon as the government permits.

Normally all these steps happen discretely. Phase 1 is successful, then comes Phase 2. Success at one step leads to funding for the next step. Normally, a company wouldn't start full-scale commercial production until it became clear that a product would win government approval—several years after Phase 1 trials.

But in the depths of April 2020, it became clear that normal timelines wouldn't work in this emergency. Government officials and industry executives were coming around to the view that it would be better to start production of as many vaccine doses as possible in advance. It was better to have to throw them out if the vaccines failed in trials than to wait to find out a vaccine works before scaling production and distribution.

In Moderna's ten-year life, it had never produced more than one hundred thousand doses of all vaccines and drugs it was working on in a year, and all the doses it had produced were for testing in clinical trials. Its new Norwood plant had the capacity to make about 100 million vaccine doses per year. Before 2020, it looked like it would be a long time before Moderna would stretch to that capacity.

But by April, Moderna's Covid-19 vaccine was the first in the United States to enter human testing, and one of about eight vaccines globally in human testing (with more than one hundred other potential vaccines in the pipeline). National health ministers and other government officials from various countries were starting to call Moderna to inquire about getting access to doses. Moderna realized it would need much more capacity than what the Norwood plant could deliver immediately. "The only way to stop this pandemic is vaccinating hundreds of millions, or billions of people," Bancel said in an interview in April 2020.

That would take a massive infusion of cash. Though Moderna had been a wizard at fundraising in its ten-year existence, it still had a much smaller reserve of cash and investments than your average Big Pharma company. It had no marketable products to generate revenue to fund development and manufacturing for the Covid-19 vaccine. It needed much more money.

But as much as government officials wanted to be first in line to get doses, few wanted to fund the process of creating those doses, to Bancel's frustration. We need doses, they were saying, but we can't send cash up front without human study results and such uncertainty over the new technology. Moderna tried to sway government officials by sharing clinical data for its other vaccines—such as CMV—which it hoped would validate the technology. But governments were still taking a wait-and-see approach.

Bancel also tried asking private foundations for funding but got no backers. Not even the Bill & Melinda Gates Foundation, which had supported Moderna a few years earlier. "We did ask them," Bancel recalled. "I spent many meetings trying to convince them. I spent weekends calling their leadership."

"We had no data," he said. "We were not getting the traction we needed to start to get payments and be able to buy raw materials."

Bancel feared that delays in securing more outside funding would push back the availability of sufficient quantities of its vaccine by several months. "The feeling was really eating us alive emotionally." Bancel began to feel demoralized by his unsuccessful efforts. It was a low point. "I was getting no help financially," Bancel said. "I was super down. I felt like a massive failure."

The first good news on the funding front came later in April when Moderna managed to sign a contract with the US Biomedical Advanced Research and Development Authority, BARDA, the same government agency that gave money to Moderna in 2016 to develop a Zika vaccine. BARDA had taken the lead on funding Covid-19 vaccine development, providing more than $450 million to Johnson & Johnson, and $30 million to Sanofi, which was partnering with GlaxoSmithKline on a vaccine. BARDA pledged up to $483.3 million to Moderna, a huge sum for a small biotech that should have signaled how advanced and promising Moderna's work was.[2]

For US officials, the deal was a risk, given that they had no evidence at the time of success in Phase 1 trials, but it was also a down payment on ensuring the United States had access to domestically produced doses of a vaccine (the Moderna contract required domestic production of a Covid-19 vaccine, though it didn't stop Moderna from lining up additional overseas manufacturing).[3] Soon after, the recently departed BARDA director Rick Bright told Congress, "We did everything possible to ensure that those investments were in companies that would build capacity in the United States to manufacture those vaccines. We had to get in line first, even when the money wasn't fully there to complete the development program."[4]

Effectively, BARDA took the risk other governments wouldn't when Bancel asked for up-front funding from them.

For Moderna, the contract meant speed. It planned a move to round-the-clock production, upping production from ten weekly shifts (two a day five days a week) to twenty-one shifts (three a day, seven days a week). The company also hired 150 new employees to accelerate development and testing, and to prepare for the manufacturing scale-up. It would bring the company's total workforce up to about 1,000. Upgrading the workforce was no longer a problem either. Even before the successful Phase 1 results, vaccine specialists at Big Pharma companies were expressing interest in jumping their ships to join Moderna.

"We can aggressively fund the best and largest clinical study that we can do," CEO Bancel said in an interview on the day the BARDA funding was announced. "We can fund the manufacturing process so we can make as much product as we can."

In normal times, the company could choose to try to build new plants of its own to meet the demand for more doses, but the virus was raging. It needed capacity faster, so Moderna sought out a contract manufacturing partner from the industry's thriving subsector of companies that do nothing but contract with drug companies to make their products.

One such contractor was Lonza, a Swiss company with a plant an hour north of Moderna's own plant in Norwood. Lonza owned a global network of about fifty manufacturing sites. Bancel targeted the company and reached out to chairman and interim CEO Albert Baehny via

Zoom call to discuss a partnership in which Moderna would transfer its manufacturing technology to Lonza to make the vaccine, to augment Moderna's in-house production. The conversations were risky, Bancel said, given they had no contract in place at all.

"It was totally unusual compared to how everybody does business, which is, agree on terms and then start working," Bancel said. He didn't have time for that.

The two men hit it off immediately and got a deal done quickly, in which Lonza would use its Portsmouth, New Hampshire, plant and a plant in Visp, Switzerland, to manufacture Moderna's Covid-19 vaccine. The Portsmouth plant would augment domestic production of vaccine doses for the United States The Swiss plant, nestled in the Alps, would supply Europe and other regions.[5]

Lonza was an established contract drug manufacturer, but there was some risk. It had never made a vaccine before. And now it would attempt to make a vaccine using a largely unproven technology it had never worked with before. "This is a challenge," Baehny said in early May.

The aggressive fundraising was being done in the depths of a severe lockdown with surging sickness and profound uncertainty.

Like so many companies, Moderna sent much of its staff home in March. Bancel worked from an office in his home in Boston. He established a routine of getting up at 4 or 5 every morning and going for a run along the Charles River—feeling safe outdoors and able to keep his distance from other people. Back at his house, he would shower, make tea, and read the *Wall Street Journal* and the *Financial Times*. Then, long stretches in his office, video calls with colleagues and others all day long. His wife sometimes brought meals into his office. He tried to make a point of taking a break and dining with his family before going back into his office. For five months, seven days a week, this was his routine, until he started to go back to Moderna's Kendall Square offices in August.

Other plans were canceled. A trip to Paris in mid-March to celebrate Bancel's father's eightieth birthday was off. He went to New York to bring his daughter home from college. Back in France, his brother got Covid-19 and lost his sense of smell for a month. Bancel and his friends scrapped their custom of meeting for dinner once a month, rotating houses.

Tal Zaks, the chief medical officer, was working from home and alarmingly losing weight. Trained as a cancer doctor, Zaks was a self-described pessimist, and he saw his weight loss as a worrisome sign. He went to see a gastroenterologist and got a colonoscopy. The doctor didn't see anything concerning. The doctor asked Zaks if he was under a lot of stress. Yes, Zaks replied, he was trying to develop a Covid-19 vaccine to end the pandemic. But he also found that highly fulfilling, which he felt mitigated the stress. Was he getting enough sleep? Zaks thought he was, but his wife let him know that he was waking up with night sweats and terrors two to three times a night, and he just wasn't remembering. Eventually, Zaks was forced to take steps to cut down on stress and improve his sleep. No calls from 6 p.m. to 8 p.m. No work on Saturdays.

Juan Andres, head of manufacturing and technical operations, lost his mother-in-law and an uncle to Covid-19. Amid the grief, it was motivation to keep working on the vaccine as quickly as possible. He said, "This situation is personal right now."

BARDA funding and the Lonza partnership were a start, but Moderna's leaders still felt constrained in how much they could invest to ensure that the manufacturing buildup was as rapid as possible. They knew they needed to lock in supply contracts from vendors for other critical supplies like storage bags and filters used in the manufacturing process. They needed more money.

Bancel went to the Moderna board with his dilemma. He proposed another stock offering to raise the financing. Noubar Afeyan, Moderna's chairman, wasn't sure. It was a difficult decision because there was no guarantee the financing would lead to a successful product that delivered a return to investors. And he was uncertain about whether there would be more demand for Moderna shares. Three months before this meeting, after all, the market had priced Moderna shares below its IPO price.

"There was quite a bit of debate and discussion at the board level," Afeyan said. "If things didn't go our way, we'd pay a steep price. Yet we thought there was an obligation."

Ultimately, the board approved pursuing the new financing, and the timing worked out when the Phase 1 results came back looking so promising. A price of $20 at the start of February had transformed into $76 per share. Speed being of the essence, investment bank Morgan Stanley served as the sole book-running manager, purchasing all the shares in the offering, in contrast to Moderna's IPO, when several banks participated. Moderna got $1.3 billion from the offering and now more cash to buy raw materials and manufacturing equipment and to hire new workers.

Even at this higher price, the stock was attracting investors who, in Moderna, saw hope, including those who were once skeptical. Michael Caldwell, the Driehaus portfolio manager in Chicago who had opted not to invest in the IPO a couple years before, bought in in May 2020. Covid-19 vaccine aside, the company's recent positive data for its CMV vaccine looked promising, too. Caldwell began to read transcripts of Moderna's earnings conference calls and investor presentations, and then listened to recordings of them to see if the executives' tone of voice sent any messages. He became convinced that Moderna executives were telegraphing that there were strong signs the Covid-19 vaccine was going to work (though as a diligent biotech investor he was likely aware of the scientists preaching caution—that Moderna had just reached base camp on a hike of Everest). Caldwell may have missed out on the cheaper IPO price in 2018 (in hindsight he thought it was folly of him to dismiss Moderna's emphasis on vaccines), but he was hoping that getting in at $76 to $80 in mid-2020 would still prove to be a good move.

With positive results and more money in hand, Moderna was hurtling toward its end goal of getting a vaccine to market and inoculating hundreds of millions, or billions. It had an idea of how it could get there, but that idea was about to be reshaped, at warp speed.

9

Warp Speed

BY THE EARLY 1950S, THE POLIOMYELITIS VIRUS, WHICH
had been around for many years, was causing frightening outbreaks
in the United States that left thousands of people—usually children—
paralyzed or dead. One of polio's most famous victims, Franklin Delano
Roosevelt, had spearheaded the launch of what would become the March
of Dimes Foundation in the 1930s to raise money for research that was
largely conducted in academic labs and funded with private donations
over many years.[1]

The March of Dimes funded Jonas Salk's work at the University of
Pittsburgh, finally leading in the early 1950s to a polio vaccine. Parents
rushed to volunteer their children for field trials of the vaccine, and the
results showed that it was highly effective at protecting them from the
ravages of the disease.

Salk and his backers explored patenting the vaccine, but ultimately
didn't, and he famously quipped, "Could you patent the sun?" Instead,
several drug companies helped manufacture the Salk vaccine, almost
entirely without incident. There was one serious mishap in the manufacture of some defective batches, which caused polio in many vaccine
recipients before the problem was identified and corrected, but otherwise the mass vaccination campaign was a success. With the addition of
a second polio vaccine developed by Albert Sabin a few years later—an

oral formulation that could be coated onto sugar lumps, to the delight of children—polio cases plunged. Seven-year-old Shannon Cox and his two siblings were among more than 286,000 people in the Fort Worth, Texas, area who lined up to get the Sabin vaccine on a *single day* in 1962, at clinics set up in schools and other public buildings. The kids had seen the effects of polio firsthand—their parents used crutches and leg braces because they had gotten polio when they were younger, when no vaccine was available. Cox grew up polio-free to become a radiation oncologist in Austin, Texas. During the pandemic of 2020, at age sixty-five, he looked back at that childhood memory and saw no reason why something similar couldn't be repeated for Covid-19. "Looking at the long history of vaccine development was reassuring," he recalled. Routine polio vaccinations all but eliminated the virus in the United States by the late 1970s, and by 2017, the total number of reported cases of polio in the world was twenty-two.

Not all efforts were so successful. In 1976, a "swine flu" strain circulated at a military base in New Jersey, infecting about five hundred soldiers and killing one. US government officials feared it had potential to spread more widely and be perhaps as potent as the flu strain that caused a lethal global pandemic in 1918. The federal government funded the development of a vaccine targeting the strain and started a campaign to vaccinate tens of millions of people in the bicentennial year. But after more than 40 million Americans received the new vaccine, doctors saw concerning side effects. More than four hundred people who received the vaccine developed Guillain-Barré syndrome, a rare neurological disorder that can cause paralysis. The risk was rare but serious enough at the individual level that the government halted the vaccination campaign soon after it was detected. What's more, the swine flu never became a pandemic that year. Many concluded the government had overreacted to the flu strain, and that the rush to develop a vaccine contributed to the safety problems.[2]

A swine flu emerged again in 2009, and this one did cause a pandemic, hitting children and younger adults particularly hard. The US government helped tweak the design of existing flu vaccines to target this pandemic strain and worked with manufacturers to ramp up production of doses (including the use of millions of fertilized chicken eggs to grow the virus needed for the vaccine). The United States and other countries scrambled to purchase doses so they could immunize their populations, staging clinics in schools.[3] To a degree, the effort worked because transmission of the virus declined by winter, and there didn't appear to be any major vaccine safety issues this time. But once the pandemic waned, some countries canceled purchase orders from vaccine manufacturers, leaving companies like Novartis AG feeling burned by the experience.[4] They had rushed to make many doses at the governments' urging, only to be told that they wouldn't be buying all of them after all.

That experience was on the minds of pharmaceutical executives in 2020 as they considered whether to join the Covid-19 vaccine hunt. Would the hunt for a Covid-19 vaccine resemble the triumphant conquest of polio, would it be dogged by problems like the 1976 swine flu vaccine, or would they go all in only to be left with unbought inventory whacking their bottom line?

In April 2020, while Moderna waited anxiously for Phase 1 results and Stéphane Bancel was out looking for much-needed money, Moncef Slaoui, the Moderna board member and a veteran vaccine researcher, took a phone call from the head of a biotech trade group. The caller wanted to gauge Slaoui's interest in advising an emerging plan in the Trump administration. With the pandemic descending to new depths of suffering and death, and the accompanying economic destruction it was causing, some administration officials thought it was time for a Manhattan Project–like plan for a vaccine that would round up a team of experts and give them money and resources to work with drug companies to find an effective vaccine against the deadly coronavirus, all within one year.

Slaoui thought it was feasible, but he wasn't too interested in getting involved. "I'm not aligned with this administration," he told his caller.

That was an understatement. Slaoui was born in Morocco. Growing up in the 1960s and 70s he was deeply bothered by the inequalities in the authoritarian kingdom. As a university student in Belgium, he joined a Marxist student-activist organization committed to overthrowing the government of Morocco. This made him a target for Moroccan authorities. In the end, he abandoned the cause after his father told him that if he really wanted to change the world, he'd be better off doing something else because "if you're dead or disappeared you're not going to change anything." That's when Slaoui decided to study immunology, returning to Belgium to earn a PhD. He would go on to study and work in the pharmaceutical industry in the United States, including nearly thirty years at GlaxoSmithKline, much of it in vaccine research.

When Slaoui retired from GSK in 2017, Noubar Afeyan and Stéphane Bancel recruited him to join Moderna's board. They knew Slaoui's reputation and experience would add to Moderna's cachet. He knew of Moderna's technology from his time as head of R&D at GSK. He was skeptical about whether it would work, partly because he wasn't certain the company could mitigate the negative immune-system reactions to the use of mRNA as a treatment for disease. Even after joining Moderna's board and chairing its product-development committee, Slaoui retained some skepticism. "I wouldn't join the board if I didn't believe the technology could deliver, but I was 50-50 this is going to really work," he said.

Still, he liked Afeyan's strategic approach to building the company. He thought Bancel was "very motivated, very driven," though sometimes to the point of being overly aggressive. He sometimes worried that Bancel's tendency to alienate people would hurt Moderna's reputation. He occasionally counseled other Moderna leaders on how to deal with Bancel.

Slaoui, mostly bald and with striking dark eyebrows, considered himself an independent director, comfortable raising questions about Moderna's direction. At one point, he told the board that Moderna might have bitten off more than it could chew by launching more than twenty different drug and vaccine projects. Moderna might be spreading itself too thin, growing too fast, he said.

Finally, by the end of 2019, Slaoui was a true believer. The tipping point was that fall's release of positive results of a clinical trial of Moderna's cytomegalovirus (CMV) vaccine. "That was the big aha moment for me," Slaoui said. "I moved from being a supportive but inquisitive board member to being completely sero-converted." (This is Slaoui's attempt at vaccinological humor: sero-conversion is the transition to the presence of antibodies in the blood, a sign of either infection or vaccination.)

Slaoui was a registered Democrat and didn't like Trump's style. And politics aside, Slaoui's years of industry experience had made him wary of getting entangled in government bureaucracy. Still, the situation was dire, and after Slaoui spoke about it with his wife, he began to open up to the idea of helping out. Maybe lending his expertise to fight the pandemic was more important than politics.

US Department of Health and Human Services officials invited Slaoui to Washington in May to meet with the secretary, Alex Azar, who was a former executive with drugmaker Eli Lilly, and Jared Kushner, Trump's son-in-law and adviser at the White House. They asked him to help lead what Azar initially called "Manhattan Project 2" to find and deploy a vaccine as fast as possible. Eventually the project was renamed Operation Warp Speed, a name that came from an FDA vaccine reviewer, Peter Marks, a Star Trek buff. But for a project that envisioned injecting new vaccines into the arms of hundreds of millions of people, the name wasn't exactly reassuring from a safety perspective.

Slaoui said he would take the job if there was no political interference, and the second-guessing on his decisions was kept to a minimum. He could be held accountable when it was all over, he said.

The administration agreed and invited him back to Washington for an announcement at the White House on May 15. In the Rose Garden, Trump announced that Slaoui would be chief scientist for Operation Warp Speed, and the chief operating officer would be General Gus Perna, a four-star general spearheading logistics for the US Army. Slaoui would be a contract government employee, paid a nominal sum of $1.

It was an unlikely moment for the onetime Marxist and immigrant, standing in the Rose Garden next to—and joining forces with—an

American army general and a capitalist American president who wanted to slash immigration and who had once bemoaned the immigrants who came from "shithole countries."[5]

Operation Warp Speed would corral resources and expertise of numerous federal agencies to develop, manufacture, and distribute safe and effective Covid-19 vaccines for the United States as quickly as possible. "That means big, and it means fast, a massive scientific, industrial, and logistical endeavor, unlike anything our country has seen since the Manhattan Project," Trump said. The operation would have about $10 billion at its disposal, allocated by Congress in pandemic funding bills.[6]

Trump made this announcement at a time when the spread of the coronavirus was slowing down from its devastating pace in April. That's not to say things were good. Slowdown meant that an average of about fourteen hundred Americans were dying from Covid-19 every day, down from more than two thousand in mid-April. Though he vowed to deliver a vaccine, Trump also talked about ending lockdown restrictions and reopening the country well before a vaccine would become available. And if Operation Warp Speed didn't produce an effective vaccine, "we are going to be like so many other cases where we had a problem come in, it will go away at some point, it will go away." Schools should reopen in the fall, he said.

Slaoui dropped a tantalizing hint at the Rose Garden about the early results of the first human study of Moderna's vaccine. "Mr. President, I have very recently seen early data from a clinical trial with a coronavirus vaccine. And this data made me feel even more confident that we will be able to deliver a few hundred million doses of vaccine by the end of 2020," Slaoui said. These were the data that Moderna would announce in more detail a few days later, showing that the vaccine induced immune responses.

Slaoui's forecast of a few hundred million doses by the end of 2020 was one of the earliest in a series of overly optimistic predictions about vaccine supply from Trump administration officials and advisers throughout the year. The actual supply available when vaccines were authorized in late 2020 would be much smaller.

The creation of Operation Warp Speed was a recognition that several federal agencies were taking steps on their own toward the same goal, and it would be better to unite them in a broad push. It didn't start the process of federal support of Covid-19 vaccines, but it organized and accelerated it, said Paul Mango, who was the deputy chief of staff for policy in the Department of Health and Human Services (HHS). Bringing the efforts together helped the government decide quickly which of the dozens of vaccines in development had the best shot at working safely and yielding millions of doses, Mango said.

It was also an acknowledgment and recognition that Covid-19 was a serious threat and that the only way out of the pandemic was a vaccine. This reality, and the behind-the-scenes actions on the ground by Operation Warp Speed and the companies it worked with, often stood in contrast to the rhetoric of Trump and his allies in an election year. They still minimized the threat of Covid-19, comparing it with seasonal flu and claiming with little or no evidence that unproven drugs made for other diseases could cure people sickened by the virus. Or they claimed that the natural immunity among people who survived infections would eventually lead to "herd immunity," a community-level protection that would finally conquer the virus, whether an effective vaccine was found or not. Left unsaid was that a vaccine-free path to herd immunity would mean many more preventable deaths.

The reality was that the need for a Covid-19 vaccine was as urgent as any in the past century—the polio epidemic, Ebola, Zika, or the swine flu outbreaks of 1976 and 2009. By the end of May 2020, one hundred thousand people in the United States were dead from Covid-19. In three months, more people had died from Covid-19 than deaths in a typical *year* from influenza, pneumonia, and suicide combined.[7] Though some states were starting to lift lockdown restrictions, economic activity was still depressed, particularly in the travel and hospitality industry. Millions of schoolchildren remained stuck at home for the remainder of the school year, enduring distance learning. A vaccine was the only answer to getting back to normal, in addition to saving lives.

HHS gave Slaoui and other Operation Warp Speed officials office space in HHS headquarters, the Hubert H. Humphrey Building near the Capitol in Washington. They designated point people to work with each of the companies selected to be part of the effort.

Slaoui resigned from Moderna's board to lessen the conflict of interest in his oversight of a federal effort to advance several vaccines that included Moderna's. But he still owned valuable Moderna shares and stock options, and his stake jumped in value by more than $2 million when Moderna announced the positive Phase 1 vaccine study results, sparking criticism from Democratic politicians, including Senator Elizabeth Warren and government watchdog groups, who demanded he unload it. How could Slaoui objectively serve the public in leading this new vaccine project when he could financially benefit from his own decisions?

The next day, he divested himself of more than $10 million worth of Moderna stock options to head off concerns, and he said he would donate to cancer research the gain in the value of his stake since his appointment to Operation Warp Speed days earlier.[8]

Operation Warp Speed would never fully escape the deeply enmeshed politics of an election year and an administration sending mixed messages. The spat over Slaoui's stockholdings was just a taste of the problems that hung over the effort.

And the incident fueled mounting questions about the personal enrichment of industry executives as their companies developed Covid-19 drugs and vaccines, most with government funding. From the start of 2020 until May, Moderna executives, directors, and a handful of larger shareholders had sold shares or exercised stock options worth a combined $197 million.[9] Tal Zaks, the chief medical officer, and CFO Lorence Kim were among the biggest sellers. Kim made $19.8 million by exercising options on May 18 (the Phase 1 positive results day) alone, and Tal Zaks made $9.8 million doing the same on the next day. Most of these sales were part of preprogrammed stock-trading plans for executives, set up in advance to avoid an executive making a transaction based on non-public information about the company. An executive might, for instance, specify a stock price or a date that would trigger the sale, and the amount to be sold, and then let the transactions unfold automatically without regard to any change in a company's fortunes.

In Kim's case, he had a limited time frame to exercise his Moderna stock options, because he was on his way out. Moderna had already announced that Kim, the CFO since 2014, would be leaving the company in August.[10] Kim was the money guy for a company in fundraising mode to invest in its experimental drugs. Now, it needed a different kind of CFO, as it was on the cusp of having its first commercial product. With product revenue and more of a global reach, Moderna needed a CFO with more experience. Kim told Bancel he was also struggling with his New York-to-Boston commute. He left on good terms, but it seemed clear that this was another case of CEO Bancel trying to upgrade the workforce.

Tal Zaks, the chief medical officer, also had a limited time left with Moderna, though this fact was less public than Kim's planned departure.

Zaks never expected a long run. Soon after Zaks started at Moderna in 2015, Stéphane Bancel took him aside and said, "I hope you understand that being the CMO at Moderna means you are the *current* CMO," Zaks recalled. Message received. When Moderna started working on the Covid-19 vaccine in early 2020, Bancel told Zaks that the chief medical officer role would be changing. Another workforce upgrade, as Zaks's experience as CMO was about advancing experimental projects through the pipeline and managing the rapid-fire launch of human studies. Now, Bancel wanted a CMO with more experience overseeing commercial products globally.

But he couldn't just turn over the job at the moment, with the vaccine project going full bore and Zaks deeply involved in overseeing it. In March of 2020, Moderna entered into an executive retention agreement with Zaks. If he stayed on as chief medical officer through the end of September 2021, he would receive a $1 million bonus.[11] That gave Bancel the time to create a transition. After signing the agreement, Zaks amended a preprogrammed trading plan to sell his equity at regular intervals, irrespective of stock price. He didn't know at the time that the price would have more than tripled. Zaks said he never expected to make much money from joining Moderna, and the trading plan, he said, was a way to ensure he could support his family.

Moderna's insiders felt that the sales were entirely appropriate—they were preprogrammed trading plans not tied to any company news. And several Moderna executives had taken salary cuts to join the company, accepting options that were intended as incentives to build a more valuable company over the long run, or buying Moderna shares with their own savings when the stock price was lower. Now, the company was more valuable.

Still, Moderna, mindful of the scrutiny and the criticism, eventually took steps to try to limit the stock sales, if for no other reason than because of optics. In August, the company disclosed that its executives and directors agreed they wouldn't instigate any new preset trading plans or add shares to existing plans. They also agreed not to make additional, unscheduled sales of stock on the open market. Moderna said it took these steps "to avoid any distraction as we pursue our mission."[12]

Preexisting trading plans were grandfathered in, though, and insiders continued to sell. In December, after Moderna's vaccine was authorized, the company lifted the restrictions.

One of Moncef Slaoui's first jobs with Warp Speed was to whittle down the list of vaccine candidates from more than one hundred in development to a handful of the best candidates worthy of a massive infusion of money and support.

One sorting mechanism was to look at how the vaccines were made.

One of the oldest ways of making a vaccine was to use a killed or weakened version of the virus itself and introduce it into the body in such a way that the body learned to fight it while not making the person sick from it. Flu, polio, and measles vaccines used this method.

Slaoui and others at Operation Warp Speed didn't want to go this route. It would require growing large amounts of the new coronavirus, which could take many months. And it would introduce a security threat in a raging pandemic, Slaoui felt.

Instead, the group focused on three other approaches and picked two efforts for each approach to hedge bets in case one didn't pan out. One category was protein-based vaccines, which sent proteins from the virus (not the whole virus) into the body to trigger an immune response, a design used for the hepatitis B shot. For these, Operation Warp Speed backed work at Novavax, a small Maryland biotech, and France's Sanofi (the latter in partnership with Slaoui's old employer, GSK). Novavax had spent years trying to hone its vaccine-making technology but still hadn't delivered a product approved by government regulators. Sanofi was an established vaccine maker.

Another category they supported was the less-proven viral-vector vaccines. These used an unrelated virus that caused common colds, an adenovirus, to carry DNA instructions into the body to trigger the immune response needed to fight the coronavirus. Here, Slaoui backed Johnson & Johnson and AstraZeneca (the latter in partnership with the University of Oxford in the United Kingdom).

The third category was mRNA, and Moderna was the clear frontrunner. But Slaoui and his team also tapped a rival mRNA project that was quickly advancing. In March, Pfizer, one of the biggest drug companies in the world, known for its Lipitor anti-cholesterol drug and Viagra pills for erectile dysfunction, formed a partnership with the small German biotech BioNTech to develop an mRNA-based Covid-19 vaccine.

BioNTech was founded in Mainz, Germany, in 2008, two years before Moderna. The founders were husband and wife Ugur Sahin and Özlem Tureci, both children of Turkish immigrants. Its history looked a lot like Moderna's. The company's early focus was to use mRNA to develop new cancer treatments.[13] Like Moderna, BioNTech formed partnerships with several Big Pharma companies. BioNTech hired Katalin Karikó, the mRNA pioneer from Penn, in 2013 to serve as a senior vice president in R&D, and in 2017, licensed the Penn patents based on the Karikó and Weissman research, just as Moderna did the same year.

Pfizer and BioNTech first started working together in 2018 to develop mRNA-based flu vaccines. When the Covid-19 pandemic hit in 2020, it was a logical next step for the companies to focus on the new virus.

Like Moderna, BioNTech started moving on potential vaccines in January, soon after the genetic sequence of the virus became available, in an effort it called "Project Lightspeed." By the time it formalized a partnership with Pfizer, BioNTech already had a candidate vaccine, code-named BNT162.

Also like Moderna, BioNTech hadn't yet successfully started selling any products. They were already rivals in developing mRNA technology, and now they would face off in trying to harness that technology to end a global pandemic.

Pfizer brought some muscle to BioNTech's project. Its primary high-selling entry in the vaccine space was the pneumococcal vaccine Prevnar, a multibillion-dollar product that Pfizer didn't develop initially, but rather gained through its 2009 acquisition of Wyeth. Pfizer also had a global manufacturing network and large, revitalized R&D and regulatory operations. And lots of cash.

Moderna agreed to cooperate with Operation Warp Speed in part because it had to. It needed the money. Pfizer, and thus BioNTech, showed less interest. Pfizer knew it would be unavoidable to work with the FDA for approval of its vaccine, but the company's executives didn't want to get overly involved with the government for fear it would slow them down. "We didn't accept the federal government funding solely for the reason we wanted to be able to move as quickly as possible with our vaccine candidate into the clinic," Pfizer's chief business officer, John Young, said during a congressional committee hearing on the vaccines in July 2020.[14]

Operation Warp Speed continued to count the Pfizer/BioNTech vaccine as one of the two mRNA vaccines it was supporting, and ultimately it would strike an agreement to purchase doses from Pfizer and provide some other assistance. But for most of 2020, the feds weren't as involved in the Pfizer effort as they were in Moderna's.

Ten-year-old Moderna remained a front-runner in the Covid-19 vaccine hunt, but now found itself in something like a cage match, going up against much older, much bigger, much more well-heeled competitors: Johnson & Johnson, AstraZeneca, Pfizer, Sanofi, and GlaxoSmithKline. Merck would enter the hunt, too. Among the front-runners, only Novavax was a fair comp for Moderna in its size and status.

Moderna flirted with the idea of teaming up with Big Pharma partners on its Covid-19 vaccine as BioNTech had. "We were trying to figure out, did we want to do this alone, or with other folks?" Moderna Chairman Noubar Afeyan recalled. In particular, the company wanted help with running vaccine clinical trials outside the United States.

One potential partner was Merck. Like BioNTech with Pfizer, Moderna had a preexisting research partnership with Merck, and in early 2020 executives from both companies began to talk about extending the partnership to Covid-19.

"We spoke with them many times about whether it was appropriate to partner with them about any aspect of it," recalled Roger Perlmutter, who was head of Merck's R&D at the time. Ultimately, they didn't reach a deal. Merck was flirting with others at the same time: it explored partnering with the University of Oxford, but negotiations fell apart when some of the Oxford researchers objected to proposed terms. Oxford eventually partnered with AstraZeneca. Merck subsequently partnered with a nonprofit vaccine group on an experimental vaccine and acquired another biotech company to develop a second Covid vaccine but scrapped both projects when early human testing produced poor results. Moderna also had brief discussions with GlaxoSmithKline and Sanofi about Covid-19 vaccine partnerships, Bancel said.

As they discussed potential deals, Moderna's leaders began to feel a disconnect between the potential partners and its own ambitions. Some of these companies seemed like they were hedging. Yes, they'd partner in case it worked, but they still doubted mRNA could work. Others seemed too skittish about getting burned, fearing they might produce massive amounts of product that was never purchased, which happened with the 2009 swine flu vaccine. Still others wanted to treat Moderna like their own outsourced research and take more control over the project than Moderna was willing to cede.

So, Moderna's leaders would go it alone, with only the emerging partnership with the federal government to help fill that void.

May and June 2020 were dedicated to setting up large Phase 3 clinical trials of the front-running vaccine efforts. The idea was to start a series of trials in the summer with thousands of subjects that could yield answers on efficacy by the fall, with the potential for FDA authorization and availability of doses by the end of the year.

Initially, the director of the NIH, Francis Collins, envisioned conducting a single, large clinical trial in which vaccines from Moderna, Sanofi, J&J, and Pfizer could all be part of the same "master protocol" and each of which would be compared with a shared group of placebo recipients.[15] But the vaccines were on different timetables, and both Moderna and Pfizer didn't want to wait. (The World Health Organization also was pushing for a single international trial that could compare multiple vaccines, but some vaccine companies were hesitant to get involved because they perceived the organization to be anti-industry.)

One of the first things Moderna had to figure out before starting its Phase 3 trial was the right dose level for its vaccine. In its successful Phase 1 trial sponsored by NIAID, Moderna tested three doses: 25 micrograms, 100 micrograms and 250 micrograms. The highest dose seemed to increase side effects, like the fever and chills that sent Ian Haydon in Seattle to urgent care. That dose was eliminated. The 100-microgram dose induced similar levels of antibodies to the 250-microgram dose, and a higher level of antibodies than the 25-microgram dose. It seemed just right for the Phase 3 study.

But there was a snag. Moderna could opt for a less-well-tested 50-microgram dose. If they could cajole a similar immune system response out of the 50 dose as the 100, it would double the supply of vaccine, and in a pandemic emergency, vaccinating many people as quickly as possible would be critical to defeating the fast-spreading virus.

This issue sparked a lively internal debate. Some, including company president Stephen Hoge, wanted a 50-microgram dose, which he thought was probably sufficient for protection while doubling supply (and increasing revenue). Others thought it was more important to make the most effective vaccine possible. And they didn't know whether the 50-microgram dose would behave more like the less effective 25-microgram dose, or the more effective 100-microgram dose. And they were competing with other companies. The known potency of 100 micrograms seemed a better option to some.

"It was clear that we would be expected to demonstrate efficacy," Tal Zaks said. "I didn't want to risk losing 10 percent to 20 percent on efficacy for the sake of having a lower dose."

Zaks, who had been suffering from profound stress throughout the year, felt a heavy weight when he recommended proceeding with the 100-microgram dose, a weight that stayed with him after the decision was made. "The stakes were huge," Zaks said. "We just have to decide whether we want to double our capacity and our revenue right off the bat . . . and the ability to protect twice as much of humanity."

Ultimately, Hoge and others came around to his recommendation, and Moderna chose the 100-microgram dose. At the time, they figured, efficacy seemed more important than supply since so many companies were projecting to have large supplies of their shots.

"It's a very hard decision to have made, and I don't know if we're ever going to know we made the right choice," Hoge later said.

Another hurdle was who would manage the large Phase 3 trials.

For several years, Moderna had worked with a Wilmington, North Carolina–based contract research organization with the unremarkable name Pharmaceutical Product Development, or PPD, to run the clinical trials of its vaccines and drugs. PPD was a mainstay for top drug companies, lining up the doctors, clinics, patients, and volunteers needed to run a trial. Though it had never run a trial this big with PPD, Moderna expected to continue with the company on this venture.

Federal officials had other ideas. They wanted NIAID, Anthony Fauci's institute, to be involved in running the Moderna trial. NIAID intended to repurpose trial sites used for its large-scale HIV vaccine trials, not just for Moderna's vaccines but for others that were being backed by Warp Speed.

Federal officials had realized that their idea for a single large trial for all vaccines wouldn't work, but they still wanted some standardization across the trials so they could reliably compare results. If they could create similar designs across multiple trials, it would guide later decisions about which vaccines to purchase, or who should get which vaccines. If Moderna's vaccine, for example, turned out to be more effective among older adults than J&J's, government officials could recommend its use in that population.

In late May, Moncef Slaoui held a two-hour virtual briefing with Warp Speed companies about the large Phase 3 trials. "We are preparing to run what may turn out to be the largest and fastest field efficacy trials ever . . . in history," Slaoui wrote in the invitation to the meeting. It was a packed agenda, in which each company would take a turn discussing its plans and the government would discuss how it planned to repurpose sites in its HIV vaccine-trial network. "This is an aggressive agenda that will require that each party comes very well prepared and focused on the key points that can help make these trials a success operationally."

Officials from Pfizer—though they were leery of getting too involved with the feds—and Johnson & Johnson gave PowerPoint presentations. But Moderna hadn't yet finalized its plans with PPD, the contract research organization, and didn't put together a slide deck. Chief medical officer Zaks suggested on the call that Moderna and PPD could handle the bulk of the Moderna vaccine trial and didn't need much help from NIAID or its clinical-trial network.

Zaks didn't object in principle to involving NIAID's repurposed vaccine trials network in Moderna's clinical trial. But he did fear it would slow down the process. Moderna had positive Phase 1 results in hand, a new infusion of cash, and an experienced clinical-trials partner in PPD. Zaks wondered if it was still worth it to accept the federal funding and the conditions that came with it.

The Warp Speed officials didn't know all this and were surprised by Zaks's posture on the call.

Two days later, Zaks and Stephen Hoge reconnected with Slaoui and Larry Corey, who oversaw the vaccine trial network the feds wanted to repurpose in the Phase 3 Covid trials. Corey wanted Moderna's Phase 3 trial protocol to specify how people who became infected during the trial would be treated medically. Zaks told them that would be too difficult to do consistently across more than one hundred locations that would be used for the trial. Those decisions should be left up to an individual's regular doctor.

More disagreement, and more surprise from the federal officials at Zaks's position.

Federal officials were losing their patience with Zaks. "His style was very direct and difficult, but it wasn't landing well with the rest of the operation," said Slaoui, who knew Zaks from his time on Moderna's board. Tony Fauci was on the group call in which Zaks said Moderna wouldn't need much help from NIAID. Word got back to Zaks that Fauci was furious that Zaks would question the role of NIAID in the trials.

Zaks had left the impression on the Warp Speed team that Moderna would proceed with a large clinical trial however it wanted to, ignoring the fact that it was receiving a half-billion dollars in taxpayer funding, with maybe more to come. Moderna needed to ease up and accept that NIAID and the clinical-trial network it funded were going to be involved.

Whether or not Zaks realized he had overplayed his hand, he at least knew it was time to be conciliatory. He emailed Fauci and Corey and apologized for his tone and sense of frustration on the call. Then he emailed Slaoui and said he would ask other R&D leaders at Moderna to become the everyday contacts for NIAID to set up the Phase 3 trial with Moderna.

"I realized we were at an impasse, and I was the embodiment of the impasse," Zaks recalled.

Moderna expected to be in more control of its own destiny, but what could the company do? Without a deep-pocketed Big Pharma partner like Pfizer, it was relying on the government as a partner. After all, government researchers had helped design its vaccine, they organized the first human study of it, and BARDA had sunk half-a-billion dollars in the company. As Tony Fauci recalled later, "Moderna relied on us a lot because they didn't have much experience." It was hard, or impossible, at this point for Moderna to say *we'll take it from here*.

A road map of the federal plan was laid out in an article in *Science* co-authored by Larry Corey, Francis Collins, Tony Fauci, and John Mascola. "To return to a semblance of previous normality, the development of SARS-CoV-2 vaccines is an absolute necessity," they wrote. "To achieve this goal, all the resources in the public, private, and philanthropic sectors need to participate in a strategic manner."[16]

Ultimately, the feds wanted thirty thousand adults in each vaccine trial—triple what Bancel had anticipated in May. That many subjects would increase the chances that some study subjects would become exposed to the virus, accelerating their time to a statistically sound answer about whether the vaccines were working. It would also increase the chances of detecting rare side effects.

For Moderna's trial, researchers would start tracking the qualified Covid-19 cases two weeks after a person received the second dose of either a vaccine or a placebo (doses would be given four weeks apart). Once a certain number of cases accrued, they would examine the data and determine whether there were fewer Covid-19 cases among vaccinated people than among unvaccinated people. All along, an independent committee would monitor safety in the trials of the Moderna vaccine and others backed by Operation Warp Speed, with independent authority to halt vaccinations if serious side effects emerged.

The trials would be staggered: Moderna's mRNA vaccine would be first, in July, followed in August by the viral vector vaccine from AstraZeneca and Oxford. September would launch a trial of Johnson & Johnson's viral vector vaccine. Novavax's and Sanofi's protein-based vaccines would come after that.[17]

Pfizer, which opted out of Warp Speed, wasn't part of that plan. The company was planning to run its own large vaccine study, to start as early as Moderna's in July.

In all, the trials would involve finding, preparing, vaccinating, and monitoring 120,000 people in six months—even more if Novavax and Sanofi got going. It would be a monumental undertaking. As a reference point, Merck's large trial of a vaccine against rotavirus, the diarrhea-causing virus that usually infects babies, enrolled 70,000 people in eleven countries. It took four years.[18]

Paul Offit, a vaccinologist at Children's Hospital of Philadelphia, helped develop that vaccine and was now helping to design the speedy Covid vaccine trials. Later, he'd be part of the committee that would approve Covid vaccines. As someone who often speaks out against mis-information spread by the anti-vaccine movement, Offit thought there was risk in the accelerated timetable for developing Covid-19 vaccines, which could erode confidence in their efficacy and safety, but he thought it was a risk that had to be taken. Given the magnitude of the suffering and death Covid had already caused, and the massive amount of suffer-ing and death experts like him knew was still to come, for Offit, it was a "break the glass" moment.

"We are paralyzed by this virus, and therefore we are willing to ac-cept a greater degree of uncertainty about the safety and efficacy before it's put out there into the general public," he said in May 2020.

There were more details to work out, and more debate and disagree-ment with the feds that took time to sort out.

For example, Moderna and federal officials had to agree on what would count as a case of Covid-19 among study subjects for the pur-poses of determining the vaccine's efficacy—which was not as easy as it sounds. So the sides debated. Moderna wanted a lower threshold—counting only more severe cases—while federal officials wanted a defi-nition that would encompass some less severe cases as well. Ultimately, they agreed that to count as a Covid-19 case, one of two scenarios must be met: Either the study participant must have had a positive nasal-swab Covid-19 test result and must have experienced at least two symptoms from a listed range of possible symptoms, including fever, chills, muscle pain, headache, sore threat, or loss of taste or smell. Or, they had to have a positive Covid-19 test plus at least one of a group of respiratory symptoms including cough, shortness of breath, or signs of pneumonia.

They also decided that researchers would keep count of asymptomatic infections and mild cases that didn't meet the primary criteria, but that those wouldn't count toward the efficacy calculation. In short, the study's focus was to determine whether Moderna's vaccine prevented a certain level of sickness from Covid-19, not whether it prevented asymptomatic infections or ones with mild symptoms. In the current pandemic emergency, the most important thing was to keep people from being hospitalized and dying. It would be great if the vaccine also prevented asymptomatic infections and mild cases, but that was treated as a secondary benefit.

Even with the plan in place, it was clear that Moderna's Phase 3 trial wasn't going to start by July 1, as Moderna hoped. The delay gave Pfizer and BioNTech time to catch up.

But Moderna was still a front-runner in the race, an unlikely position for a small startup with no products that until the mid-2010s hadn't even conducted a human trial of a drug. A company which not four months before wasn't even sure it wanted to be in the business of developing a Covid vaccine.[19]

Now, just over one hundred days later, Stephen Hoge completely reworked the narrative around Moderna as a doubted underdog driven by relentless idealists. In February, Hoge was downplaying Moderna's role in the early vaccine trials, saying "We're just one small part of this." Now, asked how Moderna came to be one of the Covid-19 vaccine front-runners, Hoge said in an email:[20]

> Honestly, I think we've been building for a moment like this—both technologically and culturally/from ethos perspective—without really knowing it.
>
>   We're a bold bunch by nature. We have had to be. Most left comfortable careers in biopharma and/or academics because they wanted to do something game changing; they wanted to push themselves. We set our own bar high enough ("a new class of medicines") that it scares us a little, and earns a healthy dose of mockery from others for being grandiose.

And we've survived by being relentless in the face of challenges or derision. We've been grinding for almost 10 years to build a platform from nothing. We've had a long line of anonymous detractors. Our people just kept going because they believed we could make a difference. We learned to be relentless; just don't quit. We broke through on the scientific platform and showed what was possible. We built a factory. We built a large pipeline. We generated a mountain of human data across a dozen clinical programs.

So when the novel coronavirus hit, we just went after it like everything else we've ever done. One day in early January Stéphane came back saying "this is going to be big deal and we have to do something now." Before most companies even considered doing something our CEO had agreed to try something unprecedented with the NIH that was fraught with risk: go from concept to clinical trial in 3 months. So our people got to work. They attacked the problem, good was never good enough, every day was a race, and 63 days later we dosed the Phase 1. By then our team was already on to the Phase 2, and is now pushing to start the Phase 3 and to manufacture millions of doses this year.

So, on your question of being a front-runner . . . There are lots of companies (J&J, Pfizer, AstraZeneca, Merck) who are now trying to stop the virus with vaccines. We all want to deliver a part of the solution. It's going to take all of us. But I sometimes marvel that each of those companies are literally 100X larger than us, and we're doing as much.

My point is, if this pandemic was measured in resources deployed we should have already been reduced to a footnote, not be a front-runner. So if [it's] not resources, then what is it? I think it's that we're a bold and relentless bunch. We've been culturally pre-disposed to tilt at a problem despite the risks or commentary. We're just going to keep going until we can't go any further because that's who we are. And if we fail . . . well, everyone's already dismissed us anyway" ☺

10

Hold On, Help Is
on the Way

SHORTLY BEFORE 7 A.M. ON JULY 27, 2020, DAWN BAKER,
a television news anchor in Savannah, Georgia, was in a patient room at
a medical clinic. She was wearing a mask. She pulled her purple jacket off
to expose her left shoulder so that a tech could slip a needle into her and
plunge Moderna's mRNA vaccine into her body.

Baker was the first person to receive Moderna's vaccine in the large
Phase 3 study. She was nervous but felt strongly about being part of the
trial. "It's really exciting to me that I could be a part of saving lives eventually, instead of just being scared and praying," Baker told CNN.[1]

Baker was the first of what Moderna and federal officials hoped would
be thirty thousand volunteers to get the vaccine or a saline solution, the
placebo (Baker only learned later that she got the actual vaccine). They
hoped that within a few months they'd have definitive evidence one
way or the other if this experimental Covid-19 vaccine truly, and safely,
worked.

"This is a significant milestone, and it comes at a remarkably rapid
pace compared to the usual pace for vaccine preparation," NIH Director
Francis Collins said on a call with reporters a few hours after Baker received her dose in late July.

But Collins was careful to balance talk of speed with comments about safety, knowing the name Operation Warp Speed didn't sit well with all, as it conjured up images of racing forward and corner-cutting in the minds of some. He said researchers would monitor safety "in the most rigorous way."

Stéphane Bancel also was on the call, quick to point out that it was also a milestone for mRNA, the drug technology he had spent the last decade trying to move forward and which had finally reached a Phase 3 trial. "I think it's an historic day for science as well," he said.

Shortly before the study started, Moderna notched another $472 million from BARDA to fund the Phase 3 trial and late-stage clinical development of the vaccine, bringing Moderna's total federal funding for the project to $955 million. Moderna said it needed the additional funding because the size of the trial, thirty thousand participants, was three times what it initially planned for.[2]

That Dawn Baker was the first study subject to receive a dose also was significant because she is Black. The coronavirus was hurting certain communities of color—including Black, Latino, and Native American people—disproportionate to their shares of the overall population. The incidence of Covid hospitalizations among Blacks and Latinos was more than double that for non-Latino white people, and the incidence of deaths was double.[3] They were at higher risk of exposure to the virus because they were more likely to live in crowded conditions or have jobs that couldn't be performed remotely. Once infected, they were at higher risk of more severe illness, in part because of higher rates of chronic underlying medical conditions such as diabetes and obesity, as well as higher barriers to receiving medical care.[4] And the vaccine trial was starting about two months after the murder of George Floyd by police sparked nationwide protests and renewed the focus on racial justice in America.

Moderna and federal officials wanted to make sure that people of color were fairly represented in the large clinical trial of the vaccine, for a few reasons. One was scientific: they wanted to find out whether the vaccine had the same effect on people of different races and ethnicities. Also, it could help build confidence among these groups if the vaccine succeeded in testing and became widely deployed.

But to achieve that diversity, they would have to overcome reluctance among some communities of color to participate in the research—reluctance that was fueled by historical injustices in medical research. One infamous example was the Tuskegee study, in which the federal government left hundreds of Black men untreated for syphilis between 1932 and 1972.[5] There was also Henrietta Lacks, the Black woman whose cervical cancer cells were turned into an immortal cell line used for medical research long after her 1951 death, but without her consent and, for many years, without her descendants' knowledge.[6]

"We have every right and reason to be apprehensive and mistrusting," said Dr. James E. K. Hildreth, president and chief executive of Meharry Medical College, a historically Black medical school in Nashville, Tennessee. Hildreth, an immunologist who had done HIV research, served as a member of the Food and Drug Administration advisory panel that evaluated the Covid-19 vaccines during 2020. "Even today, Black patients don't feel like they're treated with dignity," he said in an interview.

Moderna and federal officials also managed the study for other demographic facts that had become evident in how the disease attacked. Covid-19 was proving much more dangerous to older adults and those with chronic health conditions. In July of 2020, for example, there were 5,709 Covid-19 deaths among Americans ages fifty to sixty-four, more than double the number of deaths of people under fifty.[7] Moderna and federal officials set a goal that at least 25 percent of study participants would either be sixty-five and older or at risk from a chronic health condition if they were under sixty-five.

Geography was another important factor. Study sites were best in locations where the virus was spreading fastest. Such locations could speed up answers about whether those who received the vaccine had lower disease rates than those who received a placebo, because study participants were more likely to encounter the virus in their everyday lives (study subjects were never intentionally infected with coronavirus after getting the vaccine or placebo).

When the Moderna trial started, the number of infections had abated in some earlier hot spots like Seattle, New York, and Boston, while it surged in places that had largely escaped the brunt of the spring surge. Cases were rising in places like Texas and Florida, which had lifted restrictions sooner than other states and were digging in their heels on staying open. The rate of positive cases surged in Florida to about 15 percent of those tested, and Disney World still proceeded with plans to reopen in July.[8] While the virus's spread was bad for the residents of these high-transmission states, it made Florida ideal as a vaccine trial site. What's more, people who were at higher risk of infection in these places, like grocery workers and first responders (not to mention Disney World workers), would be ideal study subjects.

"No one wants to see people get infected and suffer and even die," NIAID's Anthony Fauci said. "But if in fact that is occurring, we could get an answer to vaccine efficacy and safety much more quickly. It's a double-edged sword."[9]

As a result, Moderna set up its Phase 3 study to recruit volunteers at fifteen sites in Texas, where the virus was surging, versus only three in all of New York State, where cases were down.

Overall, one hundred designated clinical-trial sites were busy recruiting volunteers. Some were major academic hospitals like Penn's in Philadelphia and the Brigham and Women's Hospital in Boston. Others were clinics run by small companies that specialize in running vaccine studies. Some were part of the feds' HIV clinical-trial network that was repurposed for Covid-19 studies. Others were lined up by Moderna or its contractors. Their tasks were to help recruit volunteers, administer doses, record potential side effects, and conduct follow-up visits to draw blood samples, all while maintaining social distancing and preventing the spread of disease among staff and volunteers. These sites were all monitored by Moderna and the FDA, which conducted inspections of a sample of sites in clinical trials. Researchers had to adhere to the trial protocol and standards for conducting clinical research.

Benchmark Research, a firm based in Austin, Texas, that operated several of the study sites, tried to recruit volunteers by word of mouth and by running online advertisements on sites like Facebook and Instagram, said Mark Lacy, chief executive. Time to recruit was tight. "Absolutely, no question, it's the toughest project we've ever taken on," Lacy said a few weeks before the trial started. "We are entering uncharted territory."

At the University of Pennsylvania in Philadelphia, researchers hired additional staff to help with the trial. They reached out to faith-based organizations and labor unions to recruit people of color and workers on the front lines to participate in the study. The Penn doctor overseeing the study there, infectious-disease specialist Ian Frank, was mindful of one of the challenges of recruiting subjects: limited safety information about the vaccines. The only human safety data were from one small study. "People will have to participate in some regard with a leap of faith and the hope that the products will be safe," Frank said that July.

Safety indeed remained a big unknown. More data had come in from Moderna's Phase 1 study earlier in the spring, and it was mostly positive. Data showed that all forty-five people, ages eighteen to fifty-five, in the first portion of the study exhibited the desired immune response (the second portion of the trial was in adults older than fifty-five but results weren't ready yet). The data also revealed that the antibody levels remained elevated nearly two months after the second dose. And the trial showed that about 40 percent of the people receiving the 100-microgram dose had fever after the second dose, and most vaccine recipients also had other minor symptoms like injection-site pain and fatigue.[10] Researchers described them as manageable, temporary side effects related to the vaccine's induction of an immune response. Tal Zaks said in July 2020, "You're paying a price in some symptoms to educate the immune system to prepare a defense against the coronavirus."

Still, it was a small study, and researchers remained concerned about other side effects that might emerge. One worry was a rare complication known as disease enhancement, when the vaccine makes a person more susceptible to the disease the vaccine is meant to protect against, which had emerged in vaccines for other respiratory conditions like dengue. Researchers were monitoring for it, though they felt the design of Moderna's vaccine would mitigate the risk.[11]

Dr. Frank from Penn was aware of some of the public mistrust of a vaccine development process that was moving at "warp speed." He understood why people might not trust the process. But with public resistance to lockdowns and other public-health measures growing, he saw no other way out of the pandemic. "People are getting sick, and people are dying, and people are staying at home and the economy is hurting, and people's lives are turning upside down," he said. "The only practical way out of this in this country is an effective vaccine. And we need to work as quickly as possible to show these products are going to work or not work."

Mistrust aside, asking thirty thousand people to participate in a *placebo*-controlled clinical trial was a tall order. No one would know in advance whether they were getting the actual vaccine or the placebo. Would it be worth it to go through two injections, follow-up visits, and blood draws, only to find out you got a placebo that had zero chance of preventing Covid-19?

Recruiters saw patterns among those willing to participate. Older adults were less hesitant, which made sense. They were at highest risk of severe illness and death. And many could remember the devastating impact of diseases like polio that vaccines vanquished.

Gregory Rummo taught chemistry at Palm Beach Atlantic University in Florida and wanted to contribute to battling the pandemic, so he volunteered for the Moderna clinical trial. "It's a minimal something, but it's something I can do," he said, surely echoing the sentiments of many participants. His motives weren't entirely altruistic; he was hoping that the vaccine would protect him, though he didn't know if he would get a placebo instead.

For most of July 27, after Dawn Baker got her shot, Moderna basked in the glow of being the first in the United States to enter a Phase 3 trial of a Covid-19 vaccine. It stayed a front-runner—until that same night, when Pfizer and its partner BioNTech announced the start of their own Phase 3 trial. Their study began in the United States but would expand overseas to include about 120 locations.[12]

Now Moderna was neck-and-neck with Pfizer and BioNTech. And the

Pfizer/BioNTech vaccine had a built-in speed advantage: They were giv-ing doses three weeks apart, not four, like Moderna. What's more, Pfizer and BioNTech would start counting Covid-19 cases among study subjects seven days after the second dose, versus fourteen days after the second dose for the Moderna vaccine. With trials starting on the same day, this meant Pfizer and BioNTech had a good chance of finding out whether their vaccine safely worked before Moderna did.

Pfizer and BioNTech had already beat Moderna to a supply contract, too. The federal government already agreed to pay $1.95 billion to secure 100 million doses of the Pfizer/BioNTech vaccine. This implied a per-dose price of $19.50, or $39 per person vaccinated with the two-dose series. The federal government would provide the vaccines free of charge to Americans.[13]

By vaccine standards, this pricing was modest. The hepatitis B vac-cine for children costs about $25 per dose, while the combined measles/mumps/rubella vaccine costs about $82 per dose. Newer vaccines were even more expensive. Pfizer's own Prevnar runs more than $200 a dose for private purchasers.[14]

Pricing became another factor in the race to a vaccine, and it came under scrutiny. Earlier in July, executives from several vaccine makers testified virtually for a House committee hearing, and they were asked about their pricing plans for their vaccines. Pfizer and Moderna both said they would set prices that would generate profits, though they suggested the profits wouldn't be extravagant.

In contrast, AstraZeneca and Johnson & Johnson said they would charge either not-for-profit or at-cost prices for their shots. AstraZeneca had also already signed a supply deal with the United States, which im-plied a price of about $4 per dose. And J&J would soon disclose that it would sell to the US government for $10 per dose.[15]

Congresswoman Jan Schakowsky, a Democrat from Illinois who was often critical of drug-industry pricing practices, made clear that there would be political consequences if prices for Covid-19 vaccines were too high. "Ensuring the safety and efficacy of Covid-19 vaccines, of course, is critical. But it will mean nothing if the price is a barrier to all Americans getting it," she said at the hearing.

Moderna hadn't yet specified its pricing plans but had hinted about it. As early as May, CEO Bancel said: "We don't want to maximize profit on this product. That is not responsible," while also noting that pricing should reflect its value. "Any vaccine put on the market, we want to think about, 'What's the value of the vaccine to society?'"

The first pricing data from Moderna came in early August, when it disclosed a few details about small-volume supply deals it had previously signed with other countries. The company didn't disclose which countries, though Canada's government announced one of the deals. The price: $32 to $37 per dose, nearly twice the Pfizer/BioNTech price for the United States. Bancel said the company was in discussions for larger-volume contracts, and that these would carry lower per-dose prices.[16]

Moderna finally reached its own supply deal with the US government in mid-August for 100 million doses at $1.525 billion, or $15.25 per dose. But factoring in the nearly $1 billion in funding that Moderna had previously received from the federal government for vaccine development and manufacturing, the initial supply really cost US taxpayers about $25 per dose. The deal carried an option for the government to purchase an additional 400 million doses from Moderna, at $16.50 per dose (not including the development funding).[17]

Moderna executives said that the price of its Covid-19 vaccine could rise when the pandemic emergency ended, but that would be a later discussion.

Bancel said that even as early as spring 2020 he began to worry more about manufacturing a vaccine than whether the vaccine would work. To fulfill its new US contract would be intense. To make the 100 million doses the government bought in, say, ninety days, it meant that Moderna and its manufacturing partners would have to make 1.1 million doses per day.

Bancel was thinking bigger than that for months. He met with Juan Andres soon after his trip to Davos the previous winter and asked Andres to start thinking about an audacious goal: make up to one billion doses of a vaccine during 2021. That would be 2.7 million doses a day, every day for 365 days, or nearly 32 doses per second for every second of the year.

Before the pandemic, Moderna had never made more than one hundred thousand doses of anything in a *year*.

Bancel's workforce upgrade in operations to Juan Andres proved crucial, not only because Andres got the Norwood plant built, but also because he had managed massive manufacturing operations before. At Novartis, he had managed a network of plants with twenty-five thousand workers. Andres, to Bancel's relief, did not think the billion-dose goal was crazy, and the two began to brainstorm.

Andres formed a routine with his team early in the year. He woke up at 6 a.m. and started calls from his house to plan the day. Then he'd commute to either the Norwood plant or headquarters in Cambridge. In-person meetings and constant texting dominated the day. Around dinnertime, he would hold in-person debriefs before heading home, doing a little more work before going to bed.

When they were making the initial batch of vaccine for the first clinical trial, there was still an airy vibe to the endeavor. It was before the surge in the United States, so Andres and his deputies greeted visitors with handshakes and wore no masks as they roamed the Norwood plant (the clean rooms were another matter—workers in those rooms always were gowned up and wore masks and gloves). The rush to make that first batch in February was serious business, but it was also fun, and company leaders were heartened by the willingness of so many manufacturing workers to put in long hours to get it done.

Sometimes, the plant workers earned unexpected recognition. Nicolas Chornet, the site head at Norwood, recalled driving back from a visit to his native Canada. The border guard asked him where he worked, and when Chornet told him the guard asked, "Aren't you the guys in the news?" Juan Andres said his family began asking more questions about his job at dinnertime, including his fifteen-year-old son. "I wasn't used to my kid thinking I did anything cool," he said.

But by March the airy vibe was disappearing. Andres shifted to mostly working from home and if he did go to a facility, it was only the

Norwood one, as workers there were deemed essential. Like others, he found himself working nonstop, given the high stakes of the task before him and the lack of a commute. "One of the issues with working from home," he said wearily that May, "is you don't have any reason to stop."

The partnership with Lonza, the contract manufacturer, sent Andres and some other Moderna employees to both Lonza plants—one in Portsmouth, New Hampshire, and one in Visp, Switzerland, to help set up new equipment and train employees to make Moderna's vaccine. One Moderna employee lived for several months in Portsmouth to help get Lonza set up. He was the designated "PIP"—person in plant.

Chornet, the Canadian who ran Norwood, volunteered to transfer to Basel, Switzerland, to work with Lonza, though the transfer meant being separated from his family. "I know it was not what he wanted to do," Juan Andres said. Another employee volunteered to manage a new overnight shift at the Norwood plant.

Boosting production is hard in any circumstance. Doing it under pandemic restrictions is absurdly difficult. Temperature checks were added to the daily routine. Protective gowns and masks became common even in office areas of the manufacturing plant. Moderna scheduled shifts to reduce density, and employees trying to collaborate on producing the vaccine were forced to keep their distance. The measures Moderna put in place were more drastic than those for many other companies, in part for worker safety, of course, but also because the company couldn't afford to lose people to sickness—which would slow down the manufacturing process.

"People are working their asses off," Andres said in early May as Moderna prepared batches of vaccine for the large Phase 3 trial. "Weekends do not exist."

Even as Phase 3 production started, Andres was looking ahead to the huge batches that would be required if—*when*—the vaccine was approved. Instead of using repurposed equipment from its trial cancer vaccine, Moderna was bringing in new equipment. An entire supply chain of obscure but crucial material was ramping up. Andres needed more DNA plasmids, genetic starter material essential to the mRNA recipe. He needed bigger plastic bags that would hold the finished vaccine product in bulk before it was parceled into vials. He needed more of the special machines that filtered unwanted substances out of the vaccine. (One thing Moderna didn't need: the coronavirus itself. The mRNA technology only used the genetic sequence from the spike protein, which was a welcome change for Andres, who was at Novartis in 2009 when the company made a vaccine using the actual flu virus, grown in eggs.)

The hunt for all this stuff was getting competitive. "This is what I call the Amazon effect," Andres said. "We are experiencing the toilet paper, the eggs, the meat shortages." The same rush to stockpile materials that happens ahead of hurricanes (and pandemics) was happening in the vaccine supply chain. Andres began to realize how important detailed forecasts would be if his suppliers were to keep up.

It was precarious business, because to make a vaccine batch, you need every material present and accounted for. "You can have ninety-nine raw materials but if one is missing you cannot make it," Andres said, but he was underselling the challenge. About six hundred items were needed for one batch of vaccine. He wanted all of it arriving at the manufacturing plant in steady cadence, not in fits and starts.

"For manufacturing, boring is fantastic music," he said, snapping his fingers. "You just boom and boom and boom."

As they worked, Andres's team took inspiration from updates about the vaccine testing. In August, Andres called his mother in Spain with good news: the data showed the vaccine produced a good immune response in older adults, something that doesn't always happen with vaccinees due to changes in older adults' immune systems.[18]

He had already lost his mother-in-law to the virus. Now he was holding back tears relaying the result to his own mother.

"I've been telling her for months, 'Hey, hold on, help is on the way.' When I got the data that our vaccine worked in the elderly as good as young people, I called her and said, 'It is looking great,'" Andres said, choking up again as he recalled the phone conversation.

By August, Moderna had added about two hundred plant workers, fifty more than its initial goal. It expanded the main production building. It brought a technical-development department from Cambridge to the Norwood site, putting it in a building across the parking lot from its plant, a building that used to house an auto-mechanic school. Here, workers in white lab coats and safety goggles tested the quality of samples of newly manufactured vaccines using a stack of high-end machines resembling rack stereos, but which cost half-a-million dollars each. They also honed their manufacturing techniques before taking their learning across the parking lot to the plant and to other manufacturing locations.

Moderna set up three main production lines in Norwood and one more at Lonza's plant in Portsmouth. Equipment continued to arrive all summer in preparation for the ramp-up to mass production of an approved vaccine. "The biggest challenge is the synchronization of everything," Andres said. "From October on, we are going to be producing in large quantities, 24/7. My biggest concern is that everything lands."

On a Friday afternoon in August, Moderna was expecting the delivery of large air-handling units that would help expand production in Norwood. Moderna had hired construction cranes to be on site to lift the large units, the size of tractor trailers, onto the roof of its plant.

But at the last minute that delivery was delayed because the supplier was unable to secure all the necessary state permits to transport oversized cargo along the route from Kansas to Massachusetts. If the units didn't get there by Sunday, Moderna would lose the cranes, and thus lose a week of production while it waited for the cranes to come back.

Frantic, Moderna executives called Operation Warp Speed officials, who put a military colonel on the job. The colonel leaned on state officials, who in turn sent state police with sirens blaring to escort the delivery to their state line, where they'd hand off the convoy to a new escort.

The precious cargo rolled into Moderna's Norwood plant Sunday morning, in time for the cranes.

Andres also got an assist from the feds via a Cold War–era law: the Defense Production Act, enacted during the Korean War to spur domestic industry to shore up the military. Later it was amended to grant powers in national emergencies. The Trump administration invoked it to try to help Moderna and other vaccine makers several times starting around September 2020, according to Paul Mango, the HHS official on Warp Speed. He said the orders essentially required that suppliers of certain raw materials and other items needed for vaccine manufacturing—including things like plastic bags, filters and lipids—give priority to the Covid-19 vaccine makers, over other customer contracts. For the most part this procedure worked to make the supply issues boring, just how Andres liked it.

Not all was harmonious between Moderna and Operation Warp Speed though. As enrollment in the Phase 3 clinical trial proceeded through the summer, it became clear to federal officials that not enough people from minority communities were being recruited. They pressed Moderna to recruit a more diverse trial population at the sites that the company controlled.

Moncef Slaoui and Tony Fauci began holding Saturday morning Zoom calls with Moderna to "help coax and advise Moderna how to get the percentage of minorities up to a reasonable level," Fauci recalled.

At first, Moderna executives expressed confidence they could hit the enrollment targets without significantly slowing down overall enrollment. But Fauci and Slaoui said they actually wanted Moderna to slow down overall enrollment in order to ensure they enrolled more minorities. Slowing down overall enrollment meant enrolling fewer new white people for a time, to give study site leaders time to find more people of color. Bancel, of course, wanted speed. Always. Moderna executives resisted the request at first, perhaps thinking in the back of their minds of their race with Pfizer and BioNtech, in which they had already lost some ground.

"That was very tense," Slaoui said. "Voices went up and emotions were very high."

Bancel ultimately agreed and instructed study sites to look for more diverse enrollees, even if that meant it would take longer to get to the thirty-thousand-person target. "We've asked those sites to work extra hard to try to reach those communities of color that have historically been underrepresented," Stephen Hoge said at the time. "If that has some impact on the pace of enrollment, we're OK with that."

As part of the effort, Moderna created a digital app for researchers running the study locations, which incorporated US Census demographic data for the surrounding community, to compare with study enrollment, according to Hamilton Bennett, a senior director at Moderna. It was Moderna's way of telling the sites, here's what your area looks like, "without having to beat them over the head," she said. Moderna, with pressure from Warp Speed, wanted the clinical sites to bring in a study population that was representative.

By early September, Moderna had twenty thousand volunteers, two-thirds of the way to the target enrollment. About 25 percent of them were from minority groups, including Black and Latino people, Moderna said. Ultimately, the slowdown worked to achieve diversity, as 37 percent of the trial's final enrollment were Black, Latino, Asian, and other minority participants. But it cost Moderna about three weeks to get there, and they hit thirty thousand volunteers in October instead of September.[19]

Later, Bancel called the decision to slow down enrollment "one of the hardest decisions I made this year."

11

Politics, Protocols, and Patents

THERE IS NO GOOD TIME FOR A PANDEMIC, BUT 2020 COULD have been one of the worst times for a pandemic. In the United States, it was an election year in a deeply divided political climate.

A rapidly developed vaccine became a cultural lightning rod. In a generation, vaccines had gone from a well-accepted public health measure to protect communities to something that represented part of your identity, based on whether you would get the vaccine or not.

An August 2020 poll found that 35 percent of Americans said they would not get a free vaccine—and the reluctance fell along party lines. Fewer than half of Republicans (47 percent) said they would get the vaccine, despite the fact that it was a Republican administration that had launched Operation Warp Speed, effectively acknowledging the vaccine was the only way out of the pandemic. Three out of five independents said they would get vaccinated. Among Democrats, 81 percent said they would get the vaccine.[1]

A confluence of factors drove these new levels of uncertainty. One was a long era of anti-vaccination activism that connected vaccines to autism, even though the research that made that link has since been completely discredited. Another factor was the "warp speed" of the Covid vaccine development. Even people who have no idea how vaccines are developed sense that it's something that probably takes a long time. And this was happening at unprecedented speed.

And, the election was coming, leading three out of five respondents to another poll to worry about premature approval of a vaccine before the scientists had fully vetted it.[2] A successful vaccine study or even the availability of a vaccine before Election Day could be a powerful campaign boost for President Trump. With Moderna and Pfizer starting large Covid-19 vaccine trials in late July, it was theoretically possible, though unlikely, that answers about effectiveness could come before the November 3 election. Even if those results weren't available, some wondered whether the Trump administration would approve one anyway.

Again, there was a political divide on this question. Only 35 percent of Republicans were concerned about a political decision to approve a vaccine, whereas 85 percent of Democrats expressed concern.

Trump did nothing to allay concerns. In early August, he said in a radio interview with Geraldo Rivera that a vaccine might be available before Election Day. It wouldn't hurt his chances of reelection, he said, before adding that he wanted something fast to save lives, not to win the election. He also started to cast aspersions on the FDA, stating in public comments and tweets—without evidence—that the agency was delaying answers from the vaccine studies, or potential authorization of vaccines, until after Election Day. Then in early September he put aside his prior allegation of FDA foot-dragging and said a vaccine could be delivered by the end of October.

Executives at Moderna and the other vaccine companies felt caught in a bind. They were taking extraordinary steps to try to deliver Covid-19 vaccines as quickly as possible, but if their speed made people feel they were unsafe, and they refused to get shots, then their work wouldn't matter. If too few people got vaccinated, the pandemic would continue unabated. More people would suffer and die.

They also had to walk a fine line between faithfully and accurately describing the progress without agitating the unpredictable Trump, who could jeopardize the help and the money the companies were getting from federal officials.

The government officials were in a tricky position, too. Peter Marks, who oversaw FDA's division that reviews and approves vaccines, vowed to resign if the Trump administration pressured the FDA to authorize a vaccine before Phase 3 clinical trials proved it was safe and effective.[3]

In early September 2020, the companies took the matter into their own hands with a remarkable move. Amid a heated race with each other to deliver the first or best vaccine, Moderna and its rivals drafted a joint statement pledging to adhere to high ethical standards and scientific principles in bringing their vaccines forward. They declared that the safety and well-being of vaccinated people was their top priority. They would only apply for FDA authorization of a vaccine if it demonstrated safety and efficacy in a Phase 3 clinical trial. "We believe this pledge will help ensure public confidence in the rigorous scientific and regulatory process by which Covid-19 vaccines are evaluated and may ultimately be approved," the pledge read. The CEOs of AstraZeneca, BioNTech, GlaxoSmithKline, J&J, Merck, Moderna, Novavax, Pfizer, and Sanofi all signed the statement.[4]

It was a shot across the bow of the Trump administration. Trump and his deputies could say what they wanted about delivering a vaccine before Election Day, but the companies would control the process.

As if to underscore the point of the joint statement, one of the leading vaccine candidates hit a delay over a safety snag. AstraZeneca—still led by Pascal Soriot, the CEO who had given Moderna its first Big Pharma partner back in 2013—had started a Phase 3 clinical trial in the United States. It was the third vaccine to enter Phase 3 in the United States after Moderna and Pfizer. But on the same day that the joint pledge was issued, AstraZeneca paused its trials because a person in a UK study developed an unexplained neurological illness.[5] The UK testing resumed several days later after government regulators there concluded it was safe, but in the United States the FDA didn't allow the US trial to restart until late October, perhaps being extra cautious to show it was as serious about safety as the companies professed to be in their pledge.

Johnson & Johnson encountered a similar setback a few weeks after starting its Phase 3 clinical trial—the fourth major vaccine study to start in the United States. One study subject experienced a rare blood-clotting disorder. It, too, paused until the FDA allowed the US portion of the study to resume in late October, on the same day as the AstraZeneca study. (Both J&J and AstraZeneca's vaccines used the viral-vector technology; health authorities later found these viral-vector Covid vaccines to be associated with an increased risk of the blood-clotting condition.)[6]

The delays effectively put AZ and J&J farther behind in the race for a US Covid-19 vaccine. It was a two-horse race between Moderna's and Pfizer's mRNA vaccines, which hadn't run into any significant safety concerns.

As summer turned to fall, questions from analysts and journalists focused largely on these two: When will you know if it works? And how effective would it be?

No one could say for sure. There's no countdown like at a football game, with a clock hitting zero and the results then final. Vaccine development is more like a baseball game—it ends when it ends. In biotech and pharma, it's called an "event-driven" clinical trial. Moderna designed the trial so that it could make a call on the vaccine's efficacy once there were 151 confirmed cases of Covid-19 among the study subjects who displayed the symptoms the trial designers had hashed out months earlier. But they weren't giving people Covid to test their hypothesis; cases had to emerge naturally as trial volunteers went about their daily lives.

An independent oversight committee would peek at the data before the threshold of 151 was reached, first at 53 cases, and then again at 106 cases. Depending on what the data told them, Moderna might be able to call its vaccine effective after those first 53 cases. Or, it might have to wait for 151. It ends when it ends. (Pfizer's study, which started the same day as Moderna's, was designed similarly, with interim glimpses at efficacy along the way to 164 confirmed cases. Pfizer also expanded its study's enrollment target to about forty-four thousand people to include more diversity and adolescents aged sixteen to seventeen.)

Adding to the uncertain timing for results: the FDA said in October it would require that at least half of the study subjects be monitored for side effects for two months after getting vaccinated before the agency would authorize a vaccine.[7] Even if Moderna and Pfizer got an answer about the vaccine's efficacy on the early side, there'd be more waiting to account for the two months of monitoring.

Bancel said the best-case scenario would be results in October, but more likely November. After a summer surge, transmission of the virus plateaued in September. "Thankfully, for the US population it has become better the last few weeks," he said, noting that while it was good for communities, it probably would push off results. "[Slower transmission] actually makes it harder for an October readout" of the vaccine's efficacy.

Every aspect of Moderna's and Pfizer's efforts was drawing attention and scrutiny. It was becoming increasingly likely that the FDA would issue an emergency-use authorization if it deemed one of the vaccines to be safe and effective. Such an authorization would speed up the review from months to weeks, or even days.

Because of this, some doctors and vaccine specialists were demanding the companies release the formal protocols—kept confidential to this point—that spelled out how the large Phase 3 clinical trials were being conducted, and how the data would be analyzed. They wanted to know more about what researchers were measuring and how many Covid-19 cases would be needed for an answer. Eric Topol, an influential physician and author, tweeted in mid-September that Pfizer and Moderna should immediately publish the protocols for the sake of transparency in medical research. Topol's tweet from September read: "Dear @Pfizer @BioNTech_Group @moderna_tx, We, the life science/medical community/public, request immediate publication of the data analysis plans for your vaccine trials. Transparency in medical research has never been more essential."[8] The *New York Times* noted that taxpayer dollars were involved and so protocols should be publicly disclosed.

In normal times, there is little demand to make such arcane documents public. Most drug companies consider the detailed designs of their clinical trials to contain proprietary information that gives them competitive advantages. They only disclose what they're required to under law, which are mostly basic details like targeted enrollment, enrollment criteria, estimated start dates, and the primary goals of a study. All of that information is posted to clinicaltrials.gov.

But in these extraordinary circumstances, and under pressure from Topol and others, Moderna decided to release its full protocol publicly.[9] It posted the 135-page protocol document for its Phase 3 trial on its website.[10] "Mostly this is a gesture to continue to gain public trust," said Walid Gellad, a physician and professor of health policy and management at the University of Pittsburgh School of Medicine.

Bancel wasn't shy in touting the move: "We believe it's very important that the scientific community and medical community has a chance to review in detail the protocol, to understand it," Bancel said. "We want to be part of the solution. As you know, we're working hard for nine months to get a safe vaccine with high efficacy to the marketplace. Credibility and transparency, we believe, are really important."

Of course, Moderna wouldn't normally do this and only did it this time under public pressure, but Bancel saw a competitive edge in moving on it once it was clear the pressure would continue. It gave Moderna a chance to claim the high ground before its competitors. Moderna would be a "leader" in transparency, Bancel said, adding that he wasn't aware of any other companies releasing their protocols. Pfizer released its own protocol not long after.

The companies weren't likely to disparage each other publicly, and they had all developed rhetoric around fighting a common enemy. They were willing to show a united front when it mattered—such as the joint letter on adhering to safety standards—but at heart they were competing as fiercely as ever. Gamesmanship like Bancel's emphasis on being a transparency leader—implying his rivals were laggards—was common. They looked for ways to distinguish their vaccines and to bolster their reputations.

Gamesmanship had also occurred before, with the very real difference in the storage requirements between the Moderna and Pfizer vaccines. Earlier in the year, Moderna had stored its vaccine at –70°C, an ultra-cold temperature that required special freezers. By Phase 3 testing, Moderna found it was possible to store the vaccine at –20°C, closer to the temperature of a household freezer. Pfizer's vaccine, however, required ultra-cold storage when it was rolled out. Moderna executives weren't averse to pointing out the difference. Moderna also didn't mind that, given the company's close collaboration with NIAID, Anthony Fauci and other federal officials generally spoke favorably of Moderna in public, something that irked Pfizer executives.

Gamesmanship spilled into the intellectual property arena, too. Moderna investors were hounding the company about its patents. Owning the mRNA technology was a core part of the business strategy for Moderna from the start—which is what brought the lawyers to Jason Schrum's basement lab and sent them to Penn to seek rights to Karikó and Weissman's work. Since then, Moderna had filed many more patent applications including ones to cover its Covid-19 vaccine, mRNA-1273.

Would other mRNA vaccines infringe upon Moderna's own patents, the analysts and investors wanted to know. Would Moderna file patent-infringement lawsuits against other companies that were making Covid-19 vaccines if they improperly borrowed from Moderna's inventions?

And could another company challenge Moderna's patents to clear the way for making a Covid-19 vaccine like Moderna's without licensing the technology?

Patent applications don't become public immediately, so it was quite possible that some competitors had beat Moderna to the punch by applying for an important mRNA invention. This possibility forced Moderna to disclose in an August 2020 securities filing that it couldn't be 100 percent sure it had all its patents lined up to protect its Covid-19 vaccine. "Therefore, we cannot be certain that we were the first to make the inventions claimed in our patents or pending patent applications, or that we were the first to file for patent protection of such inventions, including mRNA-1273. For this and other reasons, we may be unable to secure desired patent rights, thereby losing exclusivity."[11]

It wasn't an unusual filing. Patent litigation was a normal part of doing business in the pharmaceutical industry. The patents create windows, usually about ten to fourteen years, to exclusively market pharmaceutical products, a way to help companies recoup the massive investments in R&D it takes to get drugs to market. Because patents provide this locked-in exclusive market, they are extraordinarily valuable ramparts that must be defended when they're yours and attacked when they're theirs. Companies routinely sue each other, claiming infringement.

Some companies have gone to great lengths to leverage the patent. Jonas Salk famously asked, "Could you patent the sun?" to explain in the 1950s why he didn't patent his polio vaccine. Modern drugmakers, on the other hand, seem to try to patent everything under the sun. Companies will rack up dozens of patents covering a single drug to extend monopolies beyond the typical patent timeframe. AbbVie obtained more than one hundred patents for its top-selling drug Humira, an expensive treatment for rheumatoid arthritis frequently advertised on TV. When competitors tried to make generics, AbbVie sued them for infringement against some of those one hundred patents connected to the drug. These suits led to settlements under which lower-cost generic copies couldn't be sold in the United States until 2023—more than twenty years after Humira went on sale.[12] In the 2010s, a multi-company patent battle erupted in the lucrative market for hepatitis C drugs, with companies like Gilead and Merck suing each other for infringement.[13]

A similar legal battle over Covid vaccines seemed like a distinct possibility. It had already started in October 2020, when a small San Diego company called Allele Biotechnology and Pharmaceuticals sued Pfizer and BioNTech. Allele claimed that in their Covid vaccine testing, Pfizer and BioNTech were using "mNeonGreen," a fluorescent protein owned by Allele. Pfizer and BioNTech disputed the allegation and the litigation proceeded.[14]

In 2015, Moderna had filed preliminary patent applications claiming invention of mRNA vaccines for respiratory diseases including coronaviruses. In February 2020, going all in on the vaccine, Moderna filed a follow-up to the earlier applications and was granted a US patent in July for mRNA vaccines including those encoding a spike protein from a coronavirus, formulated in a lipid nanoparticle.[15]

Moderna carried other patents that broadly covered mRNA technology, regardless of whether it was related to the Covid-19 vaccine. Some covered the modification of nucleotides for the production of proteins and the use of lipid nanoparticles to usher mRNA into human cells.[16]

Some financial analysts thought this portfolio provided broad enough coverage to pose a problem for the Pfizer/BioNTech Covid-19 vaccine. Moderna might have cause to claim infringement if the Pfizer team brought a vaccine to market.

Typically, investors would push for a drug company to assert its patents and sue. But in the context of an unprecedented pandemic killing millions, the optics of a patent lawsuit were problematic, to say the least, especially from a company that had received so much taxpayer support. Moderna didn't want to be the company that hindered the availability of vaccines that could end the pandemic because it wanted money for its inventions.

So in October 2020, Moderna said that it would not enforce its Covid-19 vaccine-related patents while the pandemic continued, meaning it wouldn't seek a court injunction against selling a vaccine it believed infringed on its patents. Moderna also said that it was willing to license its patents to others after the pandemic. The company released a list of seven "representative" patents related to the Covid-19 vaccine that it wouldn't be enforcing. (Interestingly, none of them was from Karikó and Weissman at Penn, or from Derrick Rossi at Harvard. Though Moderna had licensed rights to both sets, it seemed to have obtained so many other patents of its own that it didn't see theirs as most relevant to the vaccine.)[17]

"We're quite studiously not asserting infringement," president Stephen Hoge said. "We're doing the opposite of creating that kind of anxiety for folks. We're not interested in using that IP to decrease the number of vaccines available in a pandemic."

"If this were not a pandemic," he added, "then we would absolutely use our patents to protect our inventions from others."

Zachary Silbersher, an attorney who advises investors on patent matters, translated: "When the pandemic is over, all bets are off. It is not unreasonable for Moderna to say that. If . . . a competitor is using one of Moderna's patents, Moderna needs to reserve the right to sue them."

Moderna wasn't on the offensive on all IP matters. The company continued to face questions over whether its use of lipid nanoparticles (LNPs)—the fatty shells that encased the mRNA in most of its drugs and vaccines—infringed on patents held by Arbutus Biopharma and another company, Tekmira. Moderna insisted its LNP tech was proprietary. But before the pandemic, Moderna had started a US Patent Office proceeding seeking to invalidate Arbutus's LNP patents, which a company does when it's concerned about those patents putting them in an infringing position. If one or more Arbutus patents were upheld, Moderna might one day have to pay royalties to Arbutus for sales of its own Covid-19 vaccine.[18]

The federal government also owned some patent rights. Kizzmekia Corbett and Barney Graham of NIAID's vaccine-research center were among the inventors on a patent covering modifications to stabilized coronavirus spike proteins (thus improving the immune responses). The patentholder was the United States, as represented by the secretary of Health and Human Services, Scripps Research Institute, and Dartmouth College, where some of the coinventors worked. The NIH began to license the patent to vaccine developers on a nonexclusive basis. New York University's Technology Law and Policy Clinic noted in a paper that Moderna's vaccine likely infringes upon this patent, and if the NIH were to enforce it against Moderna, the company could be on the hook for billions in royalties to the NIH.

Tension between Moderna and its collaborators at NIAID would mount later when Moderna filed its own US patent application for the mRNA sequence of its Covid-19 vaccine and left key NIAID players off the list of inventors.[19] Moderna said in a patent filing in July 2021 that NIAID had requested that John Mascola, Barney Graham, and Kizzmekia Corbett from the vaccine-research center be added as coinventors. Moderna, however, said it "reached the good-faith determination that these individuals did not coinvent the mRNAs and mRNA compositions claimed in the present application."[20] Moderna said only its scientists invented the mRNA sequence used in the vaccine. The disclosure was a surprise to government officials, who had been negotiating with Moderna about the patent filing. NIAID disagreed with Moderna, noting its close collaboration with Moderna, and NIH Director Francis Collins suggested the dispute could end up in litigation. As routine as these disputes are in pharma and biotech, this one didn't play well with the feds or the public, fifteen months into a stubborn pandemic.

Moderna tried to make nice by offering the government co-ownership of the patent, but the optics of the dispute didn't look great for Moderna. In December 2021, Moderna tried to cool things off by dropping the patent application. The company was still very much collaborating with NIAID scientists in responding to the pandemic, and Moderna said it wanted to avoid the distraction of the patent dispute.

Patent fights are a normal part of the business, but the pandemic messed with that part of the business. The typical stream of suits and settlements was mostly stopped, abnormally. The lawyers used to roaming the arena were caged up and told to wait. As the pandemic endured, they could only pace and wait.

On October 22, 2020, Moderna enrolled its 30,000th participant in its large Phase 3 trial, less than three months after it started. Already, most of the Moderna study volunteers had received their second dose of the Moderna vaccine or a placebo. About 42 percent of participants were at least sixty-five years old or had high-risk chronic conditions; 37 percent identified as Black, Hispanic, Latino, or another minority group, numbers that tracked to the proportion in the overall US population.[21]

Most people didn't understand the historic nature of what was happening. It had been just 286 days since the genetic sequence of SARS CoV-2 was posted online, and a vaccine could possibly be available in the next sixty days. "You've got to understand," NIAID's Barney Graham said, "that what we've done in the last nine months usually occurs over ten to fifteen years."

People weren't much in the mood for reflecting on scientists' excitement. The world had become deeply impatient for a vaccine. After flattening out in late August and September, new Covid cases had started surging again. President Trump, who rarely wore a mask in public, tested positive for Covid and was hospitalized for three days.[22] He recovered, but the incident led to the cancellation of the second presidential debate against former vice president Joe Biden. Politics had affected efforts to fight the virus, and now the virus was affecting politics. This surge looked like it was everywhere, not just in certain hot spots. Plans to get back to work and to school were scuttled. Sports leagues played to empty stadiums. The world grew wearier still. The most devastating, deadly wave of the pandemic was about to hit.

Bancel professed optimism, nonetheless. "The next few weeks and months are going to be quite historic for Moderna," Bancel told analysts on the company's third-quarter earnings call. If the vaccine worked, he added, it would not only deliver a Covid-19 vaccine to help end a pandemic, but it would also validate Moderna's mRNA technology. "Think about what this team could do over the next five to ten years."

12

The Power of Science

THROUGHOUT A LARGE DRUG TRIAL, ALMOST EVERYONE, including the company making the drug, is in the dark. Information is "blinded" to protect the integrity of the study. So Moderna's thirty thousand volunteers didn't know whether they got a vaccine or a placebo (some guessed vaccine after experiencing side effects, but they didn't know for sure). The doctors and nurses who administered the shots didn't know if they were giving participants the vaccine or a placebo; both had identical labels and appearances. Moderna didn't know who got what.

And no one knew if it was working. Except the DSMB.

The Phase 3 trials were monitored by an obscure committee called a Data Safety and Monitoring Board, or DSMB. Most drug trials have a DSMB to provide independent oversight. In June 2020, NIAID had appointed one DSMB for all Covid vaccine trials (except Pfizer, which, not being a full participant in Warp Speed, had its own separate DSMB). A single group watching multiple trials was less typical, but it would expedite the process here, as it would be better positioned to quickly compare efficacy data than separate DSMBs specific to each vaccine.

The Covid vaccine DSMB had eleven members from various backgrounds, including experts in vaccinology, immunology, biostatistics, epidemiology, public health, and ethics. All were deemed to have no financial relationships with the companies developing Covid-19 vaccines. Each member received an honorarium of $200 per meeting from NIAID.[1]

Little else was known about this DSMB, other than the fact that its chair was Richard Whitley, a veteran pediatric infectious-disease specialist at the University of Alabama at Birmingham. Whitley had been on DSMBs for several clinical trials and had previously served on the board of directors of drugmaker Gilead Sciences. UAB posted a press release announcing Whitley's appointment to chair the DSMB, but soon took it down, perhaps to prevent inquiries from pouring in to Whitley about his work. It was not uncommon for hedge fund managers and Wall Street analysts (and journalists, for that matter) to try to contact doctors involved in clinical drug studies to try to scrape together any bits of useful information they could.

All DSMB discussions and materials were confidential, which meant that these eleven were the only people on earth who knew what was going on in the trials. Sometimes the DSMB met on short notice when they wanted to do a rapid review of important data. The DSMB could peek at the "unblinded" data, for example, when those predetermined thresholds of positive cases were hit—for Moderna it was 53, then 106, then the final target of 151. The team would meet over videoconference to review the data, looking at infections, reactions, and reported side effects.[2] They would know who got the vaccine and who got the placebo, and how they fared. Depending on the numbers, they could make a call on the effectiveness at any one of these milestones.

In the second week of November the United States was trying to calm itself after an unsettling week that followed the intense and unprecedented events surrounding the November 3 presidential election. Joe Biden had defeated the incumbent with a record number of votes, while the Democrats held their majority in the House and gained control of the Senate. But Trump never formally conceded and began a campaign to discredit the outcome, though his efforts were overwhelmingly rejected by judges in courts across the country. His refusal to admit defeat imperiled continuity in planning for a mass vaccination campaign, as Biden's transition team was barred from meeting with Trump administration vaccine planners for a few weeks and couldn't really get started on a vaccine rollout plan.

The coronavirus was surging, with US Covid-19 cases doubled since the start of November, to about 150,000 a day. It was the front end of a deadly surge that lasted well into winter.

The virus had shaped the election. During the campaign, Biden blasted President Trump's handling of the pandemic, saying that anyone responsible for 220,000 Covid deaths should not remain president. Trump countered that the virus was fading (it was not), and that a successful vaccine was on the horizon (it seemed to be). And the election results were unknown for a week of deep uncertainty, in large part because of the massive amount of voting by mail by those who wanted to social distance.

While most of the country was still obsessively following the politics, the DSMB was not. The Moderna trial had reached a critical threshold to allow for the first interim analysis of data, so late that second week of November, they alerted NIAID and Moderna that they were ready to review some of the results. They would meet by video call on Sunday morning, November 15, 2020.

The waiting was excruciating. Saturday was "the longest day of my life," Moderna's president, Stephen Hoge said, "and I can't sleep Saturday night."[3]

Sunday morning came, and Hoge continued to wait, not knowing if this would be a fifteen-minute conclave or an all-day session. Ultimately, the DSMB met for several hours. By that afternoon, it was ready to reveal its findings to a group that included Anthony Fauci, a representative from Moderna's funding partner BARDA, and Hoge and Bancel.

When he got word that they would meet, Hoge likened it to the puff of white smoke at the Vatican that signals when Catholic cardinals have elected a new pope.

There would be no formal presentation, just a verbal summary of the results. Within minutes of the start of the call, a statistician from the DSMB got to it.

Of thirty thousand trial participants, there were ninety-five confirmed cases of Covid-19 that met their symptom criteria. The cutoff had been fifty-three cases, but the virus was surging so dramatically that the cases shot up. That was okay purely from a statistical perspective—it meant more data to evaluate.

But those ninety-five confirmed Covid-19 cases were not split evenly between the vaccine and placebo recipients. Far from it. Of the ninety-five cases, ninety were in people who had gotten the placebo, five in people who got the vaccine. The calculations get complicated from here, but the statistician said that the efficacy of the vaccine was 94.5 percent, which meant that all other things being equal among people exposed to the virus, vaccinated people were 94.5 percent less likely to get symptomatic Covid-19 than unvaccinated people, at least through a median follow-up time of seven weeks after the second dose.[4]

The DSMB recommended to Fauci and Moderna that these interim efficacy findings should be shared with study subjects, researchers, and the public. The vaccine worked.

Fauci was the first to speak: "That's astounding!"

Hoge remembers grinning widely as he processed what he heard. He remembers feeling happiness, but also deep relief. Perhaps he had practiced his anticipatory nostalgia, but in the back of his mind there still was that fear that the vaccine wouldn't work. But it did. "It was this huge home run."

The call would last ten minutes. When Bancel hung up, he told his wife and two teenage daughters. They all cried.

For Moderna, the 94.5 percent efficacy was better than hoped for and slightly better than what Pfizer and BioNTech had initially reported just a week earlier. Yes, Pfizer had beaten Moderna to an answer, revealing on November 9 that their vaccine, BNT162b2, was more than 90 percent effective in preventing Covid-19 in an interim analysis of ninety-four confirmed cases. Technically, Moderna had lost the race, but only by a step, and only because it slowed down trial enrollment earlier in the fall to achieve greater diversity in its participants.

Bancel and his team had already resigned themselves to coming in second when they slowed down enrollment, but the results more than made up for that. Given production constraints, the world would need more than one successful vaccine. Having two mRNA vaccines report interim efficacy of at least 90 percent was a strong validation of mRNA technology. If Bancel harbored any disappointment about not beating Pfizer, he didn't show it publicly. "It shows mRNA can work," Bancel said via email on the day Pfizer released its results. "Great day for the world, as we are all waiting for vaccines."

After receiving the Moderna results, Bancel took his own victory lap that evening. "This just confirmed what we have believed all along," he said. "mRNA technology could be a game changer for vaccinology. This is the proof that by investing in science for ten years and making the long-term decisions to solve those problems, one after the other, we got to the place where Moderna's technology is very robust. . . . This technology is going to save thousands of people's lives and tonight is the proof point." He said he felt "just a huge sense of happiness and hope for the world" and that was needed. More than one thousand Americans, and about ten thousand people around the world, were dying every day from Covid-19. Lockdowns and public-health restrictions—back in force as Thanksgiving approached—had devastated the economy and mental health alike.

After the initial call with the DSMB, the team pored over additional promising details from the interim data. There were no significant safety concerns and side effects were mild and short-lived. Efficacy seemed to be consistent across all subgroups in the study—by age and other demographics, though all details weren't available yet. Of eleven cases of severe Covid-19 among study subjects, all of them were in people who had gotten the placebo. No one who received the vaccine had developed severe Covid-19 as of this analysis.

"We may be in a place with a vaccine that has a big impact on the prevention of severe disease," Bancel said. "That will be an incredible win against this awful virus."

Fauci also was feeling elated. The results of the Moderna vaccine trial were "extraordinary," "impressive," "encouraging," he said just hours after the ten-minute debrief call. He would have been satisfied with 75 percent efficacy given the urgency of the pandemic. "Now this has taken it beyond my expectation," he said. "Not only is it good news for individuals receiving the vaccine, but from a public-health standpoint, when you have a 94 percent effective vaccine and you [vaccinate] a substantial fraction of the population, that's the perfect ingredient for ending the outbreak."

The surge in cases that served as a backdrop to the results underscored how urgently the vaccines were needed. "This could not have come at a better time," Fauci said. "We have not yet seen the worst of this surge. We're going into the cooler months of fall and the colder months of winter. That's when things get bad."

And he did acknowledge that there was still much that was unknown about Moderna's vaccine: how long protection would last; whether the vaccine prevented or reduced transmission of the virus from person to person; and whether more serious side effects might emerge later on. But Fauci said they would continue to learn. One step at a time.

The results, along with the Pfizer/BioNTech results from the week before, also validated his hunch, several years before, that mRNA would be an optimal rapid-response approach to outbreaks, which is what prompted the stopwatch drill in the first place. There was always that question of whether mRNA would work, and many people suspected it never would. "Well, I think this ends that argument," Fauci said. "So, this platform looks like it's a solid platform for vaccinology."

At moments like this, the world often hears from the leaders and the success seems like theirs. Larry Corey, who ran the vaccine trials network that was crucial to Moderna's Phase 3 trial, was thinking about all the thousands of people who did something that a year before would have seemed impossible. In an email to his team—other doctors and statisticians—that mixed passion and technical data, Corey effused:[5]

When you awake this morning, you will be greeted with wonderful news; news that will make all of you smile and hopefully

bring the feeling of a job well done to all of you. The initial results
of the Moderna trial will become public and the storyline will
be as remarkable and scientifically perfect as one could design
any scientific trial: that a single strand of RNA that transcribes a
prefusion protein of SARS CoV-2 when wrapped in a lipid nanoparticle elicits a highly effective immune response in adults,
among the elderly and in racially and ethnically diverse populations. The results of the trial are a vaccine efficacy . . . that has a
94.5% point estimate in reducing symptomatic COVID. . . .

With all the talk about politics interfering with vaccine development, these results are an ironclad demonstration of the power
of science. I hope all of you recognize the absolutely critical role
you all played in this. All those weekends and long days and the
stress of it all . . . to me, it all washes away any days of angst and
frustration, to see the beauty of these results and the implications
it has on our country, our families and the world. . . . As Tony
[Fauci] said to you at the last staff meeting, what a difference you
have all made.

So, this note is to say, "Job well done." I hope you can feel the
palpable sense of excitement this announcement will have and
how much this success is about what you do.

Two weeks later, on Monday, November 30, the final results of the
Phase 3 trial came in. Moderna had set a target of 151 cases for evaluation. Ultimately because of the torrent of new cases running through
the country, especially in the Midwest, where many of its test sites were,
Moderna had 196 confirmed cases of Covid-19 among study subjects to
review.[6]

The vaccine's efficacy held steady, landing at 94.1 percent. All thirty
severe cases were in the placebo group.

Vaccine specialists were delighted. It wasn't just the high efficacy, but
also the consistency of protection across subgroups and the fact that severe cases weren't being found in the vaccinated that was so powerful.

The same day those results landed, Moderna formally requested that the FDA and European regulators authorize the emergency use of its vaccine. Pfizer had recently filed a similar request after more data analysis showed that its vaccine was 95 percent effective.

A whirlwind December was set in motion, when federal agencies would be expected to review two urgently needed vaccines, hold public advisory meetings about them, and make decisions within weeks. Hoge and Moderna's leaders ramped up production on the tornado of paperwork it would need to support authorization of the vaccine, while in parallel Juan Andres managed the massive ramp-up in production of vaccine doses.

Moderna's stock price surged 20 percent, to $152.74 on the day its final results landed. The company was now worth nearly $60 billion, bigger than some drugmakers that had been selling products for years, including its neighbor in Kendall Square, biotech pioneer Biogen. Investors were confident in the company now. Morgan Stanley analysts estimated that Moderna, which in 2019 totaled $60 million in revenue, would sell $10 billion to $15 billion worth of its Covid-19 vaccine in 2021.

Even better, the Covid-19 vaccine study results boosted the prospects that mRNA technology would work for vaccines against other diseases. It could be the platform Moderna promised, turning out treatments like apps on an iPhone.[7]

But first, Moderna had to mobilize for the biggest and most urgent mass vaccination campaign in history.

13

Evidence

THE FDA SCHEDULED A DECEMBER 17 VIRTUAL MEETING OF the "Vaccines and Related Biological Products Advisory Committee," or VRBPAC, which would spend several hours hearing the evidence behind Moderna's vaccine, and then vote on whether the FDA should grant emergency-use authorization. FDA officials indicated they would make the final call within days of the December 17 vote, and Secretary of Health and Human Services Alex Azar said distribution of doses would begin as soon as possible after that. Pfizer and BioNTech were still a week ahead and would have their hearing on December 10.[1]

If all went smoothly, the mass vaccination campaign could begin before Christmas.

To people familiar with the process, a three-week FDA review seemed cartoonishly fast. The process usually took six to ten months. But in the current emergency, some Americans not familiar with the process wondered why the agency would even need three weeks. The Phase 3 trials showed the vaccines worked safely and the coronavirus was by this time in its most deadly phase, killing more than two thousand Americans every day. More than one hundred thousand Americans were in the hospital. Some schools that had reopened were shut down again. The hoped-for fall reopening never really gained purchase. The holidays would be muted. Extended-family gatherings were canceled or moved outdoors for Thanksgiving. The same was planned for Christmas. The vaccine couldn't come fast enough.

FDA commissioner Stephen Hahn defended the timeline. The agency couldn't just assume that what the companies reported about their vaccines was the final word. They had to pore over the data with a staff of people working days, nights, and weekends to make sure nothing was missed. Three weeks was absurdly fast, he noted. To go any faster would risk missing something important, and perhaps fuel doubts.[2]

"We realize there is an issue in the US around vaccine hesitancy. There have been concerns raised about the speed with which Covid-19 vaccines have been developed," Hahn told the *Wall Street Journal*. "This will meet our gold standard of safety and efficacy that the American people have come to trust."

While the FDA cranked through all of Moderna's data, the company turned to its next big challenge: building supply.

Throughout 2020, before anyone knew for sure if the leading Covid-19 vaccines would work, estimates of the supply of doses were all over the place. Moncef Slaoui, when he left Moderna's board to take the job as chief adviser to Operation Warp Speed in May, said he was confident there would be a few hundred million doses of vaccine by the end of 2020. The same month, Vice President Mike Pence said Trump wanted 100 million doses by the fall, and 300 million doses by the winter.[3] In June, HHS said Operation Warp Speed aimed to deliver 300 million doses by January 2021.[4]

Time dampened these big numbers and big promises. Trump's 300 million by the winter turned into 100 million by the end of the year when he was on the campaign trail in July and August. Also in July, a CDC official told outside experts serving on an advisory panel that there may only be 10 million to 20 million doses available when a Covid-19 vaccine is first authorized. Clearly, that would not be enough for the US population of 331 million, let alone the world.[5]

Moderna wasn't specific about what it could supply, only saying "millions of doses" until September, when the company clarified its expectations: 20 million doses for use in the United States by the end of 2020.[6]

Because Moderna's vaccine was given as two doses four weeks apart, that would be enough for 10 million people. Bancel said to investors in early December, "It's really remarkable as a company of one thousand people, that has never done a Phase 3 . . . is ready to ship before the end of the year 20 million doses and is on its way to 500 million to 1 billion next year."[7]

Pfizer and BioNTech downshifted from saying they could turn out 100 million doses (two per person) down to 50 million, half of which would be for the United States.[8] Between the two vaccines, there would be enough doses to vaccinate 22.5 million people, about 7 percent of the US population.

A rationing plan would be needed. Doses would be prioritized for some groups until enough supply was available for the general population.[9]

It wouldn't be the Hollywood version of rationing, like in the 2011 pandemic thriller *Contagion*. In the film, public-health officials use a ping-pong-ball lottery machine to choose the birth date of the first people to receive the vaccine, announced by a rear admiral played by Bryan Cranston. This would be far more science-driven, and far, far more complicated.

The group charged with figuring out the vaccination priority plan was the Advisory Committee for Immunization Practices (ACIP), a federally appointed panel that advised the CDC on vaccine policy. In normal times this group of doctors, public-health experts, and vaccinologists decided whether a newly approved vaccine should be given routinely, and at what age.

It didn't take long for a consensus to emerge that doctors, nurses, and other health care workers should get the vaccine first. They had put their lives on the line for a year treating Covid-19 patients. What's more, protecting them had the knock-on effect of preventing staff shortages from outbreaks at health care facilities.

At the same time, it seemed clear that younger, healthy adults, who were less at risk and suffered fewer severe symptoms from Covid, should be near the end of the line.

Between those poles was the tough part. Should everyone over sixty-five get in line after health care workers since they were at high risk of severe Covid-19? Or should adults of any age who had high-risk medical conditions like diabetes and obesity come next? What about workers and residents in nursing homes and other long-term care facilities? Or teachers, given the urgency to reopen schools? Where should essential workers, whose jobs required them to be exposed to people all day, be put, like grocery store workers, at risk of exposure to the virus every time a customer walked up to the deli counter or paid the cashier? And meatpacking workers, who had suffered heavy outbreaks? Police? Bus drivers?

As expected, the ACIP panel voted to recommend that 21 million health care workers get the vaccine first. But it added another three million residents of nursing homes and long-term care facilities to this first group because of the combination of their vulnerability to the virus and crowded settings they lived in.

The vote was 13-1 for this part of the plan, the lone dissenting vote from Vanderbilt infectious-disease specialist Helen Keipp Talbot, who worried that much remained unknown about the vaccine's safety in this older population, and that it might be tougher to monitor these residents for side effects.[10]

The next priority group they settled on was people seventy-five and older and essential workers such as first responders, corrections officers, and food-industry workers. After that should come people sixty-five to seventy-four years old, plus anyone sixteen and older with a high-risk medical condition.

From there, the prioritization scheme got complicated. Even as this federal vaccine committee was trying to set priorities, all fifty states, plus US territories and even some major cities, were in the process of setting their own priorities about who should get first dibs on the limited supply of doses. While most places planned to give health care workers first priority, their next priorities varied widely after that. Arizona's governor wanted teachers near the front of the line. Some states placed first responders like police and firefighters over long-term care residents. Publicly, confusion reigned on every aspect of the priority list except for who would go first and who would go last, and that confusion would endure. Lists would change; plans would shift well into 2021.

The logistics of distributing the vaccine supply compounded the confusion over prioritization. As similar as Moderna's and Pfizer/BioNTech's vaccines were chemically, they were remarkably different products.

Moderna's vaccine could be stored at −20°C (or −4°F). Pfizer's required the more challenging −70°C, which meant it needed dry ice for shipping and special freezers for storing. This made Moderna's vaccine more suitable for shipment to rural areas that would take longer to reach and would be less likely to have the equipment for ultra-cold storage.[11]

Pfizer's smallest containers held about 975 doses, whereas Moderna's came in cartons of about 100 doses each, making Pfizer's vaccine more suitable for large hospitals and densely populated areas that could get through 1,000 doses before they went bad. Once thawed, Pfizer's doses could be refrigerated for only five days before going bad, whereas Moderna's could last thirty days.

Moderna's vaccine was shipped more ready-to-use. Once thawed, vaccine administrators could draw it directly from the vial and inject it into people's arms. Pfizer's vaccine had to be mixed with a liquid called a diluent before it could be injected.

"The [Moderna] packaging was so much easier," recalled Claire Hannan, executive director of the Association of Immunization Managers, whose members are the public-health officials who run vaccination programs.

It was looking like Moderna's would be a country vaccine and Pfizer's a city vaccine. In Minnesota, for example, public-health officials planned to get the Pfizer vaccine to bigger hospitals but outlying sites might have to wait for the Moderna vaccine, which was running about a week behind Pfizer's.[12]

These logistical challenges weren't insurmountable and would prove to be less important as vaccine supplies increased and administrators of vaccine sites became more experienced. But in the early days of the vaccination campaign, the differences mattered.

On the night of Friday, December 11, 2020, the FDA cleared the Pfizer/BioNTech vaccine for anyone sixteen and older. President Trump posted a video on Twitter in which he said the vaccine was a "medical miracle," and would save millions of lives. Distribution would start immediately.[13]

The decision came one day after an all-day meeting of the FDA's vaccine-advisory committee. The committee voted 17-4 with one abstention in favor of widespread use of the vaccine. Some of the dissenters seemed particularly concerned about including sixteen- and seventeen-year-olds in the authorization. They were a lower-risk group and the data about the vaccine's effect among them was limited from the large Phase 3 trial.[14]

Next up: Moderna. As the first doses of Pfizer's vaccine were administered, the FDA summarized their assessment of Moderna's Phase 3 trial data in a fifty-four-page document to help inform the vaccine-advisory committee meeting. To most people, the summary is boring, clinical reading. Perhaps its strongest statement was: "The 2-dose vaccination regimen was highly effective in preventing PCR-confirmed Covid-19 occurring at least 14 days after receipt of the second dose." (PCR is a reference to the diagnostic test for Covid.) The vaccine was effective across age groups, genders, racial, and ethnic groups though efficacy was higher at 95.6 percent among people eighteen to sixty-four, versus 86.4 percent among those sixty-five and older.[15]

The FDA report also underscored the need for a vaccine. By this time, the coronavirus had caused more than 71 million cases of Covid-19 and claimed the lives of more than 1.6 million people worldwide. In the United States, the toll was 296,000 deaths among the more than 16 million reported Covid-19 cases, the FDA wrote.[16] Despite being less than 5 percent of the world's population, the country accounted for 23 percent of all reported cases and 19 percent of deaths.

The FDA report listed the vaccine's ingredients: synthetic mRNA encoding the pre-fusion stabilized spike protein of the coronavirus; lipids including one known as PEG, short for polyethylene glycol; salts and sugars; and other substances including buffers that are used to stabilize the pH balance. Details about the ingredients were important because people with allergies to any of the ingredients would have to avoid the vaccine or be careful about monitoring for side effects. It could also squash budding conspiracy theories and disinformation campaigns surrounding the mRNA vaccines, including a false claim that they contained microchips as part of a plot by Bill Gates or Microsoft.

The FDA said it didn't identify any safety concerns that would preclude its authorization. But it did flag some side effects that were more common in vaccine recipients than placebo recipients. About 9 percent of vaccine recipients had injection-site reactions that were classified as "grade 3," defined as severe or medically significant but not immediately life threatening. Some 16.5 percent showed fever and fatigue. Severe fatigue was more common after the second dose than after the first.

The FDA said it would recommend that vaccinated people be monitored for a condition called Bell's palsy, which weakens facial muscles, because three vaccine recipients in the Moderna study experienced it. This condition also was reported in a small number of participants in the Pfizer study.

Moderna submitted its own eighty-four-page analysis, also clinical and boring. Moderna concluded: "Considering the ongoing public health impact due to SARS-CoV-2 and lack of approved preventative vaccines, the potential benefits of mRNA-1273 outweigh the risks."[17]

All this information would be aired two days later, at the virtual FDA vaccine-advisory committee meeting on December 17. Several Moderna executives made presentations, conferencing into the call from their homes. The presentation was available to the public.

It served as a sort of master class on mRNA technology. Chief medical officer Tal Zaks took the opportunity to ease any concerns about a new vaccine technology. "Now mRNA-1273 is not our first infectious disease vaccine," he said as he scrolled through a presentation. "In fact, we've been in early phase clinical trials for the past five years conducting twelve clinical trials that have enrolled over seventeen hundred healthy volunteers. SARS-CoV-2 is the ninth virus against which our mRNA vaccines have elicited neutralizing antibodies. And we have not seen a significant safety concern in any of our trials to date."[18]

Melissa Moore spoke next. She was chief scientific officer of platform research at Moderna, and a professor at the University of Massachusetts Medical School. She explained what happened at the cellular level. Once the vaccine is injected into muscle, the immune system kicks into action. Nearby lymph nodes—small lumps stationed around the body that hold infection-fighting cells—contain specialized immune cells known as "antigen presenting cells." The mRNA gets into those cells and instructs them to make the spike protein, which then gets displayed on the cell surface. The immune system decides this is something it needs to fight and begins to produce antibodies against the spike proteins, Moore explained.

Jacqueline Miller, who had joined Moderna from GlaxoSmithKline to lead infectious-disease research earlier in the year, spoke next and summarized the various studies of Moderna's Covid-19 vaccine. She noted that the vaccine's efficacy seemed to kick in after the first dose and before the second one, but that for maximum protection, both doses should be given.

Then came questions from the doctors and experts who served on the FDA advisory committee, and hours of discussion. Why were the efficacy rates lower in older adults? (It was sample size; efficacy was largely consistent.) What about the side effects? (Manageable.) What about the people who reported facial swelling? (Related to people who had had cosmetic surgery and received dermal fillers; medication treated it.) What about the Bell's palsy cases? (Monitoring them, but consistent with what would be found in the general population.) What about pregnant and breast-feeding women, and younger recipients, for whom there wasn't much data at all? (Extensive surveillance would be put in place and the CDC would encourage self-reporting after vaccination using smartphones.)

Behind the scenes, while dozens of people were involved in conducting the FDA's review, there were fifteen "principal discipline reviewers," each responsible for different aspects of the FDA's work: clinical data, toxicology, biostatistics, manufacturing, safety, data integrity. They even reviewed the printed label that would accompany the vaccine.

They also reviewed inspections of nine of the nearly one hundred locations where the Phase 3 study was conducted. The FDA inspectors found deficiencies—the precise nature of which wasn't revealed—at two of the sites, according to an FDA document that was released after the vaccine was authorized. The concern passed quickly when they discovered that Moderna had identified and corrected the problems. To be safe, the FDA recrunched the Phase 3 study data excluding the two sites, which accounted for about 750 participants, and found only one Covid-19 case had been reported from the two sites, in a placebo recipient.

The FDA staff also evaluated Moderna's manufacturing process for the vaccine and found no problems. All these specialized reviews had occurred in the days and weeks leading up to the public advisory committee meeting.

It was a marathon meeting, eight hours of discussion by people scattered around the country, doing their best to avoid technical glitches with webcams, accidental muting, screen-sharing snags, and background noises like a passing train, barking dogs, or crying kids. It was streamed live on FDA's website and is available on YouTube (where it has had forty-seven thousand views as of December 2021).[19]

By 5 p.m., it was time for a vote. Do the benefits of Moderna's Covid-19 vaccine outweigh its risks for use in adults eighteen and older?

Before the vote, though, Paul Offit from Children's Hospital of Philadelphia, the veteran vaccinologist who helped design the trials, spoke. Months before this, Offit professed healthy skepticism about Moderna's trumpeting of its Phase 1 trial results. Dr. Offit recalled later that his mindset earlier in the year had been: "They were suffering this hubris and there would be a price to pay for that."

Now, as a voting advisory committee member, he said, "I think the question that's being asked us is, do we have enough evidence in hand to say that the benefits of this vaccine outweigh what, at the moment, as far as severe safety issues, are theoretical risks. I think the answer to that question is clearly yes."

The panel members were given two minutes to vote electronically, but there was a glitch. Someone accidentally displayed the wrong voting question, the one from a week before about whether to recommend the Pfizer/BioNTech vaccine, as if Moderna needed another reminder that Pfizer had beaten them to this moment.

When the right question was posted, the vote ended in an instant. An FDA staffer read the outcome: 20-0 in favor of the vaccine.

Some of the panel members spoke about their decision after the vote.

"I would say that the evidence that has been studied in great detail on this vaccine highly outweighs any of the issues that we've seen," said Hayley Gans, a Stanford University pediatrics professor. "And I think it really supports us being able to, with the pandemic in our background, really move forward and finally provide a safe and effective way to get to herd immunity."

"I just want to make the point that what a remarkable achievement this is and say thanks to all the scientists present and past who contributed to this," said James Hildreth, the Black scientist who had spoken out on the reasons for distrust of the medical community in minority communities. "To go from having a sequence of a virus in January to having two vaccines available in December is a remarkable achievement."

There was one FDA panel member who abstained from the vote on the Moderna vaccine. Michael Kurilla, director of the division of clinical innovation at the NIH, said he chose not to vote because he was concerned the recommendation that everyone eighteen and older could use the vaccine was too broad. He said he wasn't convinced the shot's benefits outweighed the risks in all age groups. The shot's use, he said, should be targeted to groups that faced high risk of severe Covid-19 disease.

But the 20-0 vote was the operative development. Now, it would just be a matter of hours before FDA finalized the decision.

The next night, Friday, December 18, an FDA official emailed a nine-page letter to Carlota Vinals, head of regulatory affairs for infectious diseases at Moderna. Buried eight paragraphs into the bureaucratic missive was the good news: "I am authorizing the emergency use of Moderna COVID-19 Vaccine for the prevention of COVID-19."[20]

After ten years, Moderna had produced its first product.

It was a week before Christmas, and the pandemic was raging. During the roughly forty-five months the United States was engaged in World War II, deaths of American service people averaged ninety-two hundred per month. In the month of December 2020, the coronavirus killed more than seventy-seven thousand Americans.[21] The economy was reeling. Congress closed in on a new round of coronavirus relief in the form of $600-per-person direct payments.[22] The politicization of pandemic policy didn't stop. A federal grand jury charged six men with plotting to kidnap Michigan governor Gretchen Whitmer over her coronavirus policies.[23] The Supreme Court let stand an order by Kentucky's governor to prohibit in-person school until early January in hard-hit areas, despite a challenge from a private Christian school.[24] Even as it shepherded an astonishing feat of science, the United States' image as a leader plummeted across the world.[25]

In three weeks, there would be an insurrection at the Capitol.

The vaccines were signs of hope, bright points of light on a bleak landscape, but the supply was limited. It would take a long time to get this done and it wasn't clear that enough people were going to voluntarily get the vaccine to stop further outbreaks. There was so much yet to do.

A few hours after Moderna's Covid vaccine was approved, just before 4 a.m. on a frigid winter morning in Boston, Stéphane Bancel was catching up on email. He had woken up early. I had sent him an email the night before asking him to reflect on the significance of what had transpired just hours earlier.

"Since early January, we have chased this virus," he wrote back. "We have known every day counts to save lives, to protect people. Today is a historic day because it shows that collaboration and human ingenuity can overcome the worst enemies. I am thankful to everyone who helped us."

That's what it meant for the Covid-19 pandemic.

I had also asked what it meant for Moderna, and Bancel responded: "We have been at this for ten years. Our mRNA platform is a modern approach to medicine. But it is just the beginning."

He had spent nearly a year pushing the company toward this moment, starting in the pre-pandemic vacation days in France. He gave himself a four-day break over the Christmas weekend, and crashed, sleeping until the afternoon on some days in his Boston home. "I was not a fun father and husband," he admitted, but the yearlong pressure had caught up to him.

14

Happy Tears

THE RESEARCH HOSPITAL THAT SITS ON THE BETHESDA, Maryland, campus of the National Institutes of Health is nicknamed the House of Hope. It earned the nickname because it's where patients come to try experimental drugs when they are out of other treatment options. The first chemotherapy ever tried on cancer patients was given at the House of Hope.[1]

A few days before Christmas of 2020, NIH leaders and frontline health workers came to an auditorium there to provide new hope in the darkest, deadliest hours of the pandemic to date.

"Many prayers have been lifted up over this terribly difficult year that an answer to this global pandemic might emerge from the dedicated work of our scientists," said NIH Director Francis Collins, standing on stage, wearing a mask and a dark sport coat over a black T-shirt. "I will admit that quite a few of those prayers were mine."[2]

In this bastion of medicine and science, Collins was there to say that his prayers were answered. It was four days after the FDA authorized Moderna's vaccine and more than a week after the Pfizer shot was cleared. On stage, Collins, Anthony Fauci, and Health and Human Services Secretary Alex Azar would receive first doses of the Moderna vaccine that NIH had worked on with Moderna. The week before, Vice President Mike Pence and House Speaker Nancy Pelosi received the

Pfizer vaccine. And President-elect Joe Biden got the Pfizer shot during a televised appearance the day before. (President Trump got his first dose in January at the White House, but it was done without publicity and would only be revealed weeks later, after he left office.)

Fauci followed Collins at the dais, and he was nostalgic, recalling how he once sat in the same auditorium when he first came to the NIH in 1968.

Before the leaders got their shots, a handful of the institutes' frontline health workers got theirs. "It's really to help protect my patients who I see every day who don't have Covid, to protect my colleagues who are there on the front lines with us every single day, and then to protect my family when I get home," one NIH doctor said about his desire to get the new vaccine.

Next were the big names: Azar, Fauci, and Collins. When it was Fauci's turn, he shed his suit coat and rolled up the left sleeve of his shirt. He was a couple days shy of his eightieth birthday. His NIH colleague, Colleen McGowan, who was serving as the event's emcee, said to him, "Many in our nation are saying if Dr. Fauci gets the vaccine I'm going to get the vaccine, so tell us a little bit why it's important."

"Well, for me it's important for two reasons," Fauci said through his white mask as he awaited the injection. "One is that I'm an attending physician here on the staff at the National Institutes of Health Clinical Center, and so I do see patients. But as important, or more important, is as a symbol to the rest of the country that I feel extreme confidence in the safety and the efficacy of this vaccine, and I want to encourage everyone who has the opportunity, to get vaccinated so that we can have a veil of protection over this country, that would end this pandemic."

With that, the needle went into his arm. Afterward, an NIH staffer put a Band-Aid on the injection site. Fauci rolled his sleeve down and gave a thumbs-up, to the light applause of the modest-sized, physically distanced crowd.

Fauci had by this point agreed to serve as chief medical adviser to President-elect Biden when Biden took office in January, while keeping his longtime role as NIAID director.

The event was streamed live online, and TV news segments showed clips of Fauci getting the shot. The event was meant to mark an important step in fighting the virus, but just as much to boost confidence among those who were still skeptical or nervous about a vaccine. The last to receive the vaccine at the House of Hope event was Colleen McGowan, the emcee whose day job was director of NIH's research services office. She said she was going to chronicle her vaccination "on Facebook for all my naysayer friends to show them it's safe and effective."

When the FDA authorized Moderna's vaccine, the supply chain was ready. A supply of doses was ready to go, Moderna having started manufacturing months earlier at its own plant in Norwood, Massachusetts, and at its partner Lonza's plant in Portsmouth, New Hampshire. At those sites, the finished product was placed in large, specialized plastic bags and kept at freezing temperatures, and then sent elsewhere for finishing touches. One destination was a plant in Bloomington, Indiana, operated by a contract manufacturer called Catalent. There, workers parceled out the vaccine into vials, vials were put into cartons, and cartons were packaged up for shipping.

Truck drivers working for a wholesale drug distributor, McKesson, pulled up to the Catalent plant to pick up the initial batch of doses and move them to McKesson's distribution hubs. In August, McKesson had expanded an existing vaccine-distribution contract with the CDC to include the Covid-19 vaccines. (Pfizer, not part of Warp Speed, set up its own distribution network.) McKesson also was tapped to distribute vaccine kits that contained syringes and wallet-sized vaccination record cards that would be given to every recipient.[3]

From McKesson's hubs, the vaccines were picked up by UPS and FedEx trucks. The first refrigerated truck, belonging to FedEx, left McKesson's distribution center in Olive Branch, Mississippi, around 9 a.m. on the Sunday after the shots were authorized, with boxes of the vaccine affixed with pink priority labels. That truck brought the vaccine to a

FedEx distribution hub in Memphis, Tennessee, where the boxes were sorted and sent out on trucks and planes to arrive at vaccination locations Monday morning.

The US government, Moderna's customer, managed the distribution. Overseeing it was General Gustave Perna, the head of operations for Operation Warp Speed, who decided how many doses would be allocated to vaccine sites throughout the United States each week. The CDC ran an online system in which hospitals, clinics, and other sites placed requests for doses, then were notified of their allotments.

Perna and his team decided that 5.9 million doses of Moderna's vaccine would be distributed during its first week of availability. Though small by later standards, this initial supply was a huge boost to the fledgling mass vaccination campaign. It was nearly three times the amount that Pfizer was expected to ship that week, and about double what Pfizer had shipped the week before. Moderna didn't get there first, but it was getting more out faster, initially.[4]

And because of its easier storage and handling requirements, the Moderna vaccine would be going to more locations—thirty-four hundred sites, compared with one thousand for Pfizer's.

Adding Moderna's vaccine to the arsenal "now allows us to be on the offense" against the coronavirus, General Perna told reporters the day after the Moderna shot was authorized.[5]

Moderna expected its output to increase enough to deliver 20 million doses by the end of December. And it would pick up week by week, month by month, until reaching a steady state in the spring or summer of 2021. Moderna had already agreed to deliver up to 100 million doses. More would follow. The federal government exercised an option to purchase an additional 100 million doses, for about $16.50 per dose. By summer 2021, Moderna would have produced enough to vaccinate 100 million people, more than a third of the adult US population, with two doses each (and the government would order even more doses in the new year).

A tiny fraction of the early supply of doses went to Moderna employees, contractors, and board members. The company said the vaccination would provide an additional layer of protection to workers involved in making and delivering the vaccine. In the fall, some employees had tested positive for the virus, though Moderna felt they were catching it from outside of work, not in Moderna's facilities. As for why board members would need to get vaccinated, Bancel said it was important for them to be available to approve important decisions in the vaccine effort. By this point, Moderna had about twelve hundred employees, so the number of doses needed was small. But it also meant that some people who weren't otherwise eligible under state and federal guidelines would get the vaccine, like healthy people working from home. Pfizer, with more than eighty-eight thousand employees, was only vaccinating workers as they became eligible under government guidelines.[6]

Moderna CEO Bancel's turn to get his vaccine was January 3, a Sunday, when he visited the Norwood manufacturing site, where Moderna had set up an in-house vaccine clinic, staffed by contracted nurses from a local hospital. He and his wife got vaccinated at the same time, holding hands. "It was an extraordinary feeling," Bancel later told an interviewer. "You can imagine, working ten years on the science and working nonstop for a year. And I never thought I would get a Moderna product injected in my body. And of course, given the pandemic, actually I got the first Moderna product ever, authorized by the FDA, injected into my body."[7]

In the days following, Bancel saw his knowledge of mRNA and vaccines in a new light. Now, this process that he had described to others so many times—the software of life analogy, the grandmother's recipe book—was happening inside him. "My body was turning into a little factory and making, you know, for 48 hours the spike protein and my immune system seeing it and getting super upset with it and making an antibody, that would protect me, in case I get it later," he said.

Tal Zaks and other executives also got vaccinated around that time at Norwood. Zaks recalls quizzing the nurse who was about to vaccinate him whether she had an EpiPen on hand—that was the new safety protocol at vaccine sites after there were reports of anaphylactic reactions among some early vaccine recipients. Zaks said he felt an "immense feeling of relief and excitement and pride," when he got the shot. (The nurse had an EpiPen; Zaks didn't need it.)

At first, vaccination was voluntary for Moderna employees. Later in

2021, Moderna would make Covid-19 vaccination mandatory for all US workers, with possible exemptions for religious or medical reasons.

Others involved in the two-decade long saga also got the shots. Drew Weissman and Katalin Karikó, the Penn scientists who had successfully modified mRNA to reduce inflammation, received the Pfizer/BioNTech vaccine. "I feel humbled, and happy," Karikó said. "I am more a basic scientist, but I always wanted to do something to help patients. I wasn't thinking about a vaccine or infectious disease; I was always thinking about developing mRNA for therapeutics. I'm hopeful, now that there is so much interest and excitement for this research, that it will be possible to develop and test this mRNA vaccine technology for prevention and treatment of other diseases, too." She did not say, but Karikó may have also felt some vindication, decades after her research had been largely ignored, and she had even been demoted because of her insistence on focusing on mRNA in her research.[8]

As Weissman received the dose, he thought about "working on this stuff for 20 years. It was great to finally have it in my arm," he recalled. "I basically saw it as the only way to stop this pandemic."

Derrick Rossi, the cofounder of Moderna who bitterly parted ways with the company years earlier, got vaccinated in February 2021 at Boston Children's Hospital. He got the Pfizer/BioNTech shot, providing him a laugh line as he advocated that people should get whatever vaccine they're offered. "I was happy to get vaccinated against Covid-19, that's for sure," he said.

Another high-profile vaccinee: country singer Dolly Parton. Parton had donated money to Vanderbilt's medical center that supported the institute's work on the Phase 1 study of the Moderna shot. The seventy-five-year-old received the Moderna vaccine at Vanderbilt in March 2021, documenting the occasion in a video in which she changed the lyrics to her hit "Jolene" to: "Vaccine, vaccine, vaccine, vaccine, I'm begging of you please don't hesitate. Vaccine, vaccine, vaccine, vaccine, 'cause once you're dead, then that's a bit too late."[9]

Many Americans rushed to get vaccinated; some found it to be an emotional experience. Betty Palacz went to a vaccination clinic run by the National Guard in suburban Chicago in February 2021. She brought candy for the Guard members. Choking back tears, Palacz told WGN-TV about the toll of the pandemic. "Not being able to see my great-granddaughter. And hug my daughter, my son, and my other grandson, he has Down syndrome. It's been hard." After she got her shot, she said, "I cried, and I cried, and I'm going to cry now. Happy tears."[10]

For all the celebrating, the logistics of dispersing the shots and injecting them into the arms of millions of Americans proved to be a bigger challenge than anticipated, resulting in lower-than-expected vaccinations in the early weeks. Federal officials largely left it up to state and local officials to figure out how to carry out their part of the mass vaccination campaign. Finding vaccine appointments became so difficult in some places that tech-savvy volunteers around the United States started social-media groups to help people find slots.[11] Some states kept strict eligibility criteria well into the spring, while others opened up vaccinations to the general population sooner. Federal and state officials blamed each other for the botched rollout.

The upshot was that by the start of 2021, only 15.4 million doses of both vaccines had been distributed, and of these, about 4.5 million doses had been administered to people.[12] This fell short of even reduced targets to have enough doses for 20 million Americans by the end of December. And it was just 5 percent of Operation Warp Speed's original goal of delivering 300 million doses by January 2021.

Moderna also fell slightly short of its initial goal. As of January 4, it had delivered 18 million doses, though it had promised 20 million.[13] Bancel couldn't help but wonder if the supply would have been bigger if he had managed to round up more funding in the first few months of 2020.

There were kinks to work out at the back end of the process, with tasks like filling vials at the Catalent plant, which had delayed the release of some doses.

As complicated as domestic logistics were, the international ones were even more so. Moderna and Lonza had set up a separate supply chain to make doses for other countries. This included Lonza's plant in Visp, Switzerland, which made the bulk vaccine product, as well as a Spanish company called Rovi, which handled the filling of vials and finished packaging. The non-US supply chain was a few months behind the US one.

Lonza estimated it would need about seventy workers for each of three planned production lines at Visp, and the company set about recruiting from Switzerland, Italy, Germany, and France. But when the lines came up, the company realized seventy per line wasn't enough. "We have been realizing during the ramp-up of these lines, we need more people," Albert Baehny, the Lonza chairman, said in April 2021. "We are looking after additional skilled persons. Today around the world, what is missing the most are skilled operators."

By April 2021, Moderna was informing Canada, the United Kingdom, and other countries outside the United States that it was facing a shortfall in its promised doses to them. For Canada, this meant 16 percent fewer doses than expected for the April to June time frame.[14]

Despite the setbacks, Moderna doubled down. It stuck to its target to deliver 100 million doses to the US government by March 31. And it agreed to deliver 200 million more doses by the end of July.[15] By this point, it had signed agreements to supply more than 640 million doses around the world: 300 million for the United States, plus 160 million for the European Union, 50 million for Japan, 40 million for each of Canada and South Korea, and more for other countries.

Moderna workers and partners would send Bancel pictures of milestones as the vaccine rolled out to more countries: images of the first pallet of doses coming off a plane in Japan or France. "Those moments are stronger emotional moments because those are places where I've lived and have friends and family," he said.

In the United States, the vaccine-supply crunch started to ease up in March and April. The new Biden administration had taken steps to boost the supply by expanding its contracts with the vaccine makers and continuing to use the Defense Production Act.

Much changed over the initial rollout. The Biden administration also dropped the name "Operation Warp Speed" and moved to the more tactical and less sci-fi sounding Countermeasures Acceleration Group.[16]

Moncef Slaoui resigned as chief adviser in January.[17] In March, Glaxo-SmithKline also terminated Slaoui as chair of the board of a joint venture, Galvani, because the company said it substantiated allegations that Slaoui had sexually harassed and engaged in inappropriate conduct toward a GSK employee several years earlier when Slaoui was an employee.[18] Slaoui issued a statement saying that his actions put a former colleague in an uncomfortable situation. He apologized to the employee and to his wife and family, and said he was taking a leave of absence from his professional responsibilities.[19]

In late February, the FDA authorized a third Covid-19 vaccine, from Johnson & Johnson. Initially, J&J and federal officials hoped that the new vaccine would bolster the mass vaccination effort, partly because it could be given as a single dose.[20] But use of the J&J vaccine was hampered by manufacturing problems, a lower efficacy rate (66 percent overall, versus the 94 percent-plus rate for Pfizer and Moderna) and a rare but serious blood-clotting disorder among a few vaccine recipients.[21] The same clot disorder would be seen with AstraZeneca's vaccine, which was approved for use in other countries but not the United States. Few other Western vaccines were ready for widespread use. Merck had pulled the plug on its Covid-19 vaccine program, while Sanofi and Novavax were experiencing delays.

It had taken three months for Moderna to produce its first 20 million doses of vaccine. By March 2021, Moderna had increased speed by a factor of six, turning out 40 million doses a month, with plans to hit 50 million a month soon, according to manufacturing chief Juan Andres.

Moderna laid much of the groundwork for increasing production capacity in 2020 by adding floor space and new equipment, like that police-escorted air-handling unit, to its Norwood plant and the Lonza plant. But it couldn't go to maximum capacity right out of the gate, because of the need to introduce new equipment and processes in stages, Andres explained.

Moderna was still training newly hired workers and encountering issues like equipment malfunctions and holdups in getting replacement parts such as filters.

"There has not been a single week since we started that we have not had issues," Andres said. "In making medicines, it is absolutely impossible not to have issues in the beginning. It takes time." He likened the process to a jet's trajectory—it doesn't start out at cruising speed, but it gets there.

Over time, the company had trained more employees and figured out how to address challenges like getting raw material to its plants more quickly. The company also looked for ways big and small to speed the process. The company discovered through experience, for example, that the same set of equipment that initially made five to six vaccine batches a month could yield ten batches. Andres's team also reduced the time needed to inspect and package vials. "You get better," he said.

By March, Andres felt good about the process. "We're in the zone," he said. "I like our chances to continue delivering."[22]

The vaccine's profound effect wasn't limited to public health. It transformed Moderna's balance sheet. For the first three months of 2021, Moderna booked $1.7 billion in revenue from its Covid-19 vaccine, with a profit of $1.2 billion, a massive tally for the first full quarter of sales of a new vaccine. And it was only a fraction of what was to come. Moderna said that for full-year 2021, it was expecting about $19 billion in sales of the vaccine.[23] Pfizer booked $3.5 billion in Covid-19 vaccine revenue for the first three months of the year, and at the time was projecting $26 billion in full-year 2021 sales.

The vaccine also made Moderna profitable for the first time. The costs of making the vaccine turned out to be a fraction of what Moderna charged, which ranged from $15 to $37 per dose depending on location. The total combined costs of raw materials, manufacturing personnel, payments of royalties to outside patent holders, shipping, and other manufacturing costs, on that $1.7 billion in revenue came to $193 million.

Those costs would mount as the year went on, but Moderna still expected them to be just 20 percent of expected revenue.

By April, the United States had vaccinated a big chunk of the people most eager to get vaccinated. Half of American adults had gotten at least one dose of a vaccine. States were dropping eligibility restrictions and pharmacies began to allow walk-in vaccinations.

And it looked like it was working. By Memorial Day, the average daily case count had plunged 88 percent, to below 30,000 from more than 250,000 at the peak of the winter surge. Deaths from Covid-19 were way down, too. The vaccines were saving lives—as many as 139,000 deaths were averted according to one analysis.[24] Efficacy stayed high: in real-world use, one CDC analysis found that both the Moderna and Pfizer vaccines were 90 percent effective at reducing the risk of infection.[25] Many states that still had Covid restrictions lifted them or announced plans to do so by summer. It seemed that life was beginning to return to normal, thanks to the vaccines.

But the mass vaccination campaign was now entering a tougher phase. The goal shifted from getting supply to those who demanded it, to overcoming vaccine hesitancy in millions who didn't trust the vaccine or didn't think it was necessary. Some had formed elaborate conspiracy theories about the vaccine. It was a long way from the days of the polio vaccine, when communities showed pride in contributing to public health causes.

Some people went too far in their anti-vaccination stance. In one bizarre incident in December 2020, a Wisconsin hospital pharmacist attempted to spoil hundreds of Moderna vaccine doses by taking them out of a refrigerator because he was skeptical about the shot. He later pleaded guilty to attempted tampering with consumer products and was sentenced to three years in federal prison.[26]

With an ample supply of doses, strategy shifted to persuading the holdouts by touting the benefits of vaccination or offering incentives like lotteries for the vaccinated. It would be a tough slog in some places, and some emerging safety concerns weren't helping convince the unconvinced.

The large clinical trial of Moderna's vaccine identified some adverse events, like headache and fatigue, but in real-world use reports emerged of severe allergic reactions to both Moderna's and Pfizer's vaccines. The suspected culprit was PEG (polyethylene glycol), an ingredient needed to help get the mRNA in both vaccines into human cells intact. PEG was used in other medicines and was known to trigger rare allergic reactions. The reports of severe allergic reactions with the Covid vaccines were still relatively rare, but they were enough of a concern to warrant new precautions, including longer monitoring for people with a history of allergic reactions and ensuring that EpiPens were on hand at vaccine sites. In mid-January 2021, California health officials recommended a pause in use of one lot of 330,000 Moderna vaccine doses after some people experienced severe reactions from the batch.[27]

And as more people got vaccinated, word spread about the temporary but significant side effects, like fever, headache, chills, and fatigue. For people who previously had Covid-19, these types of symptoms seemed to kick in most often after the first dose of the vaccine. For those who never had Covid-19, they came hours after getting the second dose. They often lasted for a day or two before abating. Not everyone had these types of side effects, but they were prevalent enough that hospitals began to stagger the schedule of vaccinations among health care workers so that not everyone in a single ward was laid up at home with flu-like symptoms at the same time.

In the spring of 2021, federal officials began to spot reports of inflammation of the heart muscle or its outer lining among some people receiving the vaccine. Some resulted in hospitalizations. The conditions, myocarditis and pericarditis, were spotted within days of receiving the second dose. The risk was rare, but it was still elevated among younger males versus other groups and higher than the rate you'd typically find these conditions in young men. A CDC analysis noted twenty-two to twenty-seven cases of myocarditis in men ages eighteen to twenty-nine per one million vaccine recipients (about three thousandths of 1 percent), a small number but still much higher than six cases or less per one million in other groups.[28]

Researchers thought it was possible that the mRNA vaccines were triggering a type of immune response in some people that was also causing heart inflammation. Some experts theorized it was related to the spike protein induced by the vaccine. Others thought it could be problematic injections that hit a vein.[29]

These are the kinds of cost-benefit analyses experts were wrestling with. Some infectious-disease specialists worried that even a relatively low risk of vaccine-associated myocarditis was concerning because younger males also had a low risk of getting very sick from Covid. As a comparison, one million vaccines for men sixty-five and older prevented 12,500 hospitalizations and 2,400 deaths from Covid, while vaccinating one million men eighteen to twenty-nine prevented 300 hundred hospitalizations and 3 deaths, according to statistical analysis.[30] Was that benefit greater than the cost of a small number—only between twenty-two and twenty-seven—young men developing a heart condition? Should these young men only get one dose? Or wait longer for the second dose? Some European countries restricted the use of Moderna's vaccine in young men while they investigated the risk.

Ultimately, US officials continued to recommend two doses for young men, noting that the known risks of Covid-19 itself—which can also cause myocarditis—far outweighed the risk of rare side effects such as myocarditis or pericarditis. And while there was a "likely" association between the vaccines and myocarditis, it was rare, and of those rare cases most were mild and resolved quickly.

But risk is hard for people to understand and visualize. Even as rare as this risk was, it cycled through news and social media and reinforced vaccine hesitancy positions of some young men and their parents.

In the meantime, Moderna doubled the targeted enrollment of an ongoing study of its vaccine in children under twelve, to more than twelve thousand, to better assess this risk.

In August 2021, Moderna's Japanese partner for the vaccine, Takeda, recalled three lots, totaling about 1.6 million doses, after workers at vaccination sites in Japan spotted what appeared to be foreign substances in some sealed vials. Three men died within days of receiving doses of Moderna's vaccine. Moderna investigated, along with its partner in Spain, Rovi, which had filled and finished the vials sent to Japan. Rovi found that the most likely cause of the contamination was friction between two pieces of metal in one of its production lines that was set up incorrectly, which caused stainless steel fragments to end up in the affected vaccine vials. Moderna contended there was no evidence that the deaths following vaccination were related to the vaccines, and it considered the deaths coincidental. But it would continue to investigate. The company said the presence of the metallic particles didn't pose an "undue risk." They may cause a reaction at the injection site, but were unlikely to cause further harm to people, the company said.[31]

In the big picture, the safety risks from the vaccines appeared to be low. By the end of September 2021 in the United States alone, more than 148 million doses of Moderna's vaccine had been injected into people, fully vaccinating more than 66 million of them, and including boosters for some. And the vast majority didn't experience any significant safety issues.

As mass vaccination settled in in the first half of 2021, some world leaders and advocacy groups wanted Moderna and other vaccine makers to ease up on their patent rights, at least for the time being. India and South Africa had filed a request in October 2020 with the World Trade Organization (WTO), seeking a waiver from certain patent obligations so that countries could more easily manufacture Covid-19 vaccines without running afoul of patent rights held by the companies. They and several advocacy groups urged the Biden administration to support the proposed patent waiver. NIAID itself owned a spike-protein patent which many activists wanted to be used as leverage. NIAID could, they said, use the threat of patent-infringement litigation against Moderna (which hadn't yet licensed the patent from NIAID) to pressure Moderna to share its vaccine-making technology with other countries.

In May, the Biden administration sided with the global-access advocates and against the pharmaceutical industry and supported a temporary waiver of intellectual property protections for Covid-19 vaccines to allow developing countries to make the shots.[32]

Pharma companies vehemently opposed the Biden administration stance, claiming it would undermine the IP system that enabled medical advances such as the Covid-19 vaccine in the first place. The industry lobbied hard against the move in Washington and in other capitals.[33] (For Moderna, the waiver drew support much closer to home, though: the Cambridge City Council, which in prior years had adopted resolutions congratulating its hometown company Moderna for certain milestones, adopted a new resolution in early May supporting the patent waiver and urging Moderna and Pfizer to drop their opposition.)[34]

CEO Bancel also characterized the announcement as something of a nonevent. Biden's support of the patent waiver "doesn't change anything for Moderna," Bancel said on an earnings conference call with analysts a day after the Biden administration announced its position.[35] Moderna had said the previous October that it wouldn't enforce its patents during the pandemic. And because mRNA was a new technology, there was effectively no excess manufacturing capacity, and few people who were skilled in manufacturing the vaccine. Anyone other than Moderna, Pfizer, and a handful of contractors would have neither the space nor the smarts to do this for some time.

"And so, we saw the news last night and I didn't lose a minute of sleep on the news during the night," Bancel said. The best way forward, he said, would be for Moderna and Pfizer to maximize the supply in the months ahead and to drop the idea of a patent waiver.[36] A few weeks later he said that if there had been a patent waiver ten to fifteen years ago, Moderna might not have become what it was by 2020, "and we might still be waiting for an mRNA vaccine to be authorized." Without patents in force, investors looking for returns wouldn't have jumped in and funded Moderna's growth.[37]

By the fall of 2021, the patent waiver proposal was still active at the

WTO but hadn't been implemented. Even without taking effect, the proposal called attention to a stark disparity in global vaccine allocation. Moderna had signed supply contracts primarily with wealthy countries such as the United States, Japan, and European nations. There was a program, Covax, backed by WHO and funded by many countries, that was trying to get 2 billion vaccine doses into mostly lower-income nations by the end of the year. While other vaccine suppliers like AstraZeneca had signed on, Moderna initially didn't have a supply contract with Covax.

Some groups, like anti-poverty organization Oxfam, urged Moderna to make its vaccine available beyond wealthy countries. "As a product that was funded largely by US taxpayers, Moderna's Covid-19 [vaccine] should be a people's vaccine, patent-free, mass produced, distributed fairly, and made available free of charge, to every individual on the planet, no matter where they live, rich and poor alike," a senior adviser to Oxfam said after Moderna's vaccine was authorized in December.[38]

Pressure yielded some results. In early May 2021, Moderna signed on to supply up to 500 million doses to Covax, with the initial 34 million doses slated for delivery in the last quarter of 2021.[39] This action didn't fully alleviate pressure on Moderna, as many would continue to push the company to serve developing countries. In late September 2021, activists displeased with Moderna's progress on the issue placed a pile of fake bones in front of Bancel's Beacon Hill house. Claiming credit for the act in a press conference, they accused him of choosing profits over human life by refusing to share vaccine technology with developing countries. Some doctors on the faculty of Harvard Medical School were among the protesters. Bancel wasn't happy—he viewed it as an attack on his family. And he felt their premise was off base. "I think it is pretty unfair to shame us for having delivered a vaccine and not having enough, by people who got their vaccine here in the US," he said after the stunt. "We had never commercialized a vaccine. It was clear there was not going to be vaccines for everybody in the world at the same time. We were forbidden by the government to export for a long time in 2021 and the US had bought 60 percent of our supply anyway."

The criticism, he said, made him sad. "Some forgot history and criticized us for not doing more when we did what most big vaccine companies failed to do.”[40] Bancel still didn't budge on sharing Moderna's vaccine technology, but Moderna started to take more steps in the direction of broadening access: it announced plans to build a vaccine manufacturing plant in Africa and agreed to provide 110 million doses of its Covid-19 vaccine to the African Union.[41]

With time, Bancel would bristle less at the criticism. By December 2021, Bancel had seen more variants of the virus take hold and he said [in an interview]: “I regret deeply that we didn't try to make more product. We under-planned manufacturing. That's just a sad part of where we are.” But he cut himself and Moderna some slack. He said it was difficult to foresee in early 2020 how much demand there would be for its vaccine.

The summer of 2021 brought calm, at first. New cases and deaths from Covid-19 were way down by June. Mask mandates expired, and the CDC said that fully vaccinated people didn't have to wear masks either indoors or outdoors.

Moderna dropped its own mask requirement for vaccinated employees in Cambridge and in Norwood. Some people who had been working from home for fourteen months were coming back to the office. And they had lunch and dinner options as nearby restaurants in Kendall Square reopened for indoor dining.

But Moderna was forever changed. Once packed into a few floors, the company had taken over all ten floors of its headquarters building. Returning employees found the main entrance and lobby under renovation.

I visited Bancel again at this time, sixteen months after our meeting when he had discussed the fledgling vaccine project. Bancel's office had changed, too—he now had a standing desk. A wood box with the name of an Italian wine sat nearby. The shelf of paperweights encasing symbolic vials of the company's experimental drugs and vaccines had added two: one to commemorate the start of the Phase 1 study of the Covid-19 vaccine, and a second one to mark the FDA's emergency-use authorization. Near the tchotchkes hung Bancel's paper name plate from his White House visit in March 2020, which felt so long ago.

Bancel looked relaxed. His company was a big reason why life was returning to normal. And he said he saw it coming early on. Having made a habit of checking the vaccination numbers posted online by the CDC each morning, he said he predicted life would be back to normal by April or May. It was too early to predict what would happen later in 2021, he said, but the fall/winter pandemic wave that had peaked in January was finished, he said.

Still, he was convinced that people who received the standard, two-dose Moderna vaccine would need a booster at some point to deal with the virus variants that tried to evade the vaccine, and to deal with waning antibody production over time. Maybe not everyone would need a booster—it might be best for the elderly, or those with compromised immune systems. His own seventy-two-year-old mother, he said, who had leukemia and was vaccinated in France in January, would probably be a good candidate for a booster.

Bancel wanted to expand manufacturing, too. The company had already set a target of 1 billion vaccine doses in 2021 and expected to enter 2022 at a pace that would yield 1.4 billion doses annually. But Bancel said he began to receive more calls from government officials around the world seeking additional vaccine supplies. These included countries that hadn't struck supply deals with Moderna, plus countries that wanted to expand existing deals and lock in doses for 2022. He also anticipated the boosters, and new demand if and when the vaccine was deemed safe for children.

"We need to add meaningful capacity," Bancel said, and so he did. Moderna decided to add 50 percent more production at its Norwood plant. And it would double capacity outside the United States, partly by having Lonza add more lines at its Visp, Switzerland, plant.[42]

Expansion would mean that Moderna could be positioned to deliver up to 3 billion doses in 2022.

Fifteen miles south from where Bancel sat, Moderna's manufacturing site in Norwood looked much different in June 2021 than it had in February 2020. For one thing, it was more secure. A remote-controlled metal gate kept visiting cars out of the main parking lot. Uber drivers with visitors like me weren't allowed to pull up to the main entrance.

Moderna's main production building, the one in the old Polaroid plant, had churned out most of the 200 million doses that Moderna had delivered for use in the United States since the previous December, and on its way to meeting its contracted 300 million doses for the United States by the end of July. Moderna marked the milestone by handing out blue T-shirts to employees that read "200 million doses."

Scott Nickerson, head of Moderna's manufacturing (and also an alum of Eli Lilly like Stéphane Bancel and Juan Andres), spoke with a sense of calm, as if the toughest part of the manufacturing buildup was behind him. He felt good about the ways in which Moderna had made the manufacturing process more efficient, shortening timelines and boosting output. "As you get your legs under you, you basically look for operational excellence opportunities to cut time out of your manufacturing process," he said. "You do that as you get better at what you do."

Nickerson, who reported to Andres, did have one worry: shortages of raw materials from vendors. Anything made of plastic was in short supply, he said, including "bags, tubes, and filters." He paused, then repeated himself: "Bags, tubes, and filters," as if trying to conjure them. Other vaccine makers were short, too. Novavax, the small Maryland company that was developing a promising protein-based Covid vaccine, had blamed shortages of bags, tubes, and filters for its own production delays.

For the planned expansion in its production capacity in Norwood, Moderna expected one new production line to be operational by fall and another by early 2022. Some of the steel tanks, white plastic drums, and other equipment used to make vaccines were already in place, waiting for finishing touches and validation.

Across the parking lot was the new technology-development site, housed in a former auto-mechanic school. And down a path through the woods was another building which Moderna was renovating to house future quality-control labs and clinical manufacturing. Construction workers in hard hats and neon green vests roamed the site, the droning beeps of construction vehicles moving in reverse a constant soundtrack.

"The build has been like nothing I've ever experienced, to go as fast as we did," Matt Barrows, Moderna's senior director of manufacturing with more than twenty years of experience in biotech, said. "The build was the journey and continues to be the journey."

Barrows, who reported to Nickerson, was also busy hiring new workers. Some came with experience in biotech manufacturing, some were fresh college graduates with engineering and chemistry degrees from nearby universities, including Northeastern University and Worcester Polytechnic Institute. He was happy to get to see new hires in person after a year of video interviews and remote hiring.

New and expanded contracts with contract manufacturers including Lonza and Samsung Biologics were added. Moderna locked in deals with raw materials suppliers including a little company called Aldevron in Fargo, North Dakota, which supplies the starter genetic material template, the DNA plasmids, for vaccine production.

The company opened divisions across Europe, starting in Switzerland, and a back-office support hub in Warsaw, Poland. Its executive leadership team had taken on a new look. The company hired a new chief financial officer from Amgen to replace Lorence Kim and a chief medical officer from Johnson & Johnson to replace Tal Zaks. (In the months after he left Moderna, Zaks said he had occasional Moderna nightmares, usually involving being in a room with Bancel and not meeting the demanding CEO's expectations over things like picking the right vaccine dose. Eventually, these dreams stopped, and Zaks took a job as a venture partner with biotech investment firm Orbimed.)

Moderna also created a new executive position, chief brand officer, to shape the public perception of Moderna's story and mRNA.

Flush with success, it paid to have its simple corporate logo, lowercased letters spelling its name in the Core Sans typeface, painted on the storied "Green Monster" left-field wall of Fenway Park, home of the Red Sox baseball team. (There is a typeface called "Moderna" that Moderna the company does not use.)

Moderna had become a household name. It ranked third in a poll of corporate reputations released by Axios Harris in May 2021, behind only Patagonia and Honda. Pfizer came in seventh. Moderna scored particularly well when survey respondents assessed ethics and citizenship.[43] It was an impressive showing for Pfizer, too, because, pre-pandemic, the reputation of Big Pharma had fallen so far over the years. To be topped by Moderna, though, must have felt like a jab to those at Pfizer's Manhattan headquarters.

In a virtual ceremony in May 2021, the Vatican gave a "Pontifical Hero Award" to Stéphane Bancel, citing his leadership of Moderna as it delivered a safe and effective vaccine.[44] Lebanon's ambassador to the United States awarded Noubar Afeyan the Lebanese National Order of Merit, along with six Moderna employees and a member of the board of directors who are of Lebanese descent.[45] Afeyan also gave a commencement speech to the masked members of the graduate-student Class of 2021 at Boston University. They applauded when he described Moderna as "the pioneering company in mRNA medicines, which created and developed a life-saving vaccine faster than any other in human history."[46] *Fortune* magazine named Hamilton Bennett, senior director of vaccine access and partnerships at Moderna, to its "40 under 40" list of rising executives.[47]

A foundation led by Spain's royal family gave the 2021 Princess of Asturias Award for Technical & Scientific Research to cofounder Derrick Rossi and six other scientists for their research that paved the way for the Covid-19 vaccines. Two of his fellow honorees were Katalin Karikó and Drew Weissman at Penn.[48] Karikó and Weissman also went on to receive the 2021 Lasker-DeBakey Clinical Medical Research Award, considered to be the top US biomedical research prize, and the $3 million Breakthrough Prize in Life Sciences.[49] In October, Barney Graham and Kizzmekia Corbett shared the "Federal Employee of the Year" award from a nonprofit. It was just a few months after Graham retired from the NIH and Corbett departed to become a professor at the Harvard T.H. Chan School of Public Health, where she is running a lab focused on coronavirus research.[50]

Cofounder Ken Chien was profiled on the website of the Karolinska Institutet in Sweden, where he has worked since leaving Harvard in 2013.[51] And cofounder Bob Langer, the MIT professor who continues to serve on Moderna's board, gave the commencement speech at Olin College of Engineering in Needham, Massachusetts, in the spring of 2021.

There was, of course, unofficial recognition. Poignant moments that many employees enjoyed. Matt Barrows, the manufacturing leader, sometimes wore a fleece vest with a Moderna logo stitched in. At his kids' sporting events, parents would approach him to thank him for the vaccine, and strangers in line at Dunkin' Donuts would give him literal pats on the back. Tal Zaks visited his native Israel and was having lunch near the beach north of Tel Aviv. A diner approached him and said, "Aren't you that doctor from TV who told us everything was going to be OK? Can I shake your hand and say thank you?" An Israeli university awarded Zaks an honorary degree.

Moderna was transformed. The world seemed to be on a path to recovery. Americans were preparing for a summer of relief and release.

But the coronavirus wasn't finished delivering suffering and death.

15

Delta

VIRUSES OF ALL TYPES FREQUENTLY CHANGE. THEY MUTATE as they jump from person to person. The coronavirus was no different. Throughout the pandemic, health officials tracked variants of the SARS CoV-2 virus first found in Wuhan, China, as those variants arose. None seemed a big concern, until one was flagged in the United Kingdom in December 2020, right as Moderna's vaccine neared approval. This UK variant appeared to be as much as 70 percent more transmissible. It was given the name the Alpha variant.[1]

Alpha reinforced the possibility that the virus could mutate enough to become resistant to vaccines and treatments that were designed to target the earlier, predominant strain. Or it could fizzle out. But variants would keep coming. Shortly after Alpha, researchers identified another variant circulating in South Africa. Beta.[2]

In late December—just a few days after the United States authorized its vaccine—Moderna issued a statement that it was confident the vaccine would be effective at inducing the necessary immune response against variants. The original vaccine targeted the full length of the spike protein of the coronavirus, and the new variants appeared to have mutations in the spike protein that represented less than a 1 percent difference from the original.[3]

"So, from what we've seen so far, the variants being described do not alter the ability of neutralizing antibodies elicited by vaccination to neutralize the virus," Tal Zaks said during a virtual appearance at the all-important J.P. Morgan Health Care Conference in January 2021. "My definition of when to get worried is either when we see real clinical data that suggest that people who've either been sick or have been immunized are now getting infected at significant rates with the new variants."[4]

Even if the vaccine proved less effective against a new variant, Moderna could use its mRNA technology to quickly tweak the design of its Covid-19 vaccine, to better target a variant of the virus, Zaks said. After all, the company and its federal health partners had already demonstrated the year before how quickly they could design, manufacture, and test a new vaccine.

Still, Moderna needed to run a series of tests to see if its original vaccine offered the same high level of protection against variants as it showed in the big Phase 3 clinical trial.

Moderna collaborated again with researchers from NIAID including Barney Graham and Kizzmekia Corbett. They analyzed blood samples taken from eight people who were vaccinated with Moderna's shot in the Phase 1 trial back in early 2020. They essentially mixed these blood samples with the coronavirus variants, engineered so they copied the mutations of the variants but couldn't replicate and pose a threat to lab researchers. Researchers then analyzed whether the vaccine-induced antibodies present in the human blood samples could effectively neutralize the virus variants.

The results were mixed. They suggested the vaccine worked as well against the UK Alpha variant as against the original strain of the coronavirus. That was good news. Even if the UK variant spread more easily than the original virus, Moderna's vaccine could probably mute its effects.

But the Beta variant first identified in South Africa seemed to pose a problem. The vaccine-induced antibodies had a significantly reduced neutralization effect on this strain in the lab tests.[5] "Oh shit," Bancel said when Stephen Hoge showed him the data. It wouldn't be the last time.

Moderna's leaders saw the data on a Friday in late January 2021 and spent the weekend discussing it. They hoped that a modified, variant-targeted vaccine wouldn't be needed, and that Moderna's original vaccine would suffice, even if it had a reduced neutralizing effect. But Moderna didn't want to be caught flat-footed if a variant-specific booster was needed.

They decided by the next Monday it was time to take action. They would develop a new version of the vaccine, one that more closely matched the mutations seen in the strain that circulated in South Africa, and which could potentially be given as a booster shot to better protect people who had gotten the original vaccine.[6]

"It really highlights the fact that we need to continue to stay vigilant," Moderna's president, Stephen Hoge, said. "This virus is evolving, it's changing its stripes. And we need to keep testing the new variants, and make sure the vaccine works against them."

Moderna repeated the steps it took a year earlier: it quickly designed a new variant vaccine and manufactured an initial batch for human testing, shipping it to NIAID in late February, a year to the day after it had shipped the original batch of the original vaccine. The new batch was called mRNA-1273.351, appending the "351" because researchers initially called the variant seen in South Africa "B.1.351."

"Moderna is going to keep chasing the variants until the pandemic is under control," Bancel said that day.

Moderna also developed other plans to test. It would try a third dose of its original vaccine, given several months after the second dose, to see if that booster shot would protect against variants. It would also develop a combined vaccine that targeted both the original strain and the Beta strain.

Once again, volunteers stepped up to test these various approaches. Neal Browning, the Microsoft engineer who was the second person to get Moderna's vaccine, showed up once again to volunteer. In the intervening year, he had gotten married, in a small outdoor ceremony to minimize Covid risk. Now he received a third dose of the Moderna vaccine. He felt tenderness at the injection site and a low-grade fever and chills, but the symptoms went away after several hours. He continued to visit the research site to give blood samples to be analyzed for immune responses.

By early May, Moderna had some answers. It gave booster shots—either the original vaccine or the Beta variant–targeting vaccine—to people about six to eight months after they had been vaccinated with two doses of the original vaccine. The company found that in the new analysis, both types of booster shots increased neutralizing antibodies against the Beta variant. And they increased antibodies against a related variant that had been detected in Brazil. But the newer version of the vaccine that targeted Beta induced a stronger immune response against the Beta variant than the booster shot of Moderna's original vaccine.[7]

At the time, Moderna's plan was to continue testing the different booster approaches, with an eye toward possibly getting government approval to sell the booster shot that specifically targeted the Beta variant.

But it didn't seem particularly urgent. The existing mass vaccination campaign was making good progress at the time.

Then, with the virus on the retreat in the United States, scientists discovered a new variant driving an alarming surge in India. This variant had already jumped to other countries, including the United States. Initially, it was code-named B.1.617.2. It was even more contagious than the Alpha variant and there were fears that it could evade vaccines. This was the Delta variant.[8]

The previous winter the hope provided by vaccines was juxtaposed with the deadliest virus surge in the United States. Again, in early summer 2021, the lifting of mask mandates and reopening of public life was bringing great hope and a sense of relief. And again, this would be juxtaposed with public-health officials sounding the alarm about the Delta variant. It could become the dominant strain of the virus in the United

States, they said. The best way to stop its spread, officials said, was to get more people vaccinated, with any of the three vaccines available.

By mid-June, about 55 percent of the US adult population was fully vaccinated, which was good but still left many people exposed to the new Delta variant that spread much more easily than earlier strains. And there were clear geographic vulnerabilities. The Northeast United States had higher vaccination rates than the national average, particularly in some New England states, like Vermont with its 62 percent vaccination rate. But in the South the numbers were much lower in states like Alabama, where only 30 percent were fully vaccinated.

The high proportions of unvaccinated people in those places would serve as a breeding ground for Delta. And the more the variant spread, the more it could mutate into more variants.

By late July, the effects of an ill-fated combination—stubbornly low vaccination rates in some regions, the winding down of masking and distancing, and a rapidly spreading Delta strain—were clearer. Infections, hospitalizations, and deaths were climbing again, especially in open states like Florida, which suffered one of the highest rates of Covid-19 hospitalizations, and low-vaccinated states.[9]

Doctors and nurses who thought they had put the worst of the pandemic behind them were once again scrambling to treat severely ill Covid-19 patients in intensive-care units. By the end of August, the United States was averaging about fifteen hundred Covid-19 deaths a day, versus fewer than two hundred in early July. Nearly all of the patients who ended up in the ICU were unvaccinated.

Some vaccinated people were beginning to test positive for Covid-19, too—commonly called "breakthrough" cases—and a few progressed to severe cases. The vaccines, after all, weren't 100 percent effective in the clinical trials, either. A small percentage of vaccinated people in the studies got sick with Covid. But it was becoming clear that the vaccines weren't entirely blocking transmission of the virus or stopping asymptomatic infections, as initially hoped.

Vaccinated people were better protected than unvaccinated people, even when Delta took over. In states like Massachusetts, less than

1 percent of fully vaccinated people in the state had tested positive for Covid-19 by the fall of 2021.[10] Other analysis showed that people who weren't fully vaccinated were nearly five times more likely to get infected, ten times more likely to be hospitalized and eleven times more likely to die from Covid than fully vaccinated people.

But Delta reminded people, or made them understand for the first time, that the vaccines weren't bullet-proof. New indoor mask mandates were imposed, including at schools, where educators just weeks earlier had been eager for the first normal back-to-school season in two years. No vaccine was yet authorized for children under twelve (both Moderna and Pfizer were studying that population), raising concerns that Delta would spread rapidly among them as they gathered in classrooms.

By the end of the summer, people wondered if the pandemic would ever end. Some started talking about the coronavirus as endemic, not a pandemic.

And a big slice of America was still saying "No thanks" to the vaccine.

There was no monolithic entity resisting vaccination. Some holdouts didn't view Covid-19 as a serious threat. Some felt Moderna and the other drug companies were more interested in profits than ensuring their vaccines were safe and effective. Some viewed the shots as a bigger health risk than Covid or were uncomfortable with the novelty of mRNA technology. Some opposed vaccines more generally, or they didn't like the idea of vaccine mandates. Some objected to the use of cell lines, derived from fetal tissue, in lab tests of the mRNA vaccines and in the production of the Johnson & Johnson vaccine (though the vaccines do not contain fetal tissue).[11] Misinformation campaigns on social media by anti-vaccine activists fueled mistrust.[12] Robert F. Kennedy Jr.'s Children's Health Defense Fund filed a petition to the FDA in May 2021 asking the agency to revoke authorization of Covid-19 vaccines, citing safety risks, and questioning their effectiveness. The FDA rejected the request.[13]

Helen Keipp Talbot, an infectious-disease doctor at Vanderbilt in Nashville, Tennessee, watched with disbelief as the trends worsened.

She served on the CDC's vaccine-advisory committee and in July 2021 had been involved in discussions and votes about the Covid-19 vaccines for nearly eighteen months. She tried to educate people about the benefits of the vaccine, hoping to boost the low vaccination rates in some parts of Tennessee. But her colleagues were being inundated with unvaccinated patients.

"To know they didn't have to suffer or die, is really hard to swallow," Talbot said, choking back tears on a video call in late July 2021.

The Covid vaccines, she said, were "a gift, but it was a gift that was wasted."

Some vaccinated people began to feel angry at the holdouts, blaming them for giving the virus room to spread and become more potent. Vaccines were there for the taking, free of charge and a product of American ingenuity. As the Delta variant roared, the backlash to the vaccine spurred a backlash to the holdouts. Some companies, including Chevron and CVS, said enough is enough and mandated vaccination. Others, like Delta Airlines, started docking the pay of the unvaccinated, as much as $200 a month, as the costs associated with covering a hospitalization ran to $40,000, which would send insurance premiums soaring. The Democratic governor of New Jersey had a sudden outburst at protestors that went viral on social media, when he said, "You are the ultimate knuckleheads! And because of what you are saying and standing for, people are losing their life!"

The Republican governor of Alabama said it was "time to start blaming the unvaccinated."

Patience with holdouts was nearing its end, and fewer people were holding out. Vaccination rates started to tick up as Delta spread, suggesting that some holdouts saw a new level of threat in this variant. Polls suggested resistance to vaccination was declining. In early September 2021, 17 percent said they would definitely or probably not get vaccinated, down from 32 percent at the beginning of the year.[14] Vaccination rates still varied by demographic groups and political affiliation. About

71 percent of Asian Americans had received at least one dose of a Covid vaccine by early November, versus 55 percent of whites, 53 percent of Latinos, and 48 percent of Black people.[15] And 55 percent of Republicans reported being vaccinated, compared with 60 percent of independents and 88 percent of Democrats.[16]

More pressure: President Biden ordered federal employees and many health care workers to get vaccinated and said that employers with at least one hundred workers must require them to get vaccinated or get tested for Covid weekly—a cost that would surely move many employers to just mandate vaccination.[17] Later, the Supreme Court would strike down Biden's large-employer mandate but allow the health care worker mandate to stay.

Moderna tacked, moving away from Beta to take on Delta. The deeply satisfying year of awards and pats on the back and profits was coming apart a little bit for the saviors.

"I think the Delta variant has taught us to also be incredibly humble in the face of the virus's ability to fight back and increase its transmission," Stephen Hoge said on a conference call with analysts in early August. "I mean, I think most of us would have thought SARS-CoV-2 was a pretty good infector earlier this year. Delta has shown us that it can make huge steps forward."[18]

Moderna started to develop a vaccine to target the Delta variant, but then tacked again, switching to say they believed the best near-term strategy was to offer a third, booster dose of its original vaccine, mRNA-1273 (also known as Spikevax in some countries). The company found in a study that giving such a boost (at a 50-microgram dose, or half the dose level of the original vaccine) about six months after the original vaccination could elevate neutralizing antibodies against the Delta variant.

Moderna shared the data with the FDA in hopes that the agency would approve a third 50-microgram booster shot. In August, the FDA authorized the use of third shots of the Moderna and Pfizer vaccines for certain people with compromised immune systems.

Soon after, the Biden administration revealed plans to widen the booster campaign to the general population in the fall. Some other countries, including Israel and Hungary, had started booster shot campaigns for the general population, not only to fight back at Delta but to protect against time. Anthony Fauci cited data from Israel—one of the countries to achieve high vaccination rates—showing waning immunity about six months after primary vaccination and said a third dose would bolster protection.

But the booster plan encountered skepticism, both from infectious-disease experts outside of government, and from within federal agencies, including the FDA. They argued that while some vaccinated people had gotten Covid-19, they rarely ended up with severe disease.

"I don't understand this push for a third dose right now," Paul Offit said in the early fall. Offit was the vaccinologist from Children's Hospital of Philadelphia and member of the FDA advisory committee that approved the original vaccines; he was also reviewing Pfizer's request for a booster shot authorization. The waning antibody levels Fauci cited, Offit said, were too narrow a focus. Other elements of a vaccinated person's immune system likely remained protective against severe disease. A group of scientists, including two outgoing FDA officials, published a paper in *The Lancet*, the influential medical journal, in September arguing that boosters for the general population weren't appropriate because primary vaccinations were still highly effective against severe cases.[19] By this time, there was a growing recognition that the job of the vaccines wasn't to wipe the virus off the face of the earth, but rather to ward off its most debilitating and deadly effects. Some experts bemoaned the focus on "breakthrough infections," noting that many older vaccines don't stop actual infections, but nevertheless keep people alive and out of the hospital.

Offit's side won a partial victory when the FDA advisory panel rejected a plan to give a Pfizer booster shot to everyone sixteen and older. Instead, the panel voted to recommend them only for people sixty-five and older and other adults at high risk. Committee members said there was insufficient data to support broader use, and some were still concerned about more shots for younger people who seemed to show a higher risk of myocarditis, the heart inflammation condition.[20]

Then, a few days later, the CDC issued its own recommendation for who should get boosters, which was different from the FDA's authorization. They included adults at risk of Covid from their jobs, including teachers.

President Biden received his third dose in late September.[21] After the clearance of Pfizer's booster shot in September, the FDA authorized in October booster shots from Moderna and J&J, with different and somewhat complicated eligibility requirements and dosing intervals for each. The agency also said people could "mix and match"—taking a booster of a different vaccine than the one they got originally.[22] Bancel had been talking about the likely need for a booster shot for months. Now it was a reality.

Biden's Covid-19 response team had started the year strong by increasing the supply of vaccines and getting more people vaccinated. Then it ran into the wall of vaccine hesitancy that left 70 million eligible Americans unvaccinated right as Delta started tearing through those places with the lowest vaccine rates. Biden the candidate had blasted his predecessor for a high Covid-19 death toll, but as president he was finding out how difficult it was to halt the march of the virus.

The administration's booster plans had left many confused. On top of that, some activists for fair global access to Covid-19 vaccines were saying third shots for Americans should be put off until more people around the world could get their first shots. The leader of the World Health Organization, Tedros Adhanom Ghebreyesus, called for a moratorium on booster shots at least until the end of 2021, to conserve supply of vaccines so that every country could vaccinate at least 40 percent of its population. "We do not want to see widespread use of boosters for healthy people who are fully vaccinated," he said.[23]

And still at this time, no one was sure when, or if, children would get vaccinated. The minimum age had already dropped from sixteen to twelve, but children eleven and under remained ineligible. Finally, in late October 2021, the FDA authorized Pfizer's shot for five-to-eleven-year-olds. But the FDA delayed a decision on Moderna's vaccine in adolescents because it wanted to further weigh the risk of myocarditis, and Moderna put off requesting authorization for use in kids six to eleven.[24] The risk of severe Covid-19 disease in children was much lower than in adults, but the risk wasn't zero, and the rate of Covid hospitalizations of children under eighteen ticked up as the Delta variant spread. What's more, infected children could spread the virus to others even if they didn't get very sick. Health officials and infectious-disease specialists said it would be important to vaccinate children not only to provide individual protection but also to reduce transmission and build community-wide "herd immunity" to the virus. And it would provide another level of protection for students and staff in schools.

The disruption caused by the Delta variant and the debate over booster shots left Moderna's leaders feeling exhausted and in limbo by the fall of 2021. Stéphane Bancel started the summer confident that the devastating winter wave of Covid-19 was over. He was technically correct, but then Delta buffeted the world. Confusion over boosters fueled uncertainty. Impatience over getting children vaccinated increased among some, while others viewed the prospect with deep skepticism.

People seemed less hopeful, or at least more circumspect, over promises about the future and a return to normal. For Moderna, the bloom wasn't off the rose exactly, but something had changed. Moderna's vaccine still helped protect people from the worst effects of Covid-19. But the sharp downturn in Covid-19 cases heading into summer proved to be a mirage. The vaccine would not end the pandemic as quickly as people had hoped.

By September 2021, Bancel knew the global pandemic was far from over. Grand proclamations about the vaccine were replaced with tempered outlooks. Life could return to normal "in a year," he told the Swiss newspaper *Neue Zuercher Zeitung.* Vaccine production capacity would expand to yield enough doses to cover the world's entire population by the middle of 2022, he said.

Unvaccinated people would only develop immunity by getting infected, if they survived, he said. "Those who do not get vaccinated will immunize themselves naturally, because the Delta variant is so contagious. In this way we will end up in a situation similar to that of the flu. You can either get vaccinated and have a good winter. Or you don't do it and risk getting sick and possibly even ending up in hospital."

By late 2021, Bancel knew his employees had been through a battle and it wasn't over. Even the hard-charging manager who always asked for more faster was struggling to square the work put in with the ongoing struggle. "People have hurt their health, their marriage[s], all . . . with the aim to help other people," he said.

Stephen Hoge sounded fatigued too as he described the process of dealing with variants and betting on beating back the Beta variant, only to have to shift suddenly to deal with the Delta variant. "We're trying very much to stay ahead of this virus, and you're trying to follow the science," Stephen Hoge said. "But there are often surprises. We've never been ahead of this virus."

After all the twists and turns of 2021, Hoge said it felt like "we still don't know anything, the virus is humbling us on a regular basis."

"I hope it ends, but 2021 has felt a lot like a 2020 redux, and in a lot of ways it's felt like a much harder year," Hoge said.

16

Just the Beginning

AT THE SAME TIME BANCEL AND HOGE WERE FEELING HUM-
bled by the virus and its emerging variants, in the fall of 2021, they took
a more confident tone with investors. "We know now that mRNA from
Moderna works," Stéphane Bancel said confidently just after Labor Day,
addressing analysts and investors. "For the last ten years we believed
mRNA should work. Today we know."

Bancel was supposed to be delivering his message at a New York hotel,
at an "R&D Day" that would have been Moderna's first in-person gathering with Wall Street since the start of the pandemic. Bancel was eager
to reconnect face-to-face with this constituency that held so much influence over the company's financial fortunes.[1]

But the Delta variant scuttled that. The virtual meeting meant a yellow flag was waving during what should have been a victory lap.

Bancel focused on boosters—which if they were widely approved
would be a good source of revenue. He also needed to reinforce a key
message: that Moderna was more than a Covid-19 vaccine company. It
was now developing more than thirty other experimental mRNA drugs
and vaccines targeting a range of human diseases, from influenza to
cancer to heart disease. Successes from this R&D pipeline in the years
to come would validate a new way of making medicine and keep the

revenues growing. It would cement Moderna's place in the ranks of the biggest and most important drug companies in the world.

The leaders may have been exhausted, and everyone's sense of time may have been contorted, but on reflection, Moderna's successful gamble on developing a vaccine for Disease X was as improbable as it was miraculous. It had only been about twenty months. Moderna was transformed from a little-known biotech without a product and with a herd of increasingly skeptical investors to a household name with more than eighteen hundred employees and on track to book more than $7 billion in profit for the first nine months of 2021.

Moderna's achievements seemed even more impressive when contrasted with what happened to several of its much larger rivals. Johnson & Johnson's vaccine demonstrated a much lower efficacy rate and initial supplies were constrained by contamination problems. And vaccinations with J&J's single-dose shot were paused for a few weeks while health officials reviewed the risk of a blood-clotting disorder. As a result, J&J's vaccine played a much smaller role than expected in the mass vaccination campaign. (Later in 2021, the CDC recommended adults choose the mRNA shots over J&J's because of the safety risk.) AstraZeneca's vaccine, codeveloped with Oxford, was authorized outside the United States, and the company supplied many doses globally—importantly, in many of the lower-income countries that didn't get many mRNA vaccine doses—but it was also dogged by blood-clot risks and initial manufacturing constraints, and it still wasn't cleared for use in the United States as of January 2022. Merck scrapped its Covid-19 vaccine projects and eventually agreed to help manufacture J&J's vaccine (though Merck went on to develop a promising treatment for people already sick with Covid). Sanofi hit delays in the vaccine it codeveloped with GSK. Sanofi, too, turned to an assistant role, agreeing to help Moderna make its vaccine. Novavax, the only other company among the vaccine front-runners in the United States that was smaller than Moderna, developed a vaccine that looked good in studies. But it ran into manufacturing delays and as of September 2021 it still hadn't completed its application for FDA authorization of the shot.

Only Pfizer, with its partner BioNTech, kept pace with Moderna. Indeed, Pfizer beat Moderna. It delivered the first authorized vaccine in the United States, was the first to widen its authorized use to children and first to get full approval. And ultimately Pfizer delivered more doses. Pfizer's own immigrant CEO, Albert Bourla, made a smart bet by teaming up with BioNTech, and then pushed his workers relentlessly, just as Stéphane Bancel pushed his, to deliver a vaccine in record time.[2] Pfizer also developed an effective Covid-19 antiviral that was authorized later in 2021, setting up a 2022 in which Pfizer's expected sales for Covid-19 alone would dwarf total-company sales for many of its rivals.

But the fact that Moderna drafted on Pfizer, just a week behind on some early milestones, is somewhat astonishing given the difference in scale of the two companies. At the front of the pandemic, Moderna had no products to sell, less than $2 billion of cash and investments, and only eight hundred employees.[3] Pfizer had $52 billion in annual revenue and eighty-eight thousand employees.[4]

For much of 2021, and to most of the world, the Pfizer and Moderna vaccines were viewed as generally similar. They progressed on roughly the same timeline. They used the same technology. They had similar designs and similar efficacy rates in their Phase 3 trials. They both appeared superior to the J&J vaccine. And both outperformed another mRNA vaccine: Germany's CureVac, one of Moderna's earliest rivals. CureVac's trials reported in June 2021 efficacy of only 47 percent, prompting the company to scrap it and try developing a new shot.[5] A possible reason for the inferior performance was that CureVac's vaccine used unmodified mRNA. Pfizer and Moderna vaccines both used modified mRNA to minimize inflammation, building on what Weissman and Karikó had discovered years earlier at Penn.

If there were differences in the Pfizer and Moderna vaccines, it seemed, it came in their brand names. Where it was allowed to use a brand name, like Europe, Moderna began to brand its shot "Spikevax," nodding to the coronavirus's telltale spike protein. In the United States, it was simply "Moderna COVID-19 Vaccine," at least until the FDA granted full approval. Once Pfizer got full FDA approval in August 2021, it called its vaccine "Comirnaty"—a mashup of Covid and mRNA and immunity.

But later in 2021, research began to suggest an advantage for Moderna's vaccine over Pfizer's. A Mayo clinic study found the Moderna vaccine's effectiveness against Covid infection for the entire study period to be 86 percent, versus 76 percent for the Pfizer/BioNTech vaccine. And Moderna's vaccine was more effective at preventing Covid hospitalizations. In July, the study found, when the Delta variant surged, Moderna's vaccine fell to 76 percent effectiveness. But Pfizer's effectiveness declined to 42 percent. In Florida, where Delta was rampant, people who had gotten Moderna's vaccine had a 60 percent lower risk of infection than those who received the Pfizer/BioNTech shot.[6]

The CDC reinforced the Mayo results, finding Moderna's vaccine was 95 percent effective at preventing Covid hospitalizations, compared with 80 percent for the Pfizer/BioNTech vaccine and 60 percent for the J&J vaccine.[7] A third study in the *New England Journal of Medicine* found Moderna's vaccine 96 percent effective, versus 89 percent for Pfizer's.[8]

What could account for the differences? Potentially, dose levels and timing. Moderna shots packed in more mRNA at a higher dose to trigger immune responses. And the second Moderna dose was given four weeks after the first, versus a three-week interval for Pfizer's. That Moderna's shot was associated with higher rates of certain side effects like muscle aches than Pfizer's vaccine was consistent with the notion that the higher dose in the Moderna shot made a difference. Researchers also cited some of the chemical differences in the composition of the lipid nanoparticles for each vaccine as another potential contributing factor.

At the virtual R&D Day in September, Stephen Hoge offered investors his own assessment of why Moderna's vaccine was proving superior as the pandemic dragged on. It wasn't the science itself, per se, but the business of the science. "I think it's the difference of working on something for ten years versus a year," he said. "We've had a tremendous amount of investment in our core technology platforms. . . . It has allowed us to do things like provide a higher dose, which provides, we believe, higher tiers" of antibodies against the virus. "And higher neutralizing tiers correlated with better immunity, we believe, and ultimately, are some of

what's driving the advantage in the real-world evidence that's been reported so far."

Historians have started looking at the vaccine race with a longer lens,
and they've affixed Moderna a place in that history. It's largely Moderna
that is being credited with establishing the disruptive mRNA technology
as a viable option for vaccination—even if Moderna's original plans for
mRNA downplayed vaccination compared with other, more lucrative
therapies. And both Moderna and Pfizer are credited with the remarkable, breakneck vaccine development that seemed likely to save millions
of lives globally.

William Schaffner, an infectious-disease specialist at Vanderbilt,
called mRNA "21st century science, and that's very exciting. . . . I think
this will be proof of execution that we can very quickly develop a vaccine, test it and get it into the field."

Barton Haynes, an immunologist at Duke, wrote in the *New England
Journal of Medicine* that the vaccines were "extraordinary scientific and
medical triumphs. This happened because the scientific community was
prepared from years of technology development for other vaccines, such
as those against HIV, influenza, respiratory syncytial virus, and Zika,
and because clinical trials consortia were established that rapidly carried
out Covid-19 efficacy trials. If mRNA-LNP vaccines significantly contribute to control of the pandemic, mRNA technology has the potential to
radically change vaccine design for future viral outbreaks."[9]

Howard Markel, a medical historian at the University of Michigan
who has written about epidemics, put it more plainly: "This tops all previous vaccine history. Never before did we have such a needed vaccine
that was developed, created, and rolled out in the fog of war, or the fog
of a pandemic. It really was a Hollywood version of a pandemic, people getting sick, dying, mass panic, and then the cavalry comes in." The
Smithsonian accepted a vial from the first lot of Moderna's vaccine administered at a New York hospital, among other items that will tell the
story of the pandemic.[10]

mRNA's success made believers out of Big Pharma companies, still in the process of reinventing themselves and now facing a disruptive technology housed mostly in small biotech startups. Many Big Pharma companies were initially dismissive of mRNA (just as many scientists were). Now, Sanofi of France has made two acquisitions to venture into mRNA, including a $3.2 billion purchase of Translate Bio, a startup in Lexington, Massachusetts, with which Sanofi had been collaborating on a Covid vaccine. Pfizer said it planned to develop more mRNA-based vaccines, both in collaboration with BioNTech and on its own.

Moderna's gamble was historic. Investors and analysts at the R&D Day had recently learned how the gamble was paying off financially. The company booked global vaccine sales of $5.9 billion for the first half of the year and predicted full-year 2021 sales of $20 billion.[11] That would make Moderna's Covid-19 vaccine one of the highest-selling pharmaceutical products in the world, perhaps trailing only Pfizer's Covid-19 vaccine, which Pfizer predicted would generate $33.5 billion. (In November, Moderna would trim this full-year forecast to between $15 billion and $18 billion in vaccine sales, citing delays in shipping doses to more countries outside the United States. The same week, the much larger Pfizer, which had an established global manufacturing and distribution network entering the pandemic, boosted its full-year forecast to $36 billion.)

Moderna would crack the top twenty largest pharmaceutical companies by annual sales in its first full year of having a single commercial product, with only about eighteen hundred employees. One way to measure success in pharma is revenue per employee. At most big drug companies, a good number would be $1 million per employee. At Moderna, in 2021, it was trending toward an astonishing $10 million per employee.

Wall Street expected hefty vaccine sales from Moderna to last for a few years, even if they might decline gradually, which wouldn't be all bad. It would signal the decline and end of the pandemic. Already, by the middle of 2021, Moderna had signed contracts to supply about $12 billion worth of vaccines for 2022, with negotiations ongoing for more. Wall

Street analysts predicted that after 2021, Moderna would book Covid-19 vaccine sales of more than $30 billion through 2023.

Moderna's profit margin was strong. Costs to manufacture the vaccine were still less than 20 percent of product revenue. That allowed most of the revenue to fall to the bottom line. At the R&D Day, Bancel told analysts the company was sitting on $15 billion in cash. When all this started, in January 2020, it had a $1.3 billion reserve.

When Moderna broke offer at its IPO in 2018, Stephen Hoge felt a gut punch as the stock price plummeted from $23 to $19. He surely felt differently in August 2021, when the stock hit $497 a share, for a year-to-date gain of 378 percent, earning the company a market value of nearly $200 billion. The stock price slid down from that peak in the fall, into the mid-$200s, but investors still deemed Moderna more valuable than several large biotechs that had been churning out profitable medicines for years. It was bigger than Gilead and Regeneron in the fall of 2021. At one point in 2021, Moderna's market value dwarfed many well-known names in other industries too: UPS, Starbucks, Citigroup.

The sharp rise in Moderna's share price was aided by the stock's addition to the S&P 500 index in July 2021, compelling funds that tracked the index to buy shares. The Covid-19 vaccine's sales and profits helped too. But there was more at work, and this was often the case with Moderna in 2020 and 2021. Bad news for the world was often good news for the business. The summer surge of the Delta variant convinced many investors that the pandemic was showing signs of becoming endemic. This would increase the demand for booster shots. Because the virus was still causing sickness, and still killing thousands, Moderna's Covid-19 business looked more sustainable than before.

The higher stock price meant higher net worth for its leaders and cofounders. Stéphane Bancel's stake was worth more than $12 billion in the fall of 2021, putting him in the top two hundred of the *Forbes* billionaires list. Moderna Chairman Noubar Afeyan, together with his VC firm Flagship, owned a stake that was now worth about $10 billion. Bob

Langer from MIT owned $4.5 billion; company president Stephen Hoge owned $2 billion.[12] These riches were moving targets because the values fluctuated with movements in Moderna's stock price, but even after Moderna's shares declined in late 2021 and early 2022, the stakes were valuable enough by most people's living standards.

Even Derrick Rossi, who parted ways with Moderna years before, became wealthy enough to feel confident that he would outbid anyone in a June 2021 Canadian auction for a rare painting made by David Bowie. He got it for $108,120 Canadian dollars ($87,789 US).[13] Rossi retired from academia but stayed active in biotech. He is one of the founders of Intellia Therapeutics, a Cambridge biotech developing drugs using "CRISPR/Cas9" gene-editing technology. And he is the CEO of Convelo Therapeutics, a Cleveland, Ohio, company working on regenerative medicine.

Executives or founders at Pfizer, BioNTech, and Novavax also were enriched by the effort. They either sat on ownership stakes made more valuable on paper by their companies' work on battling Covid, or they sold portions of shares at higher prices than before the pandemic. Or both.

Such wealth creation during a pandemic that was killing millions was distasteful to some, and was made even more distasteful by the fact that it was accrued on the back of taxpayer dollars and had done little to distribute vaccine access evenly among rich and poor countries. "What a testament to our collective failure to control this cruel disease that we quickly create new vaccine billionaires but totally fail to vaccinate the billions who desperately need to feel safe," said Anna Marriott, Oxfam's Health Policy Manager. "These billionaires are the human face of the huge profits many pharmaceutical corporations are making from the monopoly they hold on these vaccines. These vaccines were funded by public money and should be first and foremost a global public good, not a private profit opportunity. We need to urgently end these monopolies so that we can scale up vaccine production, drive down prices and vaccinate the world."[14]

Tom Frieden, the former director of the CDC, blasted Moderna and Pfizer for not doing more to get their vaccine to poorer countries. It was true that Moderna and Pfizer had committed a supply of doses to be distributed through Covax or to be donated by the United States to other countries. But he thought the companies had a responsibility to transfer their Covid-19 vaccine technology to outside entities that could expand supplies for poorer countries more quickly than the companies could.[15]

The enrichment of executives like Stéphane Bancel is a by-product of a US biopharma ecosystem that rewards high risk. It's built on patents and the exploitation of patents. In the United States, a fragmented health care system without price controls, a key incentive is to invent drugs that command high prices. The system favors lucrative opportunities over ones that may do more good for more people at much lower cost.

The pricing dynamic for the Covid vaccines was somewhat muted compared to a normal drug rollout because the federal government was the sole customer, and negotiated relatively modest per-dose prices, in an emergency. But it still was a profit-making venture for the companies. Moderna and Pfizer expressly declined to make their vaccines available at not-for-profit prices despite the severity of the emergency.

Defenders of this system say that when something succeeds, saves lives, and provides a benefit to society, those who risked their money to make it happen should be rewarded. And the profits generated by today's drugs can fund development of tomorrow's medicines.

This defense leaves out who's sharing the risk with the drug companies: taxpayers. No drug company could succeed without the money poured in from NIH and the labs at universities that incubate ideas and provide basic research. A 2018 analysis found that NIH funding contributed to research associated with every one of the 210 new drugs approved by the FDA from 2010 through 2016. And government health-insurance programs are among the biggest payers for the end products.[16]

Even some industry insiders question the system. Are the rewards excessive? And do the high prices that help fuel the system put medical advances beyond the reach of many?

"The fundamental societal concern we have to have is that the industry has been enabled by mechanisms that take money from the many and give to the few," said Roger Perlmutter, the former R&D chief of Merck and Amgen who now leads a biotech startup. "And that is one contributor—it's not the largest, nothing compared to tech—to the maldistribution of resources in our country. And income inequity, asset inequity, is having a devastating impact."

Perlmutter himself is a beneficiary of this ecosystem. He understands that the biotech startup he now leads exists because venture capitalists flush with cash from pension funds and other investors are willing to cut a check and wait years for the payoff. And he knows that executives at startups often take a chance by leaving jobs with higher salaries and invest their own money in their new companies. But he questions what should count as a proportional reward.

"Is it the case that what you want is to take a small handful of people and make them absurdly wealthy?" asked Perlmutter. "Is that really what society wants?"

Howard Markel, the medical historian, again puts it more bluntly: "Of course it's ridiculous what these guys are making."

Even Ken Chien, the Moderna cofounder, began to feel some discomfort about the fortune he earned from his Moderna shares when the company met the pandemic moment. During 2021, he also began to feel that Moderna should be doing more to get its vaccine to developing countries. "I want to see Moderna step up to the plate and do more for global distribution, and not just sell the vaccine to the highest bidder," he said. "There's more than just return to shareholders here. We're not going to get rid of this thing until everyone steps up." Chien and his wife felt they had benefited from a pandemic, and it was time to give something back. They donated their Moderna shares to a nonprofit foundation they created, which will fund global health causes.

Others say this ecosystem is the best way to yield advances in medicine. Ryan Dietz, the former tech-transfer chief who first approached Derrick Rossi at his lunch presentation, said advances happen precisely because of the potential to sell a product for profit. All the years Moderna spent raising money allowed it to refine its mRNA technology to the point that when a pandemic struck, Moderna was ready to respond. "Moderna exists because there was enough venture capital to say, if we create drugs there will be a market for them," said Dietz, who did not get an ownership stake in Moderna at its creation. "And turns out, the Covid-19 vaccine wasn't anything that people conceived of, but that marketplace, that investment was absolutely necessary for the Covid-19 vaccine to exist."

Lorence Kim stayed in the ecosystem when he left Moderna in 2020. He became a venture capitalist himself, at Third Rock Ventures, the same firm that passed on Derrick Rossi's idea back in 2010. He knows that he profited when he sold his Moderna shares, and that Moderna's current leaders have become very wealthy. But he notes that every Moderna shareholder also benefited from the stock price increase.

"Executive compensation, that's a deal with shareholders," Kim said. "What is the best way to incentivize management? It's long-term incentive compensation." With stock options, "Stéphane only made money if the stock price went up. He delivered on his side of the agreement." He had a point, at least for part of Bancel's compensation. Recall that big tranche of stock options Moderna issued to Bancel at the time of the IPO in 2018, which made up a big chunk of Bancel's hefty 2018 compensation of $58.6 million. They had an exercise price of $23—the IPO price—which meant that for most of the following year they didn't have much value (in other words, he would pay more to acquire the underlying stock than he could sell it for). Moderna's stock often traded below $23 and didn't sustainably break out of that pattern until March of 2020. Until the pandemic.

It's true that Moderna benefited greatly from US taxpayer support, but Kim doesn't think that should disqualify the company from making a profit, or its executives from gaining wealth. "The point of government funding would be, did the government get value for the money it put in? It got a vaccine produced and developed. It got favorable pricing, demonstrably better pricing than other countries. For sure, the US development dollars resulted in better economics" for Moderna, he said. But "I don't think the existence of government investment should foreclose the opportunity for other stakeholders to make money. Otherwise, you'd say the government should never provide any grant to any private company."

"Nobody criticized us for selling the stock at $18, which I did," Bancel said. "The stock went up but that's not something we drove or controlled." Some people were at the company for eight to ten years and during most of that time had no liquid market to sell shares, he said. Some had 99 percent of their wealth tied up in Moderna and it made sense to set up trading plans to sell shares, he said.

As sides argue over whether the system is good or bad, right or wrong, they seem to dance around the more pertinent question that Perlmutter hinted at: How much is enough? It's not that the VC/biotech ecosystem is wrong, and risk shouldn't be rewarded, but how much is enough reward, and when does the reward start to outscale the risk and prevent good outcomes for many in return for the enrichment of a few?

Moderna did show some signs of recognizing its historic windfall. In July 2021, the company created a charitable foundation, with an initial company contribution of $50 million. Among the foundation's objectives: to advance scientific education and innovation, promote public health, and access to health care. The company also formed a partnership with a nonprofit to try to develop an mRNA treatment for an ultra-rare disease, Crigler-Najjar Syndrome Type 1, that would be given to patients at no cost.

These are not insignificant steps, but also modest when compared to the value of individual executives' stock. Consider that $50 million contribution to the charitable foundation; it equaled a small fraction of the value of Stéphane Bancel's stockholdings alone.

A big part of the rally in Moderna shares in the months leading up to the September 2021 R&D Day was a more bullish view of what would follow the Covid-19 vaccine. "The applications for this technology go way beyond vaccines," said Michael Caldwell, the Driehaus portfolio manager who sat out Moderna's IPO but later invested.

Driehaus and others also seemed to be buying into Moderna as a platform company with stellar operations. After all, the company pulled off a remarkable feat in developing and manufacturing the Covid-19 vaccine so quickly. It could do it again. "Clearly the people and their focus, the willingness to take action and charge hard, I think made a difference there," he said. "I wouldn't bet against them at this point."

In a sense, Moderna's stock had become the "Tesla of Biotech," as Jefferies analyst Michael Yee put it. Shares of Tesla, the electric-car company led by Elon Musk, soared in 2020 and 2021 on expectations that it would dominate a growing electric-vehicle market. Its market cap reached ten times that of General Motors on this promise. Moderna had similarly become a "story stock," Yee wrote in a research note in August 2021. The story was that Moderna was an "innovation and disruption technology play that will generate products rapidly, with lower risk, higher probability of success, and potential greater efficacy than older technologies."[17]

Bancel and his deputies were embracing the story at the virtual R&D Day in September 2021.[18]

Moderna, they said, would charge ahead trying to bring more mRNA vaccines to market. The designs use the same basic concept as the Covid-19 vaccine: turn the body into a pop-up protein factory that set off a desired immune response.

A top focus would be combination vaccines. There was a one-shot vaccine that would protect people against both Covid and the flu; there was a "pan-respiratory annual booster vaccine"— given once a year to protect against Covid, the flu, and a common virus called respiratory syncytial virus, or RSV, a virus that had escaped past vaccine attempts; there was a seasonal flu vaccine that would target four strains of the virus, hoping to increase the efficacy of the shots beyond the current levels of 40 percent and 60 percent, depending on the flu season.

These could be remarkable treatments. More important to investors, they were repeatable sales. Moderna saw the market for a pan-respiratory booster vaccine at least as big as the regular flu shot market, which is about 500 million doses per year. A more effective flu shot could bump up the market well beyond its $5 billion to $6 billion current size, Moderna executives said.

Bancel hinted at customizing these shots to fit viral trends in any given year, adding targeted viruses or swapping in some. It might only protect against Covid and the flu one year, but more in a different year. And it might vary year to year in the flu strain or Covid variant it targets. Targeting multiple viruses with one shot could increase convenience, making people more likely to comply with vaccine recommendations—or, as investors see it, increasing the market size.

Moderna also planned to start a clinical trial for a stand-alone RSV vaccine for people over sixty, where it would again be competing with much larger rivals, such as GlaxoSmithKline, Pfizer, and Johnson & Johnson, all of which were also developing RSV shots.

The company was also still working on its vaccine against cytomegalovirus, or CMV, the virus that can cause birth defects in babies born to infected mothers and can affect organ-transplant patients. The CMV vaccine, mRNA-1647, is more complex than the Covid vaccine. The Covid vaccine is coded to cause cells to make one protein, the spike protein. Moderna's CMV vaccine incorporates six different strands of mRNA. Five of the mRNAs are coded to induce cellular production of portions of the CMV virus known as the pentamer complex. The sixth mRNA in the vaccine is coded to cause a person's cells to make a protein from the virus known as glycoprotein B. Both the pentamer and glycoprotein B portions of the CMV virus help the virus get into various human cells to replicate—so targeting these with a vaccine could thwart viral replication and block infections.

After promising results in early studies, Moderna in October 2021 started a large Phase 3 clinical trial of the CMV vaccine.

Other vaccines were in the pipeline against Epstein-Barr virus (the cause of mononucleosis), Zika, HIV, and Nipah, the same virus that was originally going to be the focus of Moderna's "stopwatch drill" with NIAID before the news in January 2020 caused a change of plans.

Apart from preventive vaccines, Moderna also said it continued to develop mRNA products for people who were already sick with various diseases. These included vaccines and drugs to treat autoimmune disorders, heart failure, cancers including head and neck cancer, and certain rare diseases.

Personalized cancer vaccines were one of the most tantalizing research paths. They would allow doctors to take biopsies of a patient's tumor, to identify certain substances called neoepitopes, which are important to setting off the body's immune response to a tumor (often a losing battle). Moderna would then pack the genetic code for the neoepitopes into an mRNA vaccine which would supercharge the production of the neo-epitopes and an anti-cancer immune response. The "needle-to-needle" turnaround time—from biopsy collection to injection of the vaccine—would be just a few weeks.

The company paused enrollment for one study of the cancer vaccines during 2020 because it was scaling up manufacturing for the Covid-19 vaccine. Now it was resuming those trials.

Phase 2 studies picked up on the VEGF heart medicine, too—the one that traces its roots to cofounder Ken Chien's research at Harvard. The drug was designed to stimulate the production of VEGF proteins that could potentially regenerate blood vessels. Early results were released in November, showing it was safe, but more study would be needed.

If all went smoothly, Moderna could be selling several drugs and vaccines by the middle of the 2020s, and many more in the years following. Messenger RNA, which made mouse muscles glow green in lab tests two decades ago, could prevent deadly human diseases or relieve their burden for years to come. It would make Moderna a leader—and creator—of a bold future wrested from despair.

Of course, there is no guarantee that these other potential uses of mRNA will succeed. That's how drug development works. It was one thing to give mRNA in two or three doses for a vaccine, but quite another to administer mRNA repeatedly to treat a disease. Moderna would have to figure out how to deliver mRNA in a way that treated disease without triggering unwanted side effects.

It will be doing all of those things from a new home. In late 2021, Moderna broke ground on a new headquarters and research-and-development center a couple blocks down on Binney Street in Kendall Square, near IBM Watson Health, Facebook, Sanofi, and around the corner from a Tatte Bakery and Turner Construction Company. The 462,000-square foot building is set to open in 2023.[19]

It was becoming clear that the startup that made big promises about disrupting the big guys was becoming one of the big guys. On many measures, financial ones included, Moderna had closed the gap between itself and Big Pharma companies. But Bancel wouldn't say Moderna was becoming just another one of them.

"Sometimes I hear people comparing us to big pharmaceutical companies, and I just don't understand it," Bancel said, confident as ever in the business, ready to speak the language, and deliver the promise of a tech startup.

"Moderna is an information medicine-based platform company," he said. "They live in an analog world. We live in a digital world. We think this is just the beginning."

In late November, scientists in South Africa identified a new variant of concern, Omicron. This one also appeared highly contagious, though there were early signs that it was causing milder illness. Still, it had a high number of mutations, which escaped some of the potency of the vaccines.

"Oh shit," Bancel thought again when he heard about the new variant the day before Thanksgiving. "When we saw the Omicron sequence, we were shocked by how much it had drifted genetically from Delta," he recalled. He had to respond over the holiday weekend. But he decided to keep his family in the dark for a bit so they could enjoy a day at home together with a big mid-afternoon meal. His wife did most of the cooking. He went back and forth between his office and the kitchen while she prepared the meal and listened to music. In his office, he took calls and exchanged emails with colleagues and outside scientists and officials, trying to figure out what to do. But he stayed mum in the kitchen and during dinner, his effort "to protect Thanksgiving from Omicron." After dinner he told his wife the news, and then he got back to work.

On the Friday after Thanksgiving, as news spread about the new variant, Moderna executives met remotely to craft a strategy. They announced they would test whether the original vaccine was still protective against variants and start developing a modified booster shot to better target Omicron in case it was needed. For some people who had already gotten the pre-Omicron booster shot, that would mean a fourth dose of a vaccine if it came to pass. Pfizer and others reacted similarly.

Early tests showed the Pfizer and Moderna vaccines lost some potency against Omicron, but a regular booster dose should help.

Some public-health experts said the case for widespread boosters was getting stronger as winter approached and Omicron emerged. But when Moderna and other vaccine makers talked up that possibility, some people rolled their eyes. Of course they wanted to sell more boosters! This skepticism filtered into satirical pop culture. Comedy Central's *The Daily Show* posted a video of its host, Trevor Noah, pondering the thought. "On the one hand, almost all the Omicron cases have been mild so far, but on the other hand, the guy who stands to gain millions of dollars from new vaccines says we need new vaccines," he said. "Huh."

Noah then impersonated Bancel (albeit in an accent that sounded nothing like the Frenchman): "If we don't make a new vaccine this disease could be with us Ferrari, I mean, forever. Sorry I was thinking of something else." Noah continued in his own voice: "Now look, I'm not saying that the CEO of Moderna is lying. I'm not saying that at all. I'm just saying, I don't think he's the most objective source on this topic. I'll wait to hear what neutral experts say on a new vaccine like public health officials." One final dig: "Or the CEO of Johnson & Johnson. I mean, he's got nothing to gain because nobody's going to buy his vaccines either way, so I trust him." Of course, not all of his bit was literally true. Omicron did seem to be milder on average, but it would soon infect so many people that death counts rose again. And some 16 million Americans received the J&J shot, but that trailed the tallies for Moderna and Pfizer by a wide margin. Still, the whole Trevor Noah bit underscored how deeply vaccines had seeped into the national discussion and how barbed it could be, especially when people wondered about the influence of drug companies on health policy.

The company was dogged both by its role in getting vaccines to poorer nations and by patent spats. The stock was steadily falling from its near-$500 crest, getting a brief boost to the mid-$300s after Omicron arrived but then destined to fall below $200 by early 2022.

People were exhausted, and the prospect of having to change course and make an Omicron booster shot—nearly two years into the pandemic—exhausted Bancel himself. Every hour he and others at Moderna devoted to Covid meant an hour taken away from the rest of the company's pipeline. That other work didn't stop, but he conceded the Covid work was having an "indirect impact" on non-Covid work. The world felt trapped in a pandemic and Bancel felt trapped dealing with it, unable to go full bore building the platform company he envisioned.

In December 2021, Bancel was looking forward to throwing a holiday party for Moderna employees at the Museum of Science in Boston, resuming a pre-pandemic tradition. Bancel was looking forward to a chance to thank his employees, finally, in person. There had been no large Moderna gatherings since the pandemic began.

But Covid cases were climbing sharply in Massachusetts, causing the highest number of hospitalizations in ten months—in one of the most highly vaccinated states in the country. It was still very much the effects of the Delta variant causing the uptick, combined with waning immunity from vaccinations earlier in the year. But there was also Omicron looming. No one knew what it would bring.

Moderna canceled the holiday party.

Epilogue

DURING MUCH OF THE TIME I WAS WRITING THIS BOOK IN 2021, Covid-19 cases were in retreat, as more and more people gained protection from the vaccines. There were days in the spring and early summer when it seemed possible to me that by the time I turned over the manuscript, Moderna would have helped end a pandemic and moved on to turn its mRNA technology against other diseases. In short, I thought my book might have an ending—a clear date, or at least a time frame, when we all had decided that the pandemic was over.

It doesn't.

Due to the vagaries of book publishing, this book's main narrative leaves off in late 2021. As I write this epilogue in March of 2022, the pandemic continues; some say it's approaching an endemic phase. Reported Covid cases are once again in retreat, but only after several devastating waves fueled by coronavirus variants plowed through the second half of 2021. The Omicron variant proved to be a force of nature. Within weeks, it seemed as if every other household had at least one infected inhabitant. Even fully vaccinated and boosted people got infected. Holiday plans were thrown into limbo for the second year in a row, and school attendance on either side of the holidays was light.

Omicron's spread changed our experience of the pandemic and our understanding of the vaccines. The shots couldn't block infection by a variant as contagious as Omicron. In January, the daily count of new confirmed cases topped 800,000 in the United States, dwarfing the case count of the previous winter. That meant many deaths—more than 2,000 a day on average in the United States in much of January and February.

This was more than the daily toll from accidents and other diseases like diabetes and the flu.

But that didn't mean Moderna's vaccine and the Pfizer/BioNTech shot had failed. They hadn't at all. First, before Omicron emerged, one analysis estimated that Covid-19 vaccination had already prevented more than one million deaths in the United States.[1] And even after the new variant spread wildly, people were far more likely to survive infection if they were vaccinated. Overall, people who received at least the full primary vaccination were still less likely to be infected, and much less likely to die, than the unvaccinated, according to a CDC analysis. Booster shots widened the gap even more, and they were particularly effective at protecting older, more vulnerable populations from hospitalization and death. The data continue to evolve, but in nearly every case it tells a similar story: unvaccinated people were being hospitalized and dying at much higher rates than the vaccinated.

In the United States, unvaccinated people were twenty-one times more likely to die from Covid-19 than the boosted population during January 2022. At the worst point of the Omicron wave, about 6 in every 100,000 boosted adults age sixty-five and older died each week. That was a sad toll, but small compared to the 127 of every 100,000 unvaccinated seniors who were dying.[2]

As quickly as it surged, Omicron burned itself out, with case counts plunging throughout February and into March 2022. Omicron ran out of people to infect, leaving a big portion of the population immunized through either vaccination or infection, or both. People were still dying from Covid-19, as deaths lag new cases, but the daily average was dropping. In March, some of the last remaining pandemic restrictions in the United States were lifted, such as school mask requirements.

There was a sense of relief as spring 2022 approached that a post-Omicron break had arrived. Some experts think any future waves may be less damaging, thanks to immunity and the natural evolution of viruses. But many people have learned the hard way not to get their hopes up. The waves of variants created a kind of rolling fatigue among people who would see light at the end of the tunnel, only to have it snuffed, repeatedly, with new variants and their accompanying restrictions. Even with hope anew, another variant could arise and cause another surge, like the BA.2 strain of Omicron. Or there could be a seasonal resurgence of the virus, whatever the variant, indefinitely.

Covid certainly wasn't over for Moderna. Stéphane Bancel, Stephen Hoge, and their employees continued to wrestle with the virus and to seek new milestones with the vaccine. In late March, the company reported that a low-dose version of its vaccine safely induced immune responses in children under six, and Moderna's leaders thought they might finally have all the data needed to support the use of Moderna's vaccine in children under eighteen in the United States (some other countries had already allowed children to get the shot).[3] And their booster-shot strategy was still playing out. In late March, the FDA authorized a second booster dose (or fourth dose overall) of Moderna's vaccine for all adults 50 and older, as well as younger adults with compromised immune systems, at least four months after the first booster.[4] Bancel, speaking to analysts in February, predicted that eventually people would get annual boosters at the same time they get flu shots, in fall and winter. In future years, maybe a single seasonal shot would target both the coronavirus and the flu.

All of this suggested that the business of testing, manufacturing, and selling Covid-19 vaccines would keep Moderna busy for the foreseeable future. And that this would continue to be a profitable business.

It seemed likely that a price increase was in store for Moderna's Covid-19 vaccine, too. To date, the US government had bought Moderna doses for roughly $16 each. But it wasn't clear if the government would keep doing that for seasonal booster campaigns or if it would instead let vaccine purchasing and distribution revert to mostly private channels. Once the private market took over, Bancel told me in February, the price would go up, because $16 "is not the value of the vaccine."

Some more numbers help tell the story of Moderna's transformation:

- *75.7 million:* number of people in the United States vaccinated with at least two doses of Moderna's vaccine, or 23 percent of the total population, as of late March 2022

- *807 million:* number of Covid-19 vaccine doses that Moderna delivered worldwide during all of 2021

- *$17.7 billion:* Moderna's global sales of its Covid-19 vaccine for 2021

- *$12.2 billion:* Moderna's net profit in 2021

- *$641 million:* royalties from sales of the vaccine that Moderna paid to Cellscript in 2021 for the sublicense to the Penn patents that originated with Weissman's and Karikó's research

- *$21 billion:* combined value of contracts with customers for additional Covid-19 vaccine doses in 2022

- *3,000:* number of Moderna employees as of February 2022 (plus more than 650 openings on the company's jobs site)

- *$497.49:* Moderna's peak stock price, August 2021

- *$165.92:* Moderna's closing stock price, March 25, 2022

- *$66.9 billion:* Moderna's stock market capitalization as of late March 2022

The company that most people had never heard of before 2020 finally delivered on the promise of messenger RNA, churning out a product that was injected into hundreds of millions of arms around the world. The endeavor was an unprecedented windfall for the first full year of a drug company's first commercially available product.

Moderna planned to use some of the windfall to double its R&D spending to find more mRNA vaccines and drugs for a range of diseases. "What you're going to see is really a huge expansion of the pipeline," Bancel said in our February interview. "Cash is a thing we've been lacking to scale this platform and now we have it. So, we're going to invest as much as we can."

And some of the windfall went to special bonuses for employees at the manager level and below in January, including rank-and-file workers, though the company won't say how much those were. Bancel and other executives reaped the rewards with multimillion-dollar compensation packages for 2021, as detailed in a securities filing in March 2022.

But all this financial success came with a cost: among other perks that top executives received from Moderna—which may not have felt like a perk—were costs for the provision of security services to the executives or members of their households, because of a "heightened threat environment" surrounding its work on a Covid-19 vaccine. As expected for security matters, the company didn't provide specifics, such as who was making what kind of threats to whom, but Moderna said the personal safety of its leaders was "of the utmost importance."

Indeed, not all was rosy with Moderna. The same filing detailing the pay packages also revealed yet another senior personnel change—in December the company fired a senior commercial executive, Corinne Le Goff, it had hired just eleven months earlier (Moderna used the euphemism "involuntary departure"). Moderna said in the filing it needed someone with more experience in consumer and population health, but it didn't quite explain why that wouldn't have been a factor when she was hired in the first place. Le Goff declined to comment. Bancel's leadership org chart remained in flux, and old patterns of departures and constant attempts to upgrade the workforce seemed to remain.

And patent litigation was mounting. All that revenue, all those profits meant Moderna was a fat, juicy target in an industry where patent suits are a part of doing business. In March 2022, Moderna's Cambridge neighbor, Alnylam—the company once led by John Maraganore—filed a lawsuit claiming that Moderna's vaccine infringed upon an Alnylam patent covering the critical lipid nanoparticle technology that helped safely carry the mRNA into the body. A few weeks earlier, two other biotech firms had filed a similar patent lawsuit against Moderna. Moderna denied the allegations and prepared to litigate. The patent fight with the US government that was put on hold may pick up at any time, though it hadn't as of late March 2022.

Not content to constantly be hit with lawsuits, Moderna signaled it would go on the offensive. The company updated its patent pledge, saying it would never enforce its patents in lower-income countries but that it now expected its patents to be respected in wealthier countries like the United States. That could mean Moderna becomes a plaintiff in some cases in the future. Some of these disputes may take years to play out, and the lawyers, of course, will do well.

More than two years into the pandemic, Moderna had a complicated relationship with Covid-19. On the one hand, its financial fortunes were very much tied to swings in the course of the pandemic. Bancel would often remind investors there was more to Moderna than its Covid-19 vaccine, to look ahead at other potential important products. But the vaccine was still its only product, one that people still called "Moderna" despite the "Spikevax" branding the company had tried to attach to it. If investors sensed that demand for Moderna's Covid-19 vaccine was fading, the stock took a hit. Then it would jump if future demand looked stronger—say, because of a surge in cases somewhere in the world—no matter what was happening with the rest of Moderna's pipeline. If Moderna executives felt tethered to the pandemic, so did some investors and analysts. Different investors had different time horizons, and some were driving the short-term volatility, while others would have preferred to focus on the long-term potential of mRNA. Michael Yee, the Jefferies analyst, captured some of this tension in a research note in March 2022: "We see any 'wave' during 2022 to possibly drive stock resurgence—but interestingly we believe investors would really like the stock to not be so volatile around COVID and to find value from [the] rest of [the] pipeline. . . ."[5]

Moderna executives also would have liked less volatility and more value recognized for its other products in the works. On the other hand, they continued to talk up Covid-19 booster shots as an ongoing source of revenue. Bancel said during a virtual presentation to analysts in March that several countries, including the United Kingdom, Canada, and Switzerland, had already placed orders for booster doses to be delivered for 2023.

Moderna continued to face pressure to expand access to its vaccine. The anti-poverty group Oxfam owns Moderna shares and managed to place a shareholder proposal on the ballot for the company's annual shareholder meeting, scheduled for late April (a virtual shareholder meeting because of, yes, Covid). It proposed that Moderna's board look into the feasibility of transferring intellectual property and technical know-how to allow others to produce its Covid vaccine in lower-income countries. Moderna's board of directors recommended shareholders vote against the proposal, saying it has tried to increase its deliveries of doses to poorer countries, but that in some cases logistical challenges on the ground have blocked such efforts. These kinds of activist-oriented proposals rarely garner a majority of shareholder votes, but it was yet another reminder that not everyone was happy with how Moderna supplied the world with vaccine doses.

Another sign of Moderna's transformation was its role reversal in partnerships. Years earlier, little Moderna sought out big drug companies like AstraZeneca and Merck for cash, expertise, and validation of its fledgling mRNA technology. Now, with mRNA validated and a $17 billion war chest, Moderna is helping two small startups working on cutting-edge cell- and gene-editing drug technologies with tens of millions of dollars in up-front license fees. Those companies' executives may have celebrated the way Bancel, Hoge, and others did when the AstraZeneca deal put Moderna on stable financial footing. Maybe those companies see a path to go public now, too.

"If there's a lab somewhere, academic or a startup, that has a cool technology that you could plug into the Moderna platform . . . we'll be very happy to get into that business," Bancel said at an investor conference in early 2022.

In March, Bancel pledged that Moderna would take on the task of finding new vaccines against fifteen pathogens identified by global health authorities as the biggest risks. They included some that Moderna had already started work on, like Zika, and others it hadn't, like tuberculosis.

The company was relying on lists compiled by groups like the World Health Organization. By March 2022, WHO's list had changed from a few years ago. Now, Covid-19 was at the top.

But the last disease on the list hadn't changed: Disease X.

There will always be that unknown threat, what Covid once was. And for that, Moderna can only prepare so much.

Peter Loftus
March 28, 2022

Notes

Prologue

1. Rebecca Farley, "Do Pharmaceutical Companies Spend More on Marketing Than Research and Development?" PharmacyChecker.com, July 24, 2020, https://www.pharmacychecker.com/askpc/pharma-marketing-research-development/.

2. Catherine Elton, "The Untold Story of Moderna's Race for a Covid-19 Vaccine," *Boston Magazine*, June 4, 2020, https://www.bostonmagazine.com/health/2020/06/04/moderna-coronavirus-vaccine/.

3. "Health Officials Work to Solve China's Mystery Virus Outbreak," *Wall Street Journal*, January 6, 2020, https://www.wsj.com/articles/health-officials-work-to-solve-chinas-mystery-virus-outbreak-11578308757.

4. "2018 Annual Review of Diseases Prioritized under the Research and Development Blueprint," WHO Research and Development Blueprint, February 6–7, 2018, https://www.who.int/docs/default-source/blue-print/2018-annual-review-of-diseases-prioritized-under-the-research-and-development-blueprint.pdf.

5. Julie Steenhuysen and Dan Whitcomb, "Washington State Man Who Traveled to China Is First U.S. Victim of Coronavirus," Reuters, January 21, 2020, https://www.reuters.com/article/us-china-health-usa/washington-state-man-who-traveled-to-china-is-first-u-s-victim-of-coronavirus-idUSKBN1ZK2FF.

6. Matthew J. Belvedere, "Trump Says He Trusts China's Xi on Coronavirus and the US Has It 'Totally under Control,'" CNBC, January 22, 2020, https://www.cnbc.com/2020/01/22/trump-on-coronavirus-from-china-we-have-it-totally-under-control.html.

7. Larry Elliott and Graeme Wearden, "Trump Blasts 'Prophets of Doom' in Attack on Climate Activism," *Guardian*, January 21, 2020, https://www.theguardian.com/business/2020/jan/21/trump-climate-1tn-trees-davos.

8. Donna Young, "CDS Reports 1st US Case of Coronavirus; NIH Working with Moderna on Vaccine," S&P Global Market Intelligence, January 21, 2020, https://www.spglobal.com/marketintelligence/en/news-insights/trending/4urhd31MJzBeDot3X1frXw2.

9. Jessica Wang, Ellie Zhu, and Taylor Umlauf, "How China Built Two Coronavirus Hospitals in Just over a Week," *Wall Street Journal*, February 6, 2020, https://www.wsj.com/articles/how-china-can-build-a-coronavirus-hospital-in-10-days-11580397751.

Chapter 1

1. "All Nobel Prizes in Physiology or Medicine," The Nobel Prize, https://www.nobelprize.org/prizes/lists/all-nobel-laureates-in-physiology-or-medicine/.

2. Matthew Cobb, "Who Discovered Messenger RNA?" *Current Biology* 25, no. 13 (June 29, 2015): R526–R532, https://www.sciencedirect.com/science/article/pii/S0960982215006065.

3. Laura Fraser, "The Demonstration," Genentech, September 29, 2016, https://www.gene.com/stories/the-demonstration.

4. Peter Loftus, "FDA Blesses Blindness Treatment That Could Cost $1 Million," *Wall Street Journal*, December 19, 2017, https://www.wsj.com/articles/fda-approves-first-gene-therapy-to-tackle-genetic-disease-in-u-s-1513703450.

5. Elie Dolgin, "The Tangled History of mRNA Vaccines," *Nature*, September 14, 2021, https://www.nature.com/articles/d41586-021-02483-w.

6. One of Wolff's coauthors on the 1990 paper was Robert W. Malone, who had been working for the drug company Vical while collaborating with Wolff. Malone would later describe himself as "inventor of mRNA vaccines" in 2021 while raising concerns about the testing and safety of the Covid-19 vaccines; J. A. Wolff et al., "Direct Gene Transfer into Mouse Muscle in Vivo," *Science* 247 (March 23, 1990): 1465–1468; Tom Bartlett, "The Vaccine Scientist Spreading Vaccine Misinformation," *The Atlantic*, August 12, 2021, https://www.theatlantic.com/science/archive/2021/08/robert-malone-vaccine-inventor-vaccine-skeptic/619734/.

7. Peter Loftus, Jared S. Hopkins, and Bojan Pancevski, "Moderna and Pfizer Are Reinventing Vaccines, Starting with Covid," *Wall Street Journal*, November 17, 2020, https://www.wsj.com/articles/moderna-and-pfizer-are-reinventing-vaccines-starting-with-covid-11605638892.

8. Aria Bendix, "BioNTech Scientist Katalin Karikó Risked Her Career to Develop mRNA Vaccines. Americans Will Start Getting Her Coronavirus Shot on Monday," BusinessInsider.com, December 12, 2020, https://www.businessinsider.com/mrna-vaccine-pfizer-moderna-coronavirus-2020-12.

9. Katalin Karikó et al., "Suppression of RNA Recognition by Toll-like Receptors: The Impact of Nucleoside Modification and the Evolutionary Origin of RNA," *Immunity* 23, no. 2 (August 1, 2005): 165–175, https://pubmed.ncbi.nlm.nih.gov/16111635/.

10. CellScript license, June 26, 2017, https://www.sec.gov/Archives/edgar/data/1682852/000119312518323562/d577473dex108.htm.

11. "Penn Study Finds a New Role for RNA in Human Immune Response," News Release, University of Pennsylvania School of Medicine, August 23, 2005, https://www.eurekalert.org/news-releases/883761.

12. "The Nobel Prize in Physiology or Medicine," Press Release, October 8, 2012, https://www.nobelprize.org/prizes/medicine/2012/press-release/.

13. Kazutoshi Takahashi and Shinya Yamanaka, "Induction of Pluripotent Stem Cells from Mouse Embryonic and Adult Fibroblast Cultures by Defined Factors," *Cell* 126, no. 4 (August 25, 2006): 663–676, https://www.cell.com/fulltext/S0092-8674%2806%2900976-7.

14. Luigi Warren et al., "Highly Efficient Reprogramming to Pluripotency and Directed Differentiation of Human Cells Using Synthetic Modified mRNA," *Cell Stem Cell* 7, no. 5 (November 5, 2010): 618–630, https://www.ncbi.nlm.nih.gov/pmc/articles/PMC3656821/.

15. IDI would later merge into Boston Children's Hospital.

16. "Landmark Law Helped Universities Lead the Way," AUTM, https://autm.net/about-tech-transfer/advocacy/legislation/bayh-dole-act.

17. AUTM 2018 Licensing Activity Survey, https://autm.net/AUTM/media/SurveyReportsPDF/AUTM_FY2018_US_Licensing_Survey.pdf.

18. Brian Gormley, "Biotech Entrepreneur Timothy Springer Has Another Act," *Wall Street Journal*, July 19, 2017, https://www.wsj.com/articles/biotech-entrepreneur-timothy-springer-has-another-act-1500463800.

19. John Carroll, "Ironwood Raises $188M in IPO but Takes a Big Price Cut," Fierce Biotech, February 3, 2010, https://www.fiercebiotech.com/biotech/ironwood-raises-188m-ipo-but-takes-a-big-price-cut.

20. Steven Prokesch, "The Edison of Medicine," *Harvard Business Review*, March–April 2017, https://hbr.org/2017/03/the-edison-of-medicine.

21. John Wilke, "Biotech Company Is Questioned about 'Try It Out' Sales Strategy," *Wall Street Journal*, November 8, 1994, accessed via Factiva.

22. John Wilke, "PerSeptive Restates Its Results for Much of Past 2 Fiscal Years," *Wall Street Journal*, December 28, 1994, accessed via Factiva.

23. "SEC Settles Corporate Revenue Recognition and Illegal Stock Trading Case," United States Securities and Exchange Commission, February 29, 2000, https://www.sec.gov/litigation/litreleases/lr16457.htm.

24. Ron Winslow, "Perkin-Elmer to Buy PerSeptive, Seeks Role in Drug Development," *Wall Street Journal*, August 26, 1997, https://www.wsj.com/articles/SB872511484859449000.

25. Flagship Pioneering, https://www.flagshippioneering.com/about.

26. Rossi PowerPoint presentation reviewed by the author.

27. Rossi said he showed early data to GSK representatives but didn't pursue further because he was already in the process of forming what would become Moderna.

28. Flagship Pioneering, accessed November 10, 2021, https://www.flagshippioneering.com/companies/moderna.

29. From Moderna's S-1: https://www.sec.gov/Archives/edgar/data/0001682852/000119312518323562/d577473ds1.htm; Amended Form S-1 registration statement filed with the SEC, page 9: https://www.sec.gov/Archives/edgar/data/1682852/000119312518341958/d611137ds1a.htm.

30. "Safe, Efficient Method Reported for Creating and Differentiating Human Pluripotent Stem Cells," September 30, 2010, Targeted News Service, accessed via Factiva.

31. Derrick Rossi, "Modified RNAs Advance Stem Cell Field," YouTube, September 30, 2010, https://www.youtube.com/watch?v=pfYvuZdOhPs.

Chapter 2

1. "CureVac Raises EUR 27.6 Million in Financing Round," Fierce Biotech, May 10, 2010, https://www.fiercebiotech.com/biotech/curevac-raises-eur-27-6-million-financing-round.

2. It has since merged into another institution.

3. At Minnesota, Bancel focused on biochemical engineering. His thesis is titled "Topographical Imaging of Macroporous Microcarriers Using Laser Scanning Confocal Microscopy." The gist of it was that he used special microscopes and cutting-edge image-processing software—or at least, cutting-edge for the 1990s—to analyze the structure of tiny beads that are used in labs to cultivate animal cells. It was engineering but with a life-sciences bent. Stéphane Bancel and Wei-Shou Hu, "Topographical Imaging of Macroporous Microcarriers Using Laser Scanning Confocal Microscopy," *Journal of Fermentation and Bioengineering* 81, no. 5 (1996): 437–444, https://experts.umn.edu/en/publications/topographical-imaging-of-macroporous-microcarriers-using-laser-sc.

4. Stéphane Bancel, "The Other Side" speaker series, Harvard Innovation Labs, 2016: https://www.youtube.com/watch?v=-P53wVGfvjw.

5. Offer letter filed with the SEC, February 23, 2011: https://www.sec.gov/Archives/edgar/data/1682852/000119312518323562/d577473dex1012.htm.

Chapter 3

1. United States Census Bureau, https://www.census.gov/quickfacts/fact/table/cambridgecitymassachusetts/PST045219.

2. Michael Blanding, "The Past and Future of Kendall Square," *MIT Technology Review*, August 18, 2015, https://www.technologyreview.com/2015/08/18/10816/the-past-and-future-of-kendall-square/.

3. "Kendall History," Cambridge Redevelopment Authority, https://www.cambridgeredevelopment.org/redevelopment-history-of-kendall?rq=biogen.

4. Jacob Goldstein, "Sanofi-Aventis CEO on Pharma's 'Lost Decade,'" *Wall Street Journal*, January 13, 2010, https://www.wsj.com/articles/BL-HEB-28671.

5. "Top 200 Drugs by Retail Sales in 2000," DrugTopics, March 19, 2001, https://www.drugtopics.com/view/top-200-drugs-retail-sales-2000.

6. "Is It True FDA Is Approving Fewer New Drugs Lately?" FDA, https://www.fda.gov/media/80203/download.

7. "Pfizer Reports Fourth-Quarter and Full-Year 2012 Results; Provides 2013 Financial Guidance," Pfizer, January 28, 2013, https://www.pfizer.com/news/press-release/press-release-detail/pfizer_reports_fourth_quarter_and_full_year_2012_results_provides_2013_financial_guidance.

8. "GlaxoSmithKline to Plead Guilty and Pay $3 Billion to Resolve Fraud Allegations and Failure to Report Safety Data," United States Department of Justice, July 3, 2012, https://www.justice.gov/opa/pr/glaxosmithkline-plead-guilty-and-pay-3-billion-resolve-fraud-allegations-and-failure-report.

9. Jonathan D. Rockoff and Peter Loftus, "Merck to Cut 13,000 More Jobs as Patents Expire," *Wall Street Journal*, July 30, 2011, https://www.wsj.com/articles/SB10001424053111904800304576475752260745450.

10. Peter Loftus, "J&J Is Short of Cancer Drug Doxil," *Wall Street Journal*, July 21, 2011, https://www.wsj.com/articles/SB10001424053111903554904576460290484704816.

11. "Pfizer to Acquire Wyeth, Creating the World's Premier Biopharmaceutical Company," Pfizer, January 25, 2009, https://www.pfizer.com/news/press-release/press-release-detail/pfizer_to_acquire_wyeth_creating_the_world_s_premier_biopharmaceutical_company; "Merck and Shering-Plough to Merge," SEC, https://www.sec.gov/Archives/edgar/data/310158/000089882209000096/pressrelease.htm.

12. Peter Loftus, "Big Pharma's Delicate Dance on Drug Prices," *Wall Street Journal*, February 21, 2016, https://www.wsj.com/articles/big-pharmas-delicate-dance-on-drug-prices-1456110323.

13. Kenneth R. Gosselin, "Cambridge Will Gain 350 Pfizer Jobs, Many from Groton," *Hartford Courant*, February 3, 2011, https://www.courant.com/business/hc-xpm-2011-02-03-hc-pfizer-massachusetts-0203-20110202-story.html.

14. Peter Loftus, "New Kind of Drug, Silencing Genes, Gets FDA Approval," *Wall Street Journal*, August 10, 2018, https://www.wsj.com/articles/fda-approves-first-drug-based-on-gene-silencing-research-1533923359.

15. Jessica Hall and Ransdell Pierson, "Merck to Buy Sirna for $1.1 Billion in Cash," Reuters, January 19, 2007, https://www.reuters.com/article/us-sirna-merck/merck-to-buy-sirna-for-1-1-billion-in-cash-idUSWEN841420061030; John Carroll, "Merck Writes Off RNAi, Punts Sirna to Alnylam for $175M," Fierce Biotech, January 13, 2014, https://www.fiercebiotech.com/financials/merck-writes-off-rnai-punts-sirna-to-alnylam-for-175m.

16. Peter Landers, "MS Drug's Epic Journey from Folklore to Lab," *Wall Street Journal*, June 22, 2010, https://www.wsj.com/articles/SB10001424052748704256304575320714138159240.

17. Pankaj K. Mandal and Derrick J. Rossi, "Reprogramming Human Fibroblasts to Pluripotency Using Modified mRNA," *Nature Protocols* 8 (2013): 568–582, https://www.nature.com/articles/nprot.2013.019.

18. Stéphane Bancel, "What If mRNA Could Be a Drug?" TEDx Talks, December 27, 2013, https://www.youtube.com/watch?v=T4-DMKNT7xI&t=290s.

19. Damian Garde, "Moderna's Top Scientist Steps Down Amid a Billion-Dollar R&D Push," Fierce Biotech, October 13, 2015, https://www.fiercebiotech.com/r-d/moderna-s-top-scientist-steps-down-amid-a-billion-dollar-r-d-push.

20. Elie Dolgin, "The Billion-Dollar Biotech," *Nature* 522 (June 4, 2015), https://www.nature.com/articles/522026a.

21. Damian Garde, "Ego, Ambition, and Turmoil: Inside One of Biotech's Most Secretive Startups," STAT, September 13, 2016, https://www.statnews.com/2016/09/13/moderna-therapeutics-biotech-mrna/.

22. "Moderna Announces $40 Million in Financing to Advance Development of New Biotherapeutic Modality: Messenger RNA Therapeutics," Moderna, December 6, 2012, https://www.prnewswire.com/news-releases/moderna-announces-40-million-in-financing-to-advance-development-of-new-biotherapeutic-modality-messenger-rna-therapeutics-182304241.html.

23. "AstraZeneca and Moderna Therapeutics Announce Exclusive Agreement to Develop Pioneering Messenger RNA Therapeutics in Cardiometabolic Diseases and Cancer," AstraZeneca, March 21, 2013, https://www.astrazeneca.com/media-centre/press-releases/2013/astrazeneca-moderna-therapeutics-cardiometabolic-diseases-cancer-treatment-21032013.html#.

24. Ben Hirschler, "AstraZeneca Cuts Another 2,300 Jobs in Sales, Admin," Reuters, March 21, 2013, https://www.reuters.com/article/us-astrazeneca-strategy/astrazeneca-cuts-another-2300-jobs-in-sales-admin-idUSBRE92K06V20130321.

Chapter 4

1. "Battle of the Biotech Unicorns: CureVac vs. Moderna," YouTube, November 3, 2017, https://www.youtube.com/watch?v=-w7ULkppEVI.

2. Ben Miller, "Juno Therapeutics Completes $176M Fundraising Round; Bezos a Contributor," *Puget Sound Business Journal*, April 24, 2014, https://www.bizjournals.com/seattle/blog/health-care-inc/2014/04/juno-therapeutics-completes-176m-fund-raising.html.

3. "Moderna Announces License and Collaboration Agreement with Merck to Develop Messenger RNA-Based Antiviral Vaccines and Passive Immunity Therapies," Moderna, January 13, 2015, https://investors.modernatx.com/news-releases/news-release-details/moderna-announces -license-and-collaboration-agreement-merck.

4. Dan Primack, "The $3 Billion Startup That Wants to Help You to Make Medicines in Your Own Body," *Fortune*, January 8, 2015, https://fortune.com/2015/01/08/the-3-billion-startup-that-wants -to-help-you-to-make-medicines-in-your-own-cells/.

5. "Moderna Closes $450 Million Financing to Support Growth of Messenger RNA Therapeutics Platform across Diverse Therapeutic Areas," Moderna, January 5, 2015, https://www.prnewswire .com/news-releases/moderna-closes-450-million-financing-to-support-growth-of-messenger-rna -therapeutics-platform-across-diverse-therapeutic-areas-300015695.html.

6. Xinliang Fu et al., "Evidence of H10N8 Influenza Virus Infection among Swine in Southern China and Its Infectivity and Transmissibility in Swine," *Emerging Microbes & Infections* 9, no. 1 (2020): 88–94, https://www.ncbi.nlm.nih.gov/pmc/articles/PMC6968645/.

7. "Moderna Therapeutics Announces Transition to a Clinical Stage Company, Provides Business Updates and Outlines 2016 Strategic Priorities," Moderna, January 11, 2016, https://investors .modernatx.com/news/news-details/2016/Moderna-Therapeutics-Announces-Transition-to-a -Clinical-Stage-Company-Provides-Business-Update-and-Outlines-2016-Strategic-Priorities-01-11 -2016/default.aspx.

8. "Moderna Therapeutics, Through Valera, Its Infectious Disease Venture, Announces Initial Grant of up to $20 Million to Advance mRNA-Based Antibody Combination to Help Prevent HIV Infection," Moderna, January 12, 2016, https://investors.modernatx.com/news-releases/news-release -details/moderna-therapeutics-through-valera-its-infectious-disease.

9. "Moderna Announces Funding Award from BARDA for $8 Million with Potential of Up to $125 Million to Accelerate Development of Zika Messenger RNA (mRNA) Vaccine," Moderna, September 7, 2016, https://investors.modernatx.com/news-releases/news-release-details/moderna -announces-funding-award-barda-8-million-potential-125.

10. Moderna draft registration statement filed with SEC, page 269: https://www.sec.gov/ Archives/edgar/data/1682852/000095012318009220/filename1.htm.

11. Robert Weisman, "Moderna to Build $110 Million Drug Plant in Norwood," *Boston Globe*, September 21, 2016.

12. Madeleine Armstrong, "JP Morgan—Moderna Comes out of Stealth Mode," Evaluate Vantage, January 10, 2017, https://www.evaluate.com/vantage/articles/news/jp-morgan-moderna -comes-out-stealth-mode.

13. Jonathan D. Rockoff, "Startup Moderna Shows Promise in Vaccine Trial," *Wall Street Journal*, April 27, 2017, https://www.wsj.com/articles/startup-moderna-shows-promise-in-vaccine-trial -1493308801.

Chapter 5

1. Moderna stock quote, Yahoo! Finance, December 2018, https://finance.yahoo.com/quote/ MRNA/history?period1=1478649600&period2=1636416000&interval=1d&filter=history&frequency =1d&includeAdjustedClose=true.

2. Charley Grant, "Record Biotech IPO May Be Worth the $7 Billion," *Wall Street Journal*, November 12, 2018, https://www.wsj.com/articles/record-biotech-ipo-may-be-worth-the-7-billion -1542043242.

3. Moderna Form S-1 Registration Statement, page 1: https://www.sec.gov/Archives/edgar/ data/0001682852/000119312518323562/d577473ds1.htm.

4. Brian Gormley, "Biotech Startup Moderna Drops an Underwriter Ahead of IPO," *Wall Street Journal*, December 4, 2018, https://www.wsj.com/articles/biotech-startup-moderna-drops-an -underwriter-ahead-of-ipo-1543966659.

5. Matthew J. Belvedere, "George HW Bush's Funeral: Here's a Rundown of the Financial Markets That Are Open and Closed," CNBC, December 5, 2018, https://www.cnbc.com/2018/12/05/ george-hw-bushs-funeral-rundown-of-financial-markets-open-and-closed.html.

6. Jessica Menton, "Stocks Stage Recovery after Dow Drops over 700 Points," *Wall Street Journal*, December 6, 2018, https://www.wsj.com/articles/stocks-stage-recovery-after-dow-drops-over-700-points-1544075565.

7. Corrie Driebusch and Jonathan D. Rockoff, "Moderna IPO Raises over $600 Million in Rocky Market," *Wall Street Journal*, December 6, 2018, https://www.wsj.com/articles/highly-anticipated-moderna-listing-is-seen-as-test-of-new-ipos-1544092200.

8. Moderna Amended Form S-1 Registration Statement, filed with SEC, December 4, 2018, page 326: https://www.sec.gov/Archives/edgar/data/0001682852/000119312518341958/d611137ds1a.htm.

9. Johnson & Johnson proxy statement filed with SEC, March 13, 2019, page 69: https://www.sec.gov/Archives/edgar/data/0000200406/000020040619000013/a2019jnjproxy.htm#s376F35B4455D5DC6B123B793F964E000.

10. Moderna proxy statement filed with SEC, May 15, 2019, page 19: https://www.sec.gov/Archives/edgar/data/0001682852/000119312519148153/d689184ddef14a.htm#toc689184_15.

11. "Opening Bell, December 7, 2018," CNBC, December 7, 2018, https://www.cnbc.com/video/2018/12/07/opening-bell-december-7-2018.html.

12. Corrie Driebusch and Kimberly Chin, "Moderna Declines in Public-Market Debut," *Wall Street Journal*, December 7, 2018, https://www.wsj.com/articles/moderna-declines-in-public-market-debut-1544204238.

13. Moderna stock quote, Yahoo! Finance, https://finance.yahoo.com/quote/MRNA/history?period1=1478649600&period2=1636416000&interval=1d&filter=history&frequency=1d&includeAdjustedClose=true.

14. Transcript of Stéphane Bancel comments at J.P. Morgan Health Care Conference, January 13, 2000, CQ FD Disclosure, accessed via Factiva.

Chapter 6

1. Barney Graham (@BarneyGrahamMD), "1/13/20 was the day we shared our modified sequence recommendations with Moderna as requested by CEO Stéphane Bancel on January 7th, 'Let us know in real time. I will get the team aware of it and (be) ready to run when you give us a sequence,'" Twitter, January 13, 2021, 7:22 p.m., https://twitter.com/BarneyGrahamMD/status/1349512209370648578?s=20 (confirmed by Graham to author).

2. "Novel 2019 Coronavirus Genome," Virological.org, https://virological.org/t/novel-2019-coronavirus-genome/319.

3. "Severe Acute Respiratory Syndrome Coronavirus 2 Isolate Wuhan-Hu-1, Complete Genome," GenBank, NCBI, https://www.ncbi.nlm.nih.gov/nuccore/MN908947.

4. Kizzmekia S. Corbett et al., "SARS-CoV-2 mRNA Vaccine Design Enabled by Prototype Pathogen Preparedness," *Nature*, August 5, 2020, https://www.nature.com/articles/s41586-020-2622-0.

5. Transcript of President's Coronavirus Task Force news conference, February 7, 2020, via Political Transcripts by CQ Transcriptions.

6. Moderna prospectus filed with the SEC February 10, 2020, page S-9: https://www.sec.gov/Archives/edgar/data/0001682852/000119312520029948/d871325d424b5.htm.

7. Moderna 8-K filed with SEC, February 11, 2020: https://www.sec.gov/Archives/edgar/data/0001682852/000119312520033357/d877577d8k.htm.

8. World Health Organization situation report, February 7, 2020, https://www.who.int/docs/default-source/coronaviruse/situation-reports/20200207-sitrep-18-ncov.pdf.

9. "Coronavirus Disease 2019 (COVID-19) Situation Report–32," World Health Organization, February 21, 2020, https://www.who.int/docs/default-source/coronaviruse/situation-reports/20200221-sitrep-32-covid-19.pdf?sfvrsn=4802d089_2.

10. "CDC Confirms 15th Case of Coronavirus Disease (COVID-19)," Centers for Disease Control and Prevention, February 13, 2020, https://www.cdc.gov/media/releases/2020/s0213-15th-coronavirus-case.html.

11. Amy Taxin, "U.S. Evacuees 'Relieved' about Quarantine on Military Base," AP, January 31, 2020, https://apnews.com/article/health-us-news-ap-top-news-virus-outbreak-ca-state-wire-4c2e04ef113497607ff8e9302fac6a5d.

12. Suryatapa Bhattacharya, "Fear and Boredom Aboard the Quarantined Coronavirus Cruise Ship," *Wall Street Journal*, February 14, 2020, https://www.wsj.com/articles/fear-and-boredom-aboard -the-quarantined-coronavirus-cruise-ship-11581705677.

13. "Naming the Coronavirus Disease (COVID-19) and the Virus That Causes It," World Health Organization, February 11, 2020, https://www.who.int/emergencies/diseases/novel-coronavirus -2019/technical-guidance/naming-the-coronavirus-disease-(covid-2019)-and-the-virus-that-causes-it.

Chapter 7

1. "9 Coronavirus Deaths Now Reported in Washington State," NPR, March 3, 2020, https:// www.npr.org/sections/health-shots/2020/03/03/811690163/9-coronavirus-deaths-now-reported-in -washington-state.

2. Melanie Evans and Jon Kamp, "Nursing Home in Washington State Calls for More Help in Coronavirus Outbreak," *Wall Street Journal*, March 7, 2020, https://www.wsj.com/articles/nursing -home-in-washington-state-calls-for-more-help-in-coronavirus-outbreak-11583633846.

3. "Step 3: Clinical Research," FDA, January 4, 2018, https://www.fda.gov/patients/drug -development-process/step-3-clinical-research.

4. "Panel OKs Cervical Cancer Vaccine," CBS News, May 18, 2006, https://www.cbsnews.com/ news/panel-oks-cervical-cancer-vaccine/.

5. Scott Hensley and Ron Winslow, "Pipeline Problem: Demise of a Blockbuster Drug Complicates Pfizer's Revamp," *Wall Street Journal*, December 4, 2006.

6. Moderna annual report filed with SEC, February 27, 2020, page 37, https://www.sec.gov/ Archives/edgar/data/0001682852/000168285220000006/moderna10-k12312019.htm.

7. Peter Loftus, "Drugmaker Moderna Delivers First Experimental Coronavirus Vaccine for Human Testing," *Wall Street Journal*, February 24, 2020, https://www.wsj.com/articles/drugmaker -moderna-delivers-first-coronavirus-vaccine-for-human-testing-11582579099.

8. Megan Thielking and Helen Branswell, "CDC Expects 'Community Spread' of Coronavirus, as Top Official Warns Disruptions Could Be 'Severe,'" STAT, February 25, 2020, https://www .statnews.com/2020/02/25/cdc-expects-community-spread-of-coronavirus-as-top-official-warns -disruptions-could-be-severe/.

9. Transcript of Trump news conference, February 26, 2020, Political Transcripts by CQ Transcriptions, via Factiva.

10. President Trump meeting with pharmaceutical executives on coronavirus, video and transcript, C-SPAN, March 2, 2020, https://www.c-span.org/video/?469926-1/president-trump -meeting-pharmaceutical-executives-coronavirus.

11. Kizzmekia S. Corbett, "Evaluation of the mRNA-1273 Vaccine against SARS-CoV-2 in Nonhuman Primates," *New England Journal of Medicine* 383 (October 15, 2020): 1544–1555, https://www .nejm.org/doi/full/10.1056/nejmoa2024671.

12. "Protocol for Lisa Jackson et al., 'An mRNA Vaccine against SARS-CoV-2—Preliminary Report,'" *New England Journal of Medicine* 383 (October 15, 2020): 1920–1931, https://www.nejm.org/ doi/suppl/10.1056/NEJMoa2022483/suppl_file/nejmoa2022483_protocol.pdf.

13. Peter Loftus, "Recruitment Begins for First Test of Experimental Coronavirus Vaccine," *Wall Street Journal*, March 4, 2020, https://www.wsj.com/articles/recruitment-begins-for-first-test-of -experimental-coronavirus-vaccine-11583358054.

14. Joseph Walker, Peter Loftus, and Jared S. Hopkins, "Scientists Rush to Find Coronavirus Cure—But It Still Isn't Fast Enough," *Wall Street Journal*, April 6, 2020, https://www.wsj.com/ articles/inside-the-race-to-find-a-coronavirus-cure-11586189463.

15. "Coronavirus Disease 2019 (COVID-19) Situation Report–56," World Health Organization, March 16, 2020, https://www.who.int/docs/default-source/coronaviruse/situation-reports/20200316 -sitrep-56-covid-19.pdf?sfvrsn=9fda7db2_6.

16. "March 10, 2020, Presidential Primary Results," Washington Secretary of State, March 20, 2020, https://results.vote.wa.gov/results/20200310/president-democratic-party.html.

17. "NCAA Cancels Men's and Women's Basketball Championships Due to Coronavirus Concerns," NCAA, March 17, 2020, https://www.ncaa.com/live-updates/basketball-men/d1/ncaa -cancels-mens-and-womens-basketball-championships-due.

18. Eric Morath and Sarah Chaney, "U.S. Employers Cut 701,000 Jobs in March," *Wall Street Journal*, April 3, 2020, https://www.wsj.com/articles/u-s-jobs-report-likely-to-show-start-of-record-labor-market-collapse-11585906617.

19. Jared S. Hopkins, "Coronavirus Pandemic Delays Testing of New Drugs," *Wall Street Journal*, March 27, 2020, https://www.wsj.com/articles/coronavirus-upends-testing-of-new-drugs-11585301412.

20. Peter Loftus, "How Eli Lilly Developed Covid-19 Drug in Pandemic's Long Shadow," *Wall Street Journal*, November 10, 2020, https://www.wsj.com/articles/how-eli-lilly-developed-a-covid-drug-in-the-pandemics-long-shadow-11605023414.

21. "Atlanta Site Added to NIH Clinical Trial of a Vaccine for COVID-19," National Institute of Allergy and Infectious Diseases, March 27, 2020, https://www.niaid.nih.gov/news-events/atlanta-site-added-nih-clinical-trial-vaccine-covid-19.

22. "NIH Clinical Trial of a Vaccine for COVID-19 Now Enrolling Older Adults," National Institute of Allergy and Infectious Diseases, April 17, 2020, https://www.niaid.nih.gov/news-events/nih-clinical-trial-vaccine-covid-19-now-enrolling-older-adults.

23. Jennifer Levitz and Paul Berger, "'I'm Sorry I Can't Kiss You'—Coronavirus Victims Are Dying Alone," *Wall Street Journal*, April 10, 2020, https://www.wsj.com/articles/im-sorry-i-cant-kiss-youcoronavirus-victims-are-dying-alone-11586534526.

24. Rebecca Ballhaus and Jared S. Hopkins, "Trump Pushes Broader Use of Hydroxychloroquine against Coronavirus," *Wall Street Journal*, April 6, 2020, https://www.wsj.com/articles/trump-pushes-broader-use-of-hydroxychloroquine-against-coronavirus-11586194581.

25. Barney Graham (@BarneyGrahamMD), "On May 9, 2020 I got a call from Jim Chappel and Mark Denison at Vanderbilt. They had been measuring neutralizing activity of vaccinee serum against live SARS-CoV-2 in their BL3 lab. They described the results and then showed me the curves. The potency was better than expected," Twitter, May 9, 2021, 11:24 a.m., https://twitter.com/BarneyGrahamMD/status/1391413877427089413?s=20.

26. Peter Loftus, "Moderna Says Initial Covid-19 Vaccine Results Are Positive," *Wall Street Journal*, May 18, 2020, https://www.wsj.com/articles/moderna-says-initial-covid-19-vaccine-results-are-positive-11589805115.

Chapter 8

1. "Moderna Announces Pricing of Public Offering of Shares of Common Stock," Moderna, May 18, 2020, https://investors.modernatx.com/news-releases/news-release-details/moderna-announces-pricing-public-offering-shares-common-stock-0.

2. Peter Loftus, "Moderna Gets U.S. Funding for Development, Manufacturing of Experimental Coronavirus Vaccine," *Wall Street Journal*, April 16, 2020, https://www.wsj.com/articles/u-s-awards-up-to-483-million-to-moderna-to-accelerate-coronavirus-vaccine-development-and-production-11587075412.

3. BARDA contract, p. 4: https://www.hhs.gov/sites/default/files/moderna-75a50120c00034.pdf.

4. Transcript of House Energy and Commerce subcommittee on health hearing, May 14, 2020, Political Transcripts by CQ Transcriptions, via Factiva.

5. "Moderna and Lonza Announce Worldwide Strategic Collaboration to Manufacture Moderna's Vaccine (mRNA-1273) against Novel Coronavirus," Moderna, May 1, 2020, https://investors.modernatx.com/news-releases/news-release-details/moderna-and-lonza-announce-worldwide-strategic-collaboration.

Chapter 9

1. David M. Oshinsky, *Polio: An American Story* (New York: Oxford University Press, 2005).

2. R. E. Neustadt and H. V. Fineberg, *The Swine Flu Affair: Decision-Making on a Slippery Disease* (Washington, DC: National Academies Press, 1978), https://www.ncbi.nlm.nih.gov/books/NBK219595/.

3. Betsy McKay, "U.S. Urges H1N1 Shots as Supplies Surge," *Wall Street Journal*, December 23, 2009, https://www.wsj.com/articles/SB126150314633801635.

4. Jeanne Whalen, "Novartis Seeks Payment for Cancelled Orders," *Wall Street Journal*, May 6, 2020, https://www.wsj.com/articles/SB10001424052748703322204575226463473239880.

5. Alan Fram and Jonathan Lemire, "Trump: Why Allow Immigrants from 'Shithole Countries'?" AP, January 12, 2018, https://apnews.com/article/immigration-north-america-donald -trump-ap-top-news-international-news-fdda2ffob877416c8ae1c1a77a3cc425.

6. Transcript, President Donald Trump Delivers Remarks on Vaccine Development, May 15, 2020, Political Transcripts by CQ Transcriptions, via Factiva.

7. "Leading Causes of Death," Centers for Disease Control and Prevention, https://www.cdc .gov/nchs/fastats/leading-causes-of-death.htm.

8. Elizabeth Weise, "Moncef Slaoui, Ex-Pharma Exec Tapped by Trump to Lead Vaccine Group, Will Divest $10M Stock Options," *USA Today*, May 18, 2020, https://www.usatoday.com/story/news/ 2020/05/18/trumps-coronavirus-vaccine-lead-moncef-slaoui-divests-moderna-options/5215507002/.

9. Data provided to author by InsiderScore research firm.

10. Transcript of Moderna first-quarter earnings conference call, May 7, 2020, CQ FD Disclosure, via Factiva.

11. Moderna Executive Retention Agreement, filed with SEC, March 29, 2020, https://www.sec .gov/Archives/edgar/data/1682852/000119312520089933/d905037dex101.htm.

12. Moderna quarterly report filed with SEC, August 6, 2020, page 119, https://www.sec.gov/ix ?doc=/Archives/edgar/data/0001682852/000168285220000017/mrna-20200630.htm.

13. Bojan Pancevski and Jared S. Hopkins, "How Pfizer Partner BioNTech Became a Leader in Coronavirus Vaccine Race," *Wall Street Journal*, October 22, 2020, https://www.wsj.com/articles/how -pfizer-partner-biontech-became-a-leader-in-coronavirus-vaccine-race-11603359015.

14. Transcript of House Energy and Commerce subcommittee hearing, July 21, 2020, Political Transcripts by CQ Transcriptions, via Factiva.

15. Email from NIH Director Francis Collins, May 3, 2020, obtained via a Freedom of Information Act request by Jason Leopold of BuzzFeed News, page 730: https://s3.documentcloud .org/documents/20793561/leopold-nih-foia-anthony-fauci-emails.pdf.

16. Lawrence Corey et al., "A Strategic Approach to COVID-19 Vaccine R&D," *Science* 368, no. 6494 (May 11, 2020): 948–950, https://www.science.org/doi/10.1126/science.abc5312.

17. Peter Loftus, "Coronavirus Vaccine Candidates' Pivotal U.S. Testing to Start This Summer," *Wall Street Journal*, June 10, 2020, https://www.wsj.com/articles/coronavirus-vaccine-candidates -pivotal-u-s-testing-to-start-this-summer-11591781405.

18. "RotaTeq," Merck Vaccines, https://www.merckvaccines.com/rotateq/rotavirus-study/ safety-profile/.

19. Peter Loftus, "Coronavirus Vaccine Front-Runners Emerge, Rollouts Weighed," *Wall Street Journal*, May 17, 2020, https://www.wsj.com/articles/coronavirus-vaccine-frontrunners-emerge -rollouts-weighed-11589707803.

20. Email to author, June 2, 2020.

Chapter 10

1. Jacqueline Howard and Elizabeth Cohen, "Georgia News Anchor Receives First Shot in US Phase 3 Trial of a Covid Vaccine: 'I Never Thought That I'd Do Something Like This,'" CNN, July 28, 2020, https://www.cnn.com/2020/07/27/health/coronavirus-vaccine-dawn-baker-feature/index .html.

2. "Moderna Announces Expansion of BARDA Agreement to Support Larger Phase 3 Program for Vaccine (mRNA-1273) against Covid-19," Moderna, July 26, 2020, https://investors.modernatx .com/news-releases/news-release-details/moderna-announces-expansion-barda-agreement-support -larger-phase.

3. "Risk for COVID-19 Infection, Hospitalization, and Death by Race/Ethnicity," Centers for Disease Control and Prevention, November 22, 2021, https://www.cdc.gov/coronavirus/2019-ncov/ covid-data/investigations-discovery/hospitalization-death-by-race-ethnicity.html#footnote03.

4. Leo Lopez et al., "Racial and Ethnic Health Disparities Related to COVID-19," *Journal of the American Medical Association* 325, no. 8 (January 22, 2021): 719–720, https://jamanetwork.com/ journals/jama/fullarticle/2775687.

5. "The U.S. Public Health Service Syphilis Study at Tuskegee," Centers for Disease Control and Prevention, https://www.cdc.gov/tuskegee/timeline.htm.

6. Rebecca Skloot, *The Immortal Life of Henrietta Lacks* (New York: Crown, 2011).

7. "Weekly Updates by Select Demographic and Geographic Characteristics," Centers for Disease Control and Prevention, https://www.cdc.gov/nchs/nvss/vsrr/covid_weekly/index.htm.

8. "More Than 10,000 COVID-19 Cases Reported as Walt Disney World Reopens to Public," Clickorlando.com, July 11, 2020, https://www.clickorlando.com/news/local/2020/07/11/covid-19 -cases-rise-as-walt-disney-world-reopens-to-public/.

9. Peter Loftus, "Surging Covid-19 Cases in U.S., Other Countries Could Speed Up Vaccine Studies," *Wall Street Journal*, July 27, 2020, https://www.wsj.com/articles/surging-covid-19-cases-in-u -s-other-countries-could-speed-up-vaccine-studies-11595842201.

10. Lisa A. Jackson et al., "An mRNA Vaccine against SARS-CoV-2—Preliminary Report," *New England Journal of Medicine* 383 (November 12, 2020): 1920–1931, https://www.nejm.org/doi/full/10 .1056/nejmoa2022483.

11. Peter Loftus, "As Covid-19 Vaccine Development Pushes Ahead, Researchers Probe Safety," *Wall Street Journal*, July 12, 2020, https://www.wsj.com/articles/as-covid-19-vaccine-development -pushes-ahead-researchers-probe-safety-11594546201.

12. Peter Loftus and Jared S. Hopkins, "Moderna, Pfizer Coronavirus Vaccines Begin Final-Stage Testing," *Wall Street Journal*, July 27, 2020, https://www.wsj.com/articles/modernas-coronavirus -vaccine-begins-final-stage-testing-11595854440.

13. Jared S. Hopkins and Chris Wack, "Pfizer, BioNTech Get $1.95 Billion Covid-19 Vaccine Order from U.S. Government," *Wall Street Journal*, July 22, 2020, https://www.wsj.com/articles/pfizer -biontech-get-1-95-billion-covid-19-vaccine-order-from-u-s-government-11595418221.

14. "CDC Vaccine Price List," Centers for Disease Control and Prevention, https://www.cdc .gov/vaccines/programs/vfc/awardees/vaccine-management/price-list/index.html.

15. Jared S. Hopkins and Peter Loftus, "Pharma Companies Split on Coronavirus Vaccine Pricing Plans," *Wall Street Journal*, July 21, 2020, https://www.wsj.com/articles/pharma-companies-split-on -coronavirus-vaccine-pricing-plans-11595367562.

16. Peter Loftus, "Covid-19 Vaccine Makers Signal Prices," *Wall Street Journal*, August 5, 2020, https://www.wsj.com/articles/covid-19-vaccine-makers-signal-prices-11596648639.

17. Jared S. Hopkins, "Moderna Inks $1.5 Billion Coronavirus Vaccine Deal with U.S.," *Wall Street Journal*, August 11, 2020, https://www.wsj.com/articles/moderna-inks-1-5-billion-coronavirus-vaccine -deal-with-u-s-11597190519.

18. Peter Loftus, "Moderna Says Covid-19 Vaccine Shows Signs of Working in Older Adults," *Wall Street Journal*, August 26, 2020, https://www.wsj.com/articles/moderna-says-covid-19-vaccine-shows -signs-of-working-in-older-adults-11598452800.

19. "COVE Study," Moderna, October 21, 2020, https://www.modernatx.com/sites/default/files/ content_documents/2020-COVE-Study-Enrollment-Completion-10.22.20.pdf.

Chapter 11

1. Shannon Mullen O'Keefe, "One in Three Americans Would Not Get COVID-19 Vaccine." Gallup, August 7, 2020, https://news.gallup.com/poll/317018/one-three-americans-not-covid-vaccine .aspx.

2. "Poll: Most Americans Worry Political Pressure Will Lead to Premature Approval of a COVID-19 Vaccine; Half Say They Would Not Get a Free Vaccine Approved Before Election Day," KFF, September 10, 2020, https://www.kff.org/coronavirus-covid-19/press-release/poll-most -americans-worry-political-pressure-will-lead-to-premature-approval-of-a-covid-19-vaccine-half-say -they-would-not-get-a-free-vaccine-approved-before-election-day/.

3. Dan Levine and Marisa Taylor, "Exclusive: Top FDA Official Says Would Resign If Agency Rubber-Stamps an Unproven COVID-19 Vaccine," Reuters, August 20, 2020, https://www.reuters .com/article/us-health-coronavirus-vaccines-fda-exclu/exclusive-top-fda-official-says-would-resign-if -agency-rubber-stamps-an-unproven-covid-19-vaccine-idUSKBN25H03H.

4. Peter Loftus and Jared S. Hopkins, "Covid-19 Vaccine Developers Prepare Joint Pledge on Safety, Standards," *Wall Street Journal*, September 4, 2020, https://www.wsj.com/articles/covid-19-vaccine-developers-prepare-joint-pledge-on-safety-standards-11599257729.

5. Peter Loftus and Maura Orru, "AstraZeneca Pauses Covid-19 Vaccine Trial after Illness in a U.K. Subject," *Wall Street Journal*, September 9, 2020, https://www.wsj.com/articles/astrazeneca-pauses-covid-19-vaccine-trial-after-illness-in-a-u-k-subject-11599608962.

6. Peter Loftus, "Johnson & Johnson Pauses Covid-19 Vaccine Trials Due to Sick Subject," *Wall Street Journal*, October 13, 2020, https://www.wsj.com/articles/johnson-johnson-pauses-covid-19-vaccine-trials-due-to-sick-subject-11602555101.

7. Thomas M. Burton and Rebecca Ballhaus, "White House Agrees to FDA's Guidelines for Vetting Covid-19 Vaccines," *Wall Street Journal*, October 6, 2020, https://www.wsj.com/articles/white-house-agrees-to-fdas-guidelines-for-vetting-covid-19-vaccines-11602011953.

8. Eric Topol (@EricTopol), "The #SARSCoV2 vaccine companies haven't been transparent; the stakes are big. Calling @pfizer @moderna_tx, both completing enrollment in the weeks ahead, to publish their data analysis plans, stopping rules, statistical assumptions for efficacy, and DSMB roster. We need to know," Twitter, September 12, 2020, 1:05 p.m., https://twitter.com/EricTopol/status/1304828376801189890?s=20.

9. Alaric Dearment, "Moderna Publishes Phase III Covid-19 Vaccine Study Protocol as Trial Enrolls More Than 80% of Participants," *MedCity News*, September 17, 2020, https://medcitynews.com/2020/09/moderna-publishes-phase-iii-covid-19-vaccine-study-protocol-as-trial-enrolls-more-than-80-of-participants/.

10. "Clinical Study Protocol," Moderna, August 20, 2020, https://www.modernatx.com/sites/default/files/mRNA-1273-P301-Protocol.pdf.

11. Moderna quarterly report filed with SEC, August 6, 2020, page 92: https://www.sec.gov/ix?doc=/Archives/edgar/data/0001682852/000168285220000017/mrna-20200630.htm.

12. Peter Loftus and Denise Roland, "By Adding Patents, Drugmaker Keeps Cheaper Humira Copies Out of U.S.," *Wall Street Journal*, October 16, 2020, https://www.wsj.com/articles/biosimilar-humira-goes-on-sale-in-europe-widening-gap-with-u-s-1539687603.

13. Peter Loftus, "Lucrative Drug Niche Sparks Legal Scramble," *Wall Street Journal*, July 20, 2014, https://www.wsj.com/articles/lucrative-drug-niche-sparks-legalscramble-1405898259.

14. Angus Liu, "Pfizer-BioNTech, Regeneron Sued for Patent Infringement with COVID-19 Products," Fierce Pharma, October 6, 2020, https://www.fiercepharma.com/pharma/pfizer-biontech-regeneron-sued-for-infringement-allele-s-patent-their-covid-19-products.

15. United States Patent no. US 10,702,600 B1, July 7, 2020, https://www.modernatx.com/sites/default/files/US10702600.pdf.

16. United States Patent no. US 10,703,789 B2, July 7, 2020, https://www.modernatx.com/sites/default/files/US10703789.pdf.

17. Peter Loftus, "Moderna Vows to Not Enforce Covid-19 Vaccine Patents during Pandemic," *Wall Street Journal*, October 8, 2020, https://www.wsj.com/articles/moderna-vows-to-not-enforce-covid-19-vaccine-patents-during-pandemic-11602154805.

18. "Moderna Loses Key Patent Challenge," *Nature Biotechnology* 38 (September 4, 2020): 1009, https://www.nature.com/articles/s41587-020-0674-1.

19. Sheryl Gay Stolberg and Rebecca Robbins, "Moderna and U.S. at Odds over Vaccine Patent Rights," *New York Times*, November 9, 2021, https://www.nytimes.com/2021/11/09/us/moderna-vaccine-patent.html.

20. Moderna filing with the U.S. Patent and Trademark Office, August 21, 2020, https://www.nytimes.com/interactive/2021/11/09/us/moderna-patent-filing.html.

21. "Moderna Completes Enrollment of Phase 3 Cove Study of mRNA Vaccine against Covid-19 (mRNA-1273)," Moderna, October 22, 2020, https://investors.modernatx.com/news-releases/news-release-details/moderna-completes-enrollment-phase-3-cove-study-mrna-vaccine.

22. Tamara Keith et al., "Trump Takes 'Precautionary' Treatment after He and First Lady Test Positive for Virus," NPR, October 2, 2020, https://www.npr.org/sections/latest-updates-trump-covid-19-results/2020/10/02/919385151/president-trump-and-first-lady-test-positive-for-covid-19.

Chapter 12

1. Steven Joffe et al., "Data and Safety Monitoring of COVID-19 Vaccine Clinical Trials," *Journal of Infectious Diseases* 224, no. 12 (December 15, 2021): 1995–2000, https://academic.oup.com/jid/advance-article/doi/10.1093/infdis/jiab263/6278127.

2. Steven Joffe et al., "Data and Safety Monitoring of COVID-19 Vaccine Clinical Trials."

3. Stephen Hoge interview by Rand Richards Cooper ("The Moderna Era"), Amherst College, June 28, 2021, https://www.amherst.edu/amherst-story/magazine/issues/2021-summer/the-moderna-era.

4. Peter Loftus, "Moderna's Covid-19 Vaccine Is 94.5% Effective in Early Results, Firm Says," *Wall Street Journal*, November 16, 2020, https://www.wsj.com/articles/moderna-says-its-covid-19-vaccine-was-94-5-effective-in-latest-trial-11605528008.

5. Email from Larry Corey, reviewed by author.

6. Peter Loftus, "Moderna Asks Health Regulators to Authorize Its Covid-19 Vaccine," *Wall Street Journal*, November 30, 2020, https://www.wsj.com/articles/moderna-to-ask-health-regulators-to-authorize-its-covid-19-vaccine-11606737602.

7. Peter Loftus, Jared S. Hopkins, and Bojan Pancevski, "Moderna and Pfizer Are Reinventing Vaccines, Starting with Covid," *Wall Street Journal*, November 17, 2020, https://www.wsj.com/articles/moderna-and-pfizer-are-reinventing-vaccines-starting-with-covid-11605638892.

Chapter 13

1. Thomas M. Burton and Joseph Walker, "Next Stop for Covid-19 Vaccines: FDA Review," *Wall Street Journal*, November 19, 2020, https://www.wsj.com/articles/next-stop-for-covid-19-vaccines-fda-review-11605792716.

2. Thomas M. Burton, "FDA Head Defends Covid-19 Vaccine-Approval Process," *Wall Street Journal*, December 2, 2020, https://www.wsj.com/articles/fda-head-defends-covid-19-vaccine-approval-process-11606954168.

3. Transcript of Vice President Pence in roundtable with restaurant executives, May 22, 2020, Political Transcripts by CQ Transcriptions, via Factiva.

4. Department of Health and Human Services fact sheet, June 16, 2020, author's copy.

5. CDC slide presentation, July 29, 2020: https://www.cdc.gov/vaccines/acip/meetings/downloads/slides-2020-07/COVID-07-Mbaeyi-508.pdf.

6. Moderna Form 8-K filed with SEC September 18, 2020, https://www.sec.gov/ix?doc=/Archives/edgar/data/0001682852/000168285220000019/mrna-20200918.htm.

7. Transcript of Moderna appearance at Piper Sandler Healthcare Conference, December 2, 2020, CQ FD Disclosure, via Factiva.

8. Costas Paris, "Supply-Chain Obstacles Led to Last Month's Cut to Pfizer's Covid-19 Vaccine-Rollout Target," *Wall Street Journal*, December 3, 2020, https://www.wsj.com/articles/pfizer-slashed-its-covid-19-vaccine-rollout-target-after-facing-supply-chain-obstacles-11607027787.

9. Peter Loftus, "Early Coronavirus Vaccine Supplies Likely Won't Be Enough for Everyone at High Risk," *Wall Street Journal*, August 6, 2020, https://www.wsj.com/articles/early-coronavirus-vaccine-supplies-likely-wont-be-enough-for-everyone-at-high-risk-11596706202.

10. Peter Loftus, Jared S. Hopkins, and Betsy McKay, "CDC Panel Recommends Giving First Covid-19 Vaccines to Health Workers, Nursing Homes," *Wall Street Journal*, December 1, 2020, https://www.wsj.com/articles/cdc-panel-recommends-giving-first-covid-vaccines-to-health-workers-nursing-homes-11606862069.

11. Jared S. Hopkins, "Covid-19 Vaccine Race Turns Deep Freezers into a Hot Commodity," *Wall Street Journal*, September 4, 2020, https://www.wsj.com/articles/covid-19-vaccine-race-turns-deep-freezers-into-a-hot-commodity-11599217201.

12. Peter Loftus, "Moderna's Covid-19 Vaccine Could Widen Immunization Effort," *Wall Street Journal*, December 18, 2020, https://www.wsj.com/articles/modernas-covid-19-vaccine-could-widen-immunization-effort-11608287402.

13. Jared S. Hopkins and Thomas M. Burton, "Pfizer, BioNTech Covid-19 Vaccine Is Authorized in the U.S.," *Wall Street Journal*, December 11, 2020, https://www.wsj.com/articles/pfizer-biontech -covid-19-vaccine-is-authorized-in-the-u-s-11607740101.

14. Thomas M. Burton and Jared S. Hopkins, "FDA Panel Endorses Covid-19 Vaccine," *Wall Street Journal*, December 11, 2020, https://www.wsj.com/articles/fda-advisory-panel-takes-up-pfizer -biontech-covid-19-vaccine-11607596201.

15. Thomas M. Burton and Peter Loftus, "FDA Finds Moderna Covid-19 Vaccine Highly Effective," *Wall Street Journal*, December 15, 2020, https://www.wsj.com/articles/modernas-covid-19 -vaccine-is-next-in-line-for-authorization-11608028201.

16. FDA Briefing Document, Moderna Covid-19 Vaccine, page 6, https://www.fda.gov/media/ 144434/download.

17. Moderna Briefing Document submitted to FDA, https://www.fda.gov/media/144452/ download.

18. Transcript of FDA Vaccines and Related Biological Products Advisory Committee Meeting, December 17, 2020, https://www.fda.gov/media/145466/download.

19. Vaccine and Related Biological Products Advisory Committee, "Food and Drug Administration (FDA) Center for Biologics Evaluation and Research (CBER) 63rd Meeting of the Vaccines and Related Biological Products Advisory Committee," YouTube, December 17, 2020, https://www.youtube.com/watch?v=I4psAfbUtCo&t=13s.

20. FDA letter of authorization (letter of December 18 originally posted, but the site now includes an updated letter of authorization, October 20, 2021), https://www.fda.gov/media/144636/ download.

21. Nicole Acevedo, "December Was the Deadliest, Most Infectious Month since the Start of the Pandemic," NBC News, January 1, 2021, https://www.nbcnews.com/news/us-news/december-was -deadliest-most-infectious-month-start-pandemic-n1252645.

22. Alexander Bolton and Scott Wong, "Congress Close to Coronavirus Deal That Includes Stimulus Checks," *The Hill*, December 16, 2020, https://thehill.com/homenews/senate/530435 -congress-close-to-coronavirus-deal-that-includes-stimulus-checks.

23. "Federal Grand Jury Charges Six with Conspiracy to Kidnap the Governor of Michigan," United States Department of Justice, December 17, 2020, https://www.justice.gov/usao-wdmi/pr/ 2020_1217_fox_et_al.

24. Billy Kobin and Joe Sonka, "US Supreme Court Declines to Review Beshear's Order Halting In-Person Classes at Religious Schools," *Louisville Courier Journal*, December 17, 2020, https://www .courier-journal.com/story/news/education/2020/12/17/us-supreme-court-rules-kentucky-gov -beshears-person-class-ban/6490425002/.

25. Richard Wike, Janell Fetterolf, and Mara Mordecai, "U.S. Image Plummets Internationally as Most Say Country Has Handled Coronavirus Badly," Pew Research Center, September 15, 2020, https://www.pewresearch.org/global/2020/09/15/us-image-plummets-internationally-as-most-say -country-has-handled-coronavirus-badly/.

Chapter 14

1. "The NIH Clinical Center—The 'House of Hope,'" National Institutes of Health, August 17, 2017, https://www.niams.nih.gov/about/about-the-director/letter/nih-clinical-center -house-hope.

2. "Secretary Azar and Doctors Fauci and Collins Receive Covid-19 Vaccine," C-SPAN video and transcript, December 22, 2020, https://www.c-span.org/video/?507498-1/secretary-azar-doctors-fauci -collins-receive-covid-19-vaccine.

3. Peter Loftus and Charles Passy, "U.S. Starts Delivery of Moderna's Covid-19 Vaccine," *Wall Street Journal*, December 20, 2020, https://www.wsj.com/articles/u-s-starts-rollout-of-modernas -covid-19-vaccine-11608460200.

4. Jared S. Hopkins, "Pfizer to Complete First Covid-19 Vaccine Shipments in U.S.," *Wall Street Journal*, December 16, 2020, https://www.wsj.com/articles/covid-19-vaccine-latest-updates-12-16-2020 -11608142583.

5. Peter Loftus and Charles Passy, "U.S. Starts Delivery of Moderna's Covid-19 Vaccine," *Wall Street Journal*, December 20, 2020, https://www.wsj.com/articles/u-s-starts-rollout-of-modernas-covid-19-vaccine-11608460200.

6. Peter Loftus, "Moderna to Offer Its Covid-19 Vaccine to Workers, Contractors and Board," *Wall Street Journal*, December 29, 2020, https://www.wsj.com/articles/moderna-to-offering-its-covid-19-vaccine-to-workers-contractors-board-11609281794.

7. Interview with Stéphane Bancel, Science History Institute, June 7, 2021, https://www.sciencehistory.org/distillations/podcast/interview-with-stephane-bancel.

8. "University of Pennsylvania mRNA Biology Pioneers Receive COVID-19 Vaccine Enabled by Their Foundational Research," Penn Medicine News, December 23, 2020, https://www.pennmedicine.org/news/news-releases/2020/december/penn-mrna-biology-pioneers-receive-covid19-vaccine-enabled-by-their-foundational-research.

9. "Dolly Parton Sings and Gets COVID Vaccine Shot," YouTube, March 3, 2021, https://www.youtube.com/watch?v=OjbSWebA3Ko.

10. Dana Rebik, "'I'm Going to Cry Now, Happy Tears': Despite Hurdles, Seniors and Essential Workers Get Covid Vaccine Shots," WGNTV, February 4, 2021, https://wgntv.com/news/coronavirus/im-going-to-cry-now-happy-tears-despite-hurdles-seniors-and-essential-workers-get-covid-vaccine-shots/.

11. Morgan O'Hanlon, "'Scheduling Angels' Are Scouring the Internet to Book Vaccine Appointments for Strangers," *Texas Monthly*, February 24, 2021, https://www.texasmonthly.com/news-politics/scheduling-angels-are-scouring-the-internet-to-book-vaccine-appointments-for-strangers/.

12. "15.4 Million Doses of COVID-19 Vaccines Distributed, 4.5 Million Administered: U.S. CDC," Reuters, January 4, 2021, https://www.reuters.com/article/us-health-coronavirus-usa-cdc/15-4-million-doses-of-covid-19-vaccines-distributed-4-5-million-administered-u-s-cdc-idUSKBN299265.

13. "Moderna Provides Covid-19 Vaccine Supply Update," Moderna, January 4, 2021, https://investors.modernatx.com/news-releases/news-release-details/moderna-provides-covid-19-vaccine-supply-update.

14. Peter Loftus and Paul Vieira, "Vaccine Manufacturing Issues Force Moderna to Cut Supplies to Canada, U.K.," *Wall Street Journal*, April 16, 2021, https://www.wsj.com/articles/vaccine-manufacturing-issues-force-moderna-to-cut-supplies-to-canada-u-k-11618600046.

15. "U.S. Government Purchases Additional 100 Million Doses of Moderna's Covid-19 Vaccine," Moderna, February 11, 2021, https://investors.modernatx.com/news-releases/news-release-details/us-government-purchases-additional-100-million-doses-modernas.

16. "On-the-Record Press Call by Office of Science and Technology Policy Director Dr. Eric Lander and NSC Director for Global Health Security and Biodefense Dr. Beth Cameron on American Pandemic Preparedness," The White House, September 3, 2021, https://www.whitehouse.gov/briefing-room/press-briefings/2021/09/03/on-the-record-press-call-by-office-of-science-and-technology-policy-director-dr-eric-lander-and-nsc-director-for-global-health-security-and-biodefense-dr-beth-cameron-on-american-pandemic-preparedne/.

17. Jeff Mason, "Operation Warp Speed Chief Adviser Resigns, Biden's Transition Official Says," Reuters, January 12, 2021, https://www.reuters.com/article/us-health-coronavirus-slaoui/operation-warp-speed-chief-adviser-resigns-bidens-transition-official-says-idUSKBN29I097.

18. "Moncef Slaoui Departs Galvani Bioelectronics Board of Directors," GSK, March 24, 2021, https://us.gsk.com/en-us/media/press-releases/moncef-slaoui-departs-galvani-bioelectronics-board-of-directors/.

19. "Statement from Dr. Moncef Slaoui," PR Newswire, March 24, 2021, https://www.prnewswire.com/news-releases/statement-from-dr-moncef-slaoui-301255362.html.

20. Peter Loftus and Thomas M. Burton, "J&J Covid-19 Vaccine Authorized for Use in U.S.," *Wall Street Journal*, February 7, 2021, https://www.wsj.com/articles/j-j-covid-19-vaccine-authorized-for-use-in-u-s-11614467922.

21. Peter Loftus and Thomas M. Burton, "U.S. Seeks to Pause J&J Covid-19 Vaccine Use after Rare Blood-Clot Cases," *Wall Street Journal*, April 13, 2021, https://www.wsj.com/articles/u-s-seeks-to-pause-j-j-covid-19-vaccine-use-amid-clotting-reports-11618313210.

22. Peter Loftus, "Covid-19 Vaccine Manufacturing in U.S. Races Ahead," *Wall Street Journal*, March 21, 2021, https://www.wsj.com/articles/covid-19-vaccine-manufacturing-in-u-s-races-ahead-11616328001.

23. Peter Loftus and Matt Grossman, "Moderna Turns First Profit, Boosted by Its Covid-19 Vaccine," *Wall Street Journal*, May 6, 2021, https://www.wsj.com/articles/moderna-turns-first-ever-profit-boosted-by-its-covid-19-vaccine-11620302289.

24. Sumedha Gupta et al., "Vaccinations against COVID-19 May Have Averted up to 140,000 Deaths in the United States," *Health Affairs* 40, no. 9 (August 18, 2021): 1465–1472, https://www.healthaffairs.org/doi/abs/10.1377/hlthaff.2021.00619.

25. "Interim Estimates of Vaccine Effectiveness of BNT162b2 and mRNA-1273 COVID-19 Vaccines in Preventing SARS-CoV-2 Infection among Health Care Personnel, First Responders, and Other Essential and Frontline Workers—Eight U.S. Locations, December 2020–March 2021," Centers for Disease Control and Prevention, April 2, 2021, https://www.cdc.gov/mmwr/volumes/70/wr/mm7013e3.htm.

26. "Hospital Pharmacist Sentenced for Attempt to Spoil Hundreds of COVID Vaccine Doses," US Food and Drug Administration, June 8, 2021, https://www.fda.gov/inspections-compliance-enforcement-and-criminal-investigations/press-releases/hospital-pharmacist-sentenced-attempt-spoil-hundreds-covid-vaccine-doses.

27. Nouran Salahieh, "After Allergic Reactions at 1 Clinic, California Pauses Use of Large Batch of Moderna COVID-19 Vaccine," KTLA.com, January 17, 2021, https://ktla.com/news/california/after-allergic-reactions-at-1-clinic-california-pauses-use-of-more-than-330k-doses-of-moderna-covid-19-vaccine/.

28. "Use of COVID-19 Vaccines after Reports of Adverse Events among Adult Recipients of Janssen (Johnson & Johnson) and mRNA COVID-19 Vaccines (Pfizer-BioNTech and Moderna): Update from the Advisory Committee on Immunization Practices—United States, July 2021," Centers for Disease Control and Prevention, August 13, 2021, https://www.cdc.gov/mmwr/volumes/70/wr/mm7032e4.htm.

29. Peter Loftus, "Covid-19 Vaccines and Myocarditis Link Probed by Researchers," *Wall Street Journal*, November 7, 2021, https://www.wsj.com/articles/researchers-probe-link-between-covid-19-vaccines-and-myocarditis-11636290002.

30. Hannah Rosenblum, "COVID-19 Vaccines in Adults: Benefit-Risk Discussion," Centers for Disease Control and Prevention, July 22, 2021, https://www.cdc.gov/vaccines/acip/meetings/downloads/slides-2021-07/05-COVID-Rosenblum-508.pdf.

31. "Joint Statement from Moderna and Takeda on the Investigation of Suspended Lots of Moderna's Covid-19 Vaccine in Japan," Moderna, September 1, 2021, https://investors.modernatx.com/news-releases/news-release-details/joint-statement-moderna-and-takeda-investigation-suspended-lots.

32. Yuka Hayashi and Jared S. Hopkins, "U.S. Backs Waiver of Intellectual Property Protection for Covid-19 Vaccines," *Wall Street Journal*, May 6, 2021, https://www.wsj.com/articles/u-s-backs-waiver-of-intellectual-property-protection-for-covid-19-vaccines-11620243518.

33. Jared S. Hopkins and Peter Loftus, "Covid-19 Vaccine Makers Press Countries to Oppose Patent Waiver," *Wall Street Journal*, May 26, 2021, https://www.wsj.com/articles/covid-19-vaccine-makers-press-countries-to-oppose-patent-waiver-11622021402.

34. "Free the Vaccine Resolution," Cambridgema.gov, May 3, 2021, https://cambridgema.iqm2.com/Citizens/Detail_LegiFile.aspx?ID=13956&highlightTerms=Moderna.

35. Transcript of Moderna first-quarter earnings call, May 6, 2021, VIQ FD Disclosure, via Factiva.

36. Transcript of Moderna first-quarter earnings call, May 6, 2021.

37. Transcript of Moderna appearance at CECP Biopharma CEO Investor Forum, VIQ FD Disclosure, June 7, 2021, via Factiva.

38. Author's copy of Oxfam statement, December 18, 2020.

39. Bojan Pancevski, "Moderna to Deliver Covid-19 Vaccine to Hard-Hit Developing World," *Wall Street Journal*, May 3, 2021, https://www.wsj.com/articles/moderna-to-deliver-covid-19-vaccine-to-hard-hit-developing-world-11620037924.

40. Jasper G. Goodman, "Harvard Doctors Call for Expanded Global Vaccine Access Outside Moderna CEO's Home," *The Harvard Crimson*, September 30, 2021, https://www.thecrimson.com/article/2021/9/30/moderna-ceo-bones-protest/.

41. Peter Loftus, "Moderna to Build Vaccine-Manufacturing Plant in Africa," *Wall Street Journal*, October 7, 2021, https://www.wsj.com/articles/moderna-to-build-vaccine-manufacturing-plant-in-africa-11633586400; Jeff Mason, "Exclusive: African Union to Buy up to 110 Million Moderna Vaccines—Officials," Reuters, October 26, 2021, https://www.reuters.com/world/africa/exclusive-african-union-buy-up-110-million-moderna-covid-19-vaccines-officials-2021-10-26/.

42. Peter Loftus, "Moderna to Boost Covid-19 Vaccine Production to Meet Rising Global Demand," *Wall Street Journal*, April 29, 2021, https://www.wsj.com/articles/moderna-to-boost-covid-19-vaccine-production-to-meet-rising-global-demand-11619672403.

43. Sam Baker, "Axios Harris Poll 100: Pfizer, Moderna Reputations Soar Post-Vaccine," Axios.com, May 13, 2021, https://www.axios.com/pfizer-moderna-brand-reputations-fc2c023d-0c65-4302-8b64-fd6f1e183a99.html.

44. "Stéphane Bancel: The 2021 Pontifical Hero Award for Inspiration," Vatican Conference 2021, May 6, 2021, https://vaticanconference2021.org/the-2021-pontifical-hero-awardees/stephane-bancel/.

45. "The Virtual Ceremony and Decoration of Moderna's Executives and Scientists of Lebanese Descent with the National Order of Merit," The Embassy of Lebanon, February 8, 2021, http://www.lebanonembassyus.org/2021/02/08/the-virtual-ceremony-and-decoration-of-modernas-executives-and-scientists-of-lebanese-descent-with-the-national-order-of-merit/.

46. "Advanced Degree Commencement Ceremony," Boston University, May 16, 2021, https://live.bu.edu/commencement-2021/sessions/advanced-degree-commencement-ceremony/.

47. "40 Under 40," *Fortune*, https://fortune.com/40-under-40/2021/hamilton-bennett/.

48. "Katalin Karikó, Drew Weissman, Philip Felgner, Uğur Şahin, Özlem Türeci, Derrick Rossi and Sarah Gilbert," Princess of Asturias Award for Technical & Scientific Research 2021, https://www.fpa.es/en/princess-of-asturias-awards/laureates/2021-katalin-kariko-drew-weissman-philip-felgner-ugur-sahin-ozlem-tureci-derrick-rossi-and-sarah-gilbert.html.

49. "Modified mRNA Vaccines: 2021 Lasker-DeBakey Clinical Medical Research Award," Lasker Foundation, https://laskerfoundation.org/winners/modified-mrna-vaccines/; "2022 Breakthrough Prize in Life Sciences Awarded to Penn Medicine mRNA Pioneers Drew Weissman and Katalin Karikó," Penn Medicine News, September 9, 2021, https://www.pennmedicine.org/news/news-releases/2021/september/2022-breakthrough-prize-in-life-sciences-awarded-to-mrna-pioneers-drew-weissman-and-katalin-kariko.

50. "Kizzmekia S. Corbett, PhD, Barney S. Graham, MD, PhD," Partnership for Public Service, https://servicetoamericamedals.org/honorees/corbett-graham/.

51. "Olin College Holds 16th Commencement and Presents First Honorary Degree," Olin.edu, May 16. 2021, https://www.olin.edu/news-events/2021/olin-college-holds-16th-commencement-and-presents-first-honorary-degree/; "Professor Kenneth Chien about Moderna and the COVID-19-Vaccine," Karolinska Institutet, February 8, 2021, https://news.ki.se/professor-kenneth-chien-about-moderna-and-the-covid-19-vaccine.

Chapter 15

1. Jason Douglas, "U.K. Imposes Fresh Lockdowns to Curb New Covid-19 Strain," *Wall Street Journal*, December 19, 2020, https://www.wsj.com/articles/u-k-faces-fresh-lockdown-to-curb-new-covid-19-strain-11608402790.

2. Gabriele Steinhauser, Aaisha Dadi Patel, and Benjamin Katz, "Coronavirus Variant in South Africa Sparks Fear of Faster Spread, Possible Reinfection," *Wall Street Journal*, December 30, 2020, https://www.wsj.com/articles/coronavirus-variant-in-south-africa-sparks-fear-of-faster-spread-possible-reinfection-11609358056.

3. "Statement on Variants of the SARS-COV-2 Virus," Moderna, December 23, 2020, https://investors.modernatx.com/news-releases/news-release-details/statement-variants-sars-cov-2-virus.

4. Transcript of Moderna appearance at J.P. Morgan Health Care Conference, January 11, 2021, CQ FD Disclosure, via Factiva.

5. Kai Wu et al., "mRNA-1273 Vaccine Induces Neutralizing Antibodies against Spike Mutants from Global SARS-CoV-2 Variants," *bioRxiv* (January 25, 2021), https://www.biorxiv.org/content/10.1101/2021.01.25.427948v1.full.

6. Peter Loftus, "Moderna Developing Vaccine Booster Shot for Virus Strain Identified in South Africa," *Wall Street Journal*, January 25, 2021, https://www.wsj.com/articles/moderna-developing-vaccine-booster-shot-against-virus-strain-first-identified-in-south-africa-11611581400.

7. Peter Loftus, "Moderna Says Its Covid-19 Booster Shots Show Promise against Variants," *Wall Street Journal*, May 5, 2021, https://www.wsj.com/articles/covid-19-booster-shows-promise-against-variants-in-early-study-moderna-says-11620245114.

8. Brianna Abbott, "Covid-19 Delta Variant First Found in India Is Quickly Spreading across Globe," *Wall Street Journal*, June 9, 2021, https://www.wsj.com/articles/covid-19-variant-first-found-in-india-is-quickly-spreading-across-globe-11623257849.

9. Arian Campo-Flores, "Florida Leads U.S. in Covid-19 Cases as Hospitalizations Surge," *Wall Street Journal*, July 25, 2021, https://www.wsj.com/articles/florida-leads-u-s-in-covid-19-cases-as-hospitalizations-surge-11627131600.

10. "COVID-19 Cases in Fully Vaccinated Individuals," Massachusetts Department of Public Health, October 12, 2021, https://www.mass.gov/doc/weekly-report-covid-19-cases-in-vaccinated-individuals-october-12-2021/download.

11. Ian Lovett, "Covid-19 Vaccines Draw Warnings from Some Catholic Bishops," *Wall Street Journal*, March 2, 2021, https://www.wsj.com/articles/covid-19-vaccines-draw-warnings-from-some-catholic-bishops-11614722452.

12. Sam Schechner, Jeff Horwitz, and Emily Glazer, "How Facebook Hobbled Mark Zuckerberg's Bid to Get America Vaccinated," *Wall Street Journal*, September 17, 2021, https://www.wsj.com/articles/facebook-mark-zuckerberg-vaccinated-11631880296?mod=article_inline.

13. "Response Letter to Citizen Petition from FDA CBER to Children's Health Defense," Food and Drug Administration, August 23, 2021, https://www.regulations.gov/document/FDA-2021-P-0460-30085.

14. Gary Langer, "Vaccine Hesitancy Eases in Teeth of the Delta Surge: POLL," ABC News, September 5, 2021, https://abcnews.go.com/Politics/vaccine-hesitancy-eases-teeth-delta-surge-poll/story?id=79791316.

15. Nambi Ndugga, Latoya Hill, Samantha Artiga, and Sweta Haldar, "Latest Data on COVID-19 Vaccinations by Race/Ethnicity," KFF, January 12, 2022, https://www.kff.org/coronavirus-covid-19/issue-brief/latest-data-on-covid-19-vaccinations-by-race-ethnicity/.

16. Chuck Todd, Mark Murray, and Ben Kamisar, "NBC News Poll Shows Demographic Breakdown of the Vaccinated in the U.S.," NBC News, August 24, 2021, https://www.nbcnews.com/politics/meet-the-press/nbc-news-poll-shows-demographic-breakdown-vaccinated-u-s-n1277514.

17. "Path Out of the Pandemic," The White House, https://www.whitehouse.gov/covidplan/.

18. Transcript of Moderna second-quarter earnings call, August 5, 2021, VIQ FD Disclosure, via Factiva.

19. Philip R. Krause et al., "Considerations in Boosting COVID-19 Vaccine Immune Responses," *The Lancet* 398, no. 10308 (October 9, 2021): 1377–1380, https://www.thelancet.com/journals/lancet/article/PIIS0140-6736(21)02046-8/fulltext.

20. Jared S. Hopkins and Felicia Schwartz, "FDA Advisory Panel Votes against Endorsing Covid-19 Booster Shots Widely," *Wall Street Journal*, September 17, 2021, https://www.wsj.com/articles/fda-panel-to-weigh-covid-19-booster-shots-as-health-officials-debate-need-11631871003.

21. Alana Wise, "Biden Gets COVID Booster Shot and Calls on Eligible Americans to Do the Same," NPR, September 27, 2021, https://www.npr.org/2021/09/27/1040898432/biden-covid-booster-vaccine.

22. Peter Loftus and Felicia Schwartz, "Moderna and J&J Covid-19 Boosters, Mixing and Matching Authorized by the FDA," *Wall Street Journal*, October 20, 2021, https://www.wsj.com/articles/fda-authorizes-covid-19-vaccine-boosters-from-moderna-j-j-11634763535.

23. Jamey Keaten, "WHO Chief Urges Halt to Booster Shots for Rest of the Year," AP, September 8, 2021, https://apnews.com/article/business-health-coronavirus-pandemic-united-nations-world-health-organization-6384ff91c399679824311ac26e3c768a.

24. Felicia Schwartz, "FDA Delays Moderna Covid-19 Vaccine for Adolescents to Review Rare Myocarditis Side Effect," *Wall Street Journal*, October 15, 2021, https://www.wsj.com/articles/fda -delays-moderna-covid-19-vaccine-for-adolescents-to-review-rare-myocarditis-side-effect-11634315159.

Chapter 16

1. Transcript of Moderna R&D Day, September 9, 2021, VIQ FD Disclosure, via Factiva.

2. Jared S. Hopkins, "How Pfizer Delivered a Covid Vaccine in Record Time: Crazy Deadlines, a Pushy CEO," *Wall Street Journal*, December 11, 2020, https://www.wsj.com/articles/how-pfizer -delivered-a-covid-vaccine-in-record-time-crazy-deadlines-a-pushy-ceo-11607740483.

3. Moderna annual report filed with SEC, February 27, 2020, https://www.sec.gov/Archives/ edgar/data/0001682852/000168285220000006/moderna10-k12312019.htm.

4. Pfizer annual report filed with SEC, December 31, 2019, https://www.sec.gov/ix?doc=/ Archives/edgar/data/0000078003/000007800320000014/pfe-12312019x10kshell.htm.

5. Ludwig Burger, "CureVac Fails in Pivotal COVID-19 Vaccine Trial with 47% Efficacy," Reuters, June 17, 2021, https://www.reuters.com/business/healthcare-pharmaceuticals/curevacs -covid-19-vaccine-misses-efficacy-goal-mass-trial-2021-06-16/.

6. Arjun Puranik et al., "Comparison of Two Highly-Effective mRNA Vaccines for COVID-19 during Periods of Alpha and Delta Variant Prevalence," *MedRxiv* (August 6, 2021), https://www .medrxiv.org/content/10.1101/2021.08.06.21261707v1.

7. Shaun J. Grannis et al., "Interim Estimates of COVID-19 Vaccine Effectiveness against COVID-19–Associated Emergency Department or Urgent Care Clinic Encounters and Hospitalizations among Adults during SARS-CoV-2 B.1.617.2 (Delta) Variant Predominance—Nine States, June–August 2021," Centers for Disease Control and Prevention, September 10, 2021, https:// www.cdc.gov/mmwr/volumes/70/wr/mm7037e2.htm.

8. Tamara Pilishvili et al., "Effectiveness of mRNA Covid-19 Vaccine among U.S. Health Care Personnel," *New England Journal of Medicine* 385, no. 90 (December 16, 2021), https://www.nejm.org/ doi/full/10.1056/NEJMoa2106599.

9. Barton F. Haynes, "A New Vaccine to Battle Covid-19," *New England Journal of Medicine* 384 (February 4, 2021): 470–471, https://www.nejm.org/doi/full/10.1056/NEJMe2035557.

10. "Smithsonian Collects Objects from First Known U.S. COVID-19 Vaccination Effort," Smithsonian, March 9, 2021, https://www.si.edu/newsdesk/releases/smithsonian-collects-objects -first-known-us-covid-19-vaccination-effort.

11. "Moderna Reports Second Quarter Fiscal Year 2021 Financial Results and Provides Business Updates," Moderna, August 5, 2021, https://investors.modernatx.com/news-releases/news-release -details/moderna-reports-second-quarter-fiscal-year-2021-financial.

12. "The World's Real-Time Billionaires," *Forbes*, https://www.forbes.com/real-time -billionaires/#5a205ecf3d78.

13. Sarah Cascone, "A Painting Bought at a Small Town Dump for $4 Turned Out to Be by David Bowie—and It Just Sold for More Than $87,000," Artnet, June 24, 2021, https://news.artnet.com/ market/david-bowie-landfill-painting-sets-auction-record-1983293.

14. "COVID Vaccines Create 9 New Billionaires with Combined Wealth Greater Than Cost of Vaccinating World's Poorest Countries," Oxfam, May 20, 2021, https://www.oxfam.org/en/press -releases/covid-vaccines-create-9-new-billionaires-combined-wealth-greater-cost-vaccinating.

15. Tom Frieden, "Opinion: Pfizer and Moderna's mRNA Vaccines Are Our Best Chance to End This Pandemic. Break Up Their Duopoly," *Washington Post*, October 12, 2021, https://www .washingtonpost.com/opinions/2021/10/12/its-time-break-up-pfizer-modernas-duopoly-their-vaccine -technology/.

16. "Contribution of NIH funding to new drug approvals 2010-2016," Proceedings of the National Academy of Sciences, March 6, 2018, https://www.ncbi.nlm.nih.gov/pmc/articles/PMC5878010/.

17. Jefferies Group, equity research note by Michael J. Yee, et al., August 5, 2021.

18. Transcript of Moderna R&D Day, September 9, 2021, VIQ FD Disclosure, via Factiva.

19. "Moderna to Invest in New Science Center in Cambridge, MA," Moderna, September 30, 2021, https://investors.modernatx.com/news-releases/news-release-details/moderna-invest-new -science-center-cambridge-ma.

Epilogue

1. Eric C. Schneider et al., "The U.S. Covid-19 Vaccination Program at One Year: How Many Deaths and Hospitalizations Were Prevented?" The Commonwealth Fund, December 14, 2021, https://www.commonwealthfund.org/publications/issue-briefs/2021/dec/us-covid-19-vaccination-program-one-year-how-many-deaths-and.

2. "Rates of Covid-19 Cases and Deaths by Vaccination Status," Centers for Disease Control & Prevention, https://covid.cdc.gov/covid-data-tracker/?itid=lk_inline_enhanced-template#rates-by-vaccine-status.

3. Peter Loftus, "Moderna's Covid-19 Vaccine Works Safely in Young Children, Company Says," *Wall Street Journal*, March 24, 2022, https://www.wsj.com/articles/modernas-covid-19-vaccine-works-safely-in-young-children-company-says-11648036800.

4. Jared S. Hopkins and Stephanie Armour, "FDA Authorizes Second Covid-19 Booster Shot for Older Adults," *Wall Street Journal*, March 29, 2022, https://www.wsj.com/articles/fda-authorizes-second-covid-19-booster-shot-for-older-adults-11648564824.

5. Jefferies Group, research note by Michael J. Yee et al., March 24, 2022.

Index

Acknowledgments

I would like to acknowledge all the people and families who suffered the worst effects of the Covid-19 pandemic, in the United States and around the world. Among these, it's particularly heartbreaking to think of the many children who lost parents or caregivers to the coronavirus.

This book wouldn't have been possible without the generous time provided to me by so many people involved in Moderna's story and the broader Covid-19 vaccine hunt. Many of the people quoted in this book spoke to me personally, some devoting many hours. I'm grateful to everyone who took time out of their busy schedules, as most of them had more urgent tasks at hand as they responded to a global pandemic. Thanks especially to Stéphane Bancel, Stephen Hoge, Juan Andres, Tal Zaks, Lorence Kim, Noubar Afeyan, Derrick Rossi, Ken Chien, and Bob Langer. And for facilitating various Moderna interviews, thanks to Ray Jordan, Colleen Hussey, Kate Cronin, and Lavina Talukdar.

The book arose from my experience as just one member of a large team of dedicated journalists at the *Wall Street Journal*, which sprang into action in early 2020 to cover a historic pandemic. For more than two years, my colleagues on the Health and Science team and throughout the *Journal*, in bureaus around the world, worked tirelessly. We strove to meet the strong demand from readers searching for trustworthy information about this outbreak that caused so much loss and upheaval.

Much of this book comes from my own reporting, but the smart and insightful work of many of my colleagues is a critical foundation. First, I would like to thank the leader of the *Journal*'s Health and Science team, Stefanie Ilgenfritz. Stefanie has a vast knowledge of health care, a sharp eye for what makes a compelling news story, and a tendency never to settle for "good enough" from her reporters. This had us well prepared to cover every angle of the news. Her deputy, and my immediate editor, Jonathan Rockoff, is the one who first suggested I pay a visit to Moderna in early 2020, and his knowledge of the industry and editing guided much of our coverage.

I would also like to thank other journalists on the Health and Science team and elsewhere at the *Journal* with whom I worked on pandemic coverage and whose work informs this book: Jared Hopkins, Joe Walker, Melanie Evans, Anna Wilde Mathews, Betsy McKay, Felicia Schwartz, Amy Dockser Marcus, Daniela Hernández, Brianna Abbott, Denise Roland, Julie Wernau, Sarah Toy, David Freeman, Patrick Mc-Groarty, Jenny Strasburg, Jon Kamp, Tom Burton, Stephanie Armour, Greg Zuckerman, Nailah Morgan, Lydia Randall, Drew Hinshaw, Susan Pulliam, Rolfe Winkler, Bojan Pancevski, Nour Malas, Liz Beltran, Chip Cummins, Stu Woo, Tonia Cowan, Juanje Gómez, Taylor Umlauf, Meghan Petersen, Chase Gaewski, Dan Frosch, Elizabeth Findell, Brian Gormley, Robbie Whelan, Annmarie Fertoli, and Trenae Nuri. It was a pleasure and a learning experience to collaborate with all of these reporters on various projects, and I am also proud see the great work they've produced that I wasn't involved with. Thanks to all the editors on the *Journal*'s Enterprise and publishing desks who improve our stories and have saved me from making dumb mistakes. And I would like to thank a few people who have left the *Journal*'s Health and Science team in recent years but who left their imprints on the rest of us: Jeanne Whalen, Ron Winslow, and Lee Hotz. My apologies if I've forgotten anyone else who should be acknowledged.

Thanks to the *Journal*'s editor in chief, Matt Murray, and managing editor, Karen Miller Pensiero, for allowing me to pursue this book and take time off to write it.

This book also relies in part on other publications, which are cited throughout. It was particularly useful to read pieces by Damian Garde in *STAT* and Elie Dolgin in *Nature* to learn more about the prepandemic days of Moderna and mRNA research.

My *Journal* colleague Tom Gryta, who is also a book author and fellow alum of Dow Jones Newswires, introduced me to a literary agent and has given me valuable advice along the way. Several other people, both at the *Journal* and elsewhere, have shared helpful tips about the book-writing process or have lent an ear: Tripp Mickle, Dan Hurley, Jamie Reidy, David Oshinsky, Andy Whelan, Kristin Friel, and Bob Wieman.

I was lucky to be connected with my literary agent, Eric Lupfer, of Fletcher & Company. He has been invaluable from the beginning, talking over ideas and leading me through the unfamiliar process of finding a publisher. He's skilled at spotting themes and has made many helpful suggestions for the book's focus and structure. Thanks also to Kelly Karczewski at Fletcher.

Scott Berinato, senior editor at Harvard Business Review Press, deserves much credit for making this book happen. He reached out to me to gauge my interest and then spent countless hours reviewing chapters, drawing out themes, suggesting revisions, and generally whipping drafts into shape. Thanks to many others at HBR Press, including Anne Starr, David Goehring, Stephani Finks, Felicia Sinusas, Erika Heilman, Julie Devoll, Lindsey Dietrich, Brian Galvin, Alexandra Kephart, Sally Ashworth, Jon Shipley, and Akila Balasubramaniyan.

Thanks to Spencer Fuller and Faceout Studio for the wonderful cover design, and Girl Friday Productions for fact-checking. And thanks to my fellow Glensiders, Peter Kurilla and Kelly Curtis, for help on photography and website design.

It has been gratifying to receive encouragement and support from family and friends as I've taken on this project, including the members of Devil's Pool, BeerCo, the Grace and Lewis gangs from Notre Dame, the Sunday brunch crew, and friends from Glenside, Maple Glen, La Salle, St. A's, and beyond.

My siblings—Ed, Pat, Joanne, and Christine—and their families have been so encouraging since I first told them about the book plans, as has my stepfather, Jim "Poppy" Burke, and my aunt, Alice Herron. May our future family gatherings be free of masks or having to stand outside on cold, rainy days!

My father, Edward V. Loftus Sr., was an aerospace engineer and one of the smartest people I knew. When I was a boy, I asked him so many questions, and he patiently tried to answer all of them: Why are there leap years? How does a car engine work? He died of leukemia when I was 11. I suppose I never stopped asking questions because I became a journalist. His memory lives on in our hearts.

My mother, Nancy Burke, is an inspiration. She had to pick up the pieces after my dad died, while still having to raise five kids. In midlife she went to college, got a bachelor's degree, and had careers as a hospital administrator and a librarian. She has had a lifelong love of reading, which she instilled in her children by taking us to the library on a regular basis and later passed onto the next generation by getting books for her grandkids when they visited "Gram" the librarian. She has a deep reservoir of love and affection for all of us. As I've worked on this book, her support has meant the world to me.

My children—James, Nora, and Luke—have endured the difficulties of pandemic life, such as virtual school and separation from friends, all while I was putting in many hours covering the pandemic for the *Journal* and then writing this book. But I've also been amazed at how they've bounced back and found ways to adapt, thrive, and support each other. Our bonds grew stronger. They have inspired and encouraged me, too.

Finally, I simply couldn't have done this without the encouragement and help of my wife, Eileen. She is a highly talented writer and editor, and her insightful suggestions made this book better. She patiently endured countless discussions about the progress of the book and raised my spirits when I doubted myself or hit setbacks, real or imagined, all while doing her own job and being a pandemic parent. I am forever grateful for her love and support, and for believing in me.

About the Author

PETER LOFTUS is a reporter for the *Wall Street Journal*, covering the drug and medical-device industries and other health care topics. He was part of a *Journal* team that won second place in the business category of the 2020 Association of Health Care Journalists' awards for coverage of the race for a Covid-19 vaccine. In 2016 he was part of a *Journal* team that was a finalist for the Pulitzer Prize in explanatory reporting for a series of articles about rising prescription drug prices. Before joining the *Journal* in 2013, he was a reporter for Dow Jones Newswires, covering the pharmaceutical and technology industries. Before that, he worked for community newspapers in suburban Philadelphia. He graduated from the University of Notre Dame with a bachelor's degree in English and history. He lives outside Philadelphia with his wife and three children.